Devil Boats
The PT War Against Japan

William B. Breuer

★
PRESIDIO

For RUMSEY EWING
a gallant and daring Devil Boat skipper who
typified the spirit of America's sea cavalry

Copyright © 1987 by Presidio Press

Published by Presidio Press
505 B San Marin Drive, Suite 300
Novato, CA 94945-1340

This edition printed 1995

Library of Congress Cataloging-in-Publication Data

Breuer, William B., 1923–
  Devil boats.
  Includes index.
  1. World War, 1939–1945—Naval operations, American. 2. World War, 1939–1945—Campaigns—Pacific Ocean. 3. Torpedo-boats—United States. 4. World War, 1939–1945—Naval operations, Japanese. I. Title.
  D770B68 1987 940.54'26 86-17062
ISBN 0-89141-269-7 (hardcover)
ISBN 0-89141-586-6 (paperback)

Printed in the United States of America

Contents

U.S. Army Map 1944

Give me a fast ship for I intend to go in harm's way
—Adm. John Paul Jones

Foreword

Minutes after the Japanese struck at Pearl Harbor (December 7, 1941), a PT boat shot down the first enemy plane of the war, and from that point on the speedy little craft with the powerful wallops were in the thick of the fighting. This book tells of the almost nightly feats of heroism and daring performed by resourceful PT-boat skippers and crewmen, feats so incredible that they would be rejected by Hollywood script writers as unbelievable.

In the black early days of the war, a totally unprepared America was nearly driven from the Pacific. Her "fleet" in the Philippines consisted of four leaking, obsolete PT boats. But these four boats attacked warships nightly for many weeks, than broke through the Japanese ring around Corregidor to carry General MacArthur and his party to safety.

Meanwhile, General Hideki Tojo, the Japanese strongman, was conducting the speediest, most powerful blitzkrieg the world had ever known. Tojo's main objective was Australia, more than a thousand miles south of the Philippines. Seizing Australia would deprive American forces of a base from which to mount a massive counteroffensive.

Tojo's forces reached New Guinea, New Britain, and the Solomon Islands, only a stone's throw north of Australia. In this primitive region, the craft the Japanese came to call Devil Boats ventured out nightly to confront the "Tokyo Express"—warship-escorted convoys bringing in troops and supplies. The body of water where most of these savage fights took place became the graveyard for so many ships (on both sides) that it was labeled Iron Bottom Bay.

But in MacArthur's long advance back to the Philippines, the Devil Boats did far more than clash with warships a hundred times their size. PT crews landed behind Japanese lines on sabotage missions and to gain intelligence, carried Army raiding parties ashore deep in enemy territory, shot up Nipponese shore facilities and camps, dueled with coastal guns and warplanes, and rescued scores of downed Allied pilots, often while under heavy enemy gunfire.

The Devil Boats (which were heavily armed with automatic weapons) shot up and sank hundreds of motorized barges loaded with troops or supplies, bolted into enemy-held harbors to blast docks, blockaded Japanese-held islands to keep troops penned up there, scouted ahead of American warships to flash back warnings of approaching enemy fleets, and reconnoitered landing beaches prior to island invasions. All of these dramatic actions, each an epic in its own right, come alive in these pages

JOHN D. BULKELEY
Rear Admiral, U.S. Navy (Ret.)
Washington, D.C.

Author's Note

Creating this book would have been impossible without the zealous help of scores of former Devil Boat buccaneers. They probed their memories and recounted their adventures to the author in person, by telephone, and by written communication. They dug up long-forgotten combat diaries, letters, newspaper and magazine clips, maps, and official reports.

The official history of PT boats, *At Close Quarters*, by Capt. Robert J. Bulkeley, Jr., published in 1962 by the Government Printing Office served as the authentic source for place names, ranks, and time of events. *They Were Expendable* by William L. White (NY: Harcourt, 1943) provided background and details of the early weeks of the war.

PT Boats, Inc., the veterans' group based in Memphis, graciously provided numerous photos and other important assistance.

The unofficial nicknames of Devil Boats were used where possible to give life to these beloved little craft. These nicknames were often changed, so in some instances an obsolete nickname may have been used.

Events surrounding the sinking of Lt. John F. Kennedy's PT-109 were woven together from several sources, including the account by Lt. Byron "Whizzer" White, a naval intelligence officer and now a justice of the U.S. Supreme Court, and a version by William F. "Bud" Liebenow, the skipper whose Devil Boat rescued Kennedy and his crew.

Deep appreciation is expressed to Rear Adm. John Harllee, USN (Ret.) of Washington, D.C., a former PT squadron commander in the Pacific, for reading the manuscript and offering valuable suggestions and guidance.

Abbreviations for Navy ratings

Motor Machinist's Mate	MoMM
Radioman (Mate)	RM
Fireman	FN
Chief Boatswain Mate	BMC
Boatswain Mate	BM
Ship's Cook	SC
Gunner's Mate	GM
Machinist's Mate	MM
Seaman	SN
Torpedoman	TM
Quartermaster	QM
Shipfitter	SF
Electrician's Mate	EM

Introduction

For fifteen years before a woefully unprepared America was bombed into war at Pearl Harbor, the generals and admirals who had an iron grip on the Japanese government held that an armed conflict with the United States was inevitable. In 1927 the Nipponese warlords had drawn up a secret plan called the Tanaka Memorial. It was a blueprint for military conquest of vast expanses of Asia and war with America.

In the 1930s, the Japanese militarists tightened their hold on the government by the simple means of murdering anyone who stood in their way, all the while building one of the mightiest war machines the world had ever known. By 1937, the warlords were ready to strike. They cooked up a clash between Japanese troops on maneuvers and a Chinese outpost on the Marco Polo Bridge near Peiping (now Beijing) and used that as an excuse for the massive invasion of China proper.

During the next three years, President Franklin D. Roosevelt tried by diplomatic means to "bring Japan to her senses," an effort scorned by the Nipponese warlords. In the meantime, the United States continued to ship huge quantities of oil and scrap iron to Japan.

As the war in China raged, the Japanese tried repeatedly to provoke America into armed conflict. In early 1941, the ambassador to Japan, Joseph C. Grew, wrote:

American churches, schools, universities and hospitals throughout China have been bombed [by the Japanese] despite flag markings on their roofs. American missionaries and their families have been killed. There can be no doubt that these attacks were planned.

Even the deliberate sinking of the USS *Panay*, a small gunboat patrolling the Yangtze River to protect American civilians, and the 1937 machine-gunning of survivors floundering in the water failed to arouse isolationist America to her peril.

On October 17, 1940, Gen. Hideki Tojo, the strongman of the Japanese Imperial Army, became prime minister. His predecessor, a moderate who advocated restraint in dealing with the United States, had been nearly murdered and was frightened into resigning. Tojo immediately resolved to prepare for war with America, a nation he hated intensely.

Nicknamed "Razor Brain," Tojo was barely five-feet-four and wore oversized horn-rimmed glasses that gave him an owlish appearance. A man of enormous ambition and drive, Tojo had a reputation as a brilliant organizer and administrator, and as a skilled and daring military strategist. He was the principal architect of an operational plan designed to unleash throughout the Pacific the most devastating blitzkrieg in history, one that would extend the Japanese Empire from Manchuria some five thousand miles southward to Australia.

First, however, a bold sneak attack would be launched to destroy or severely cripple the United States fleet at Pearl Harbor, freeing the powerful Nipponese navy to dominate the Pacific and permitting ground forces to fan out rapidly to gobble up one Asian country after the other. General Tojo's idea was to achieve an impregnable position throughout huge expanses of Asia before the sleeping giant, America, would awaken and be capable of hitting back. Tojo's blueprint for conquest was approved by the Supreme War Council on September 6, 1941, at a meeting that broke up with shouts of "banzai!"

Plans for the attack on America's largest naval base in the Pacific had been in the works for ten years. From 1931 on, each graduating class at the Japanese naval academy had been confronted with the final examination question: "How would you carry out a surprise attack on Pearl Harbor?" It took the U.S. Navy to supply the answer. In 1932, with Japanese observers looking on, an American carrier sneaked in north of the island of Oahu, and in a predawn "raid," its planes "sank" all the ships at Pearl. Tokyo carefully recorded the details.

In the fall of 1941 when Japan's militarists had decided on war, the American people were still peacefully preoccupied at home, just as they had been during the 1920s and 1930s. True, a madman with a comic-opera mustache named Hitler had overrun most of Europe, and the Japanese army was brutalizing ancient China. But there were two broad oceans to protect the United States from these unpleasant affairs, so why worry? America's motto was: "Keep out of other people's quarrels!"

As a result of this national attitude, the United States's defenses had been allowed to slip to those of a third-rate power. Only the dedicated and relentless efforts of a hard core of professional military men prevented America from suffering an even more monumental calamity than the one that was about to strike the nation.

Among the relative handful of devoted professionals was Lt. John D. "Buck" Bulkeley who commanded the six-craft Motor Torpedo Boat Squadron 3 that, with black war clouds gathering, arrived in Manila Bay on September 28, 1941. Popularly called PT boats, these speedy "patrol-torpedo" craft, unwanted by the navy leaders, were untested and few and far between. By early December 1941, there were only twenty-nine PT boats in the entire United States Navy: six in the Philippines, twelve at Pearl Harbor, and eleven at the New York Navy Yard being fitted out for the Panama Canal Zone.

Between the two world wars, U.S. Navy brass hats had shown no interest in the development of PT boats. Curiously, during the Prohibition era, it was the illegal but flourishing bootlegging business that had been responsible for innovations the Navy later adopted. Rum runners, as they were called, had brought a few British versions of the PT boat into the United States and were using them to smuggle liquor from Canada to points along the eastern seaboard. In military fashion, the smugglers carried out experiments to improve the performance of the PTs, including the addition of more powerful engines. They developed operational procedures—such as stalking along the coast at night—that would be put into practice years later at Guadalcanal, New Guinea, New Britain, the Philippines, and elsewhere in the Pacific.

It was not until 1937 that President Roosevelt, who had been assistant secretary of the Navy in the First World War, personally saw to it that $15 million (a modest sum) was appropriated for PT boat development. But peacetime progress was methodical and slow; it was not until June 17, 1940, that the first operational PT was delivered to the Navy. During the year ahead modifications were to be incorporated, and the Navy would settle on two standard types: the Higgins 78-footer (35 tons) and the Elco 80-footer (38 tons).

Each plywood boat had a crew of about twelve men and was powered by three Packard engines. Armed with four .50-caliber machine guns and four torpedoes, the PT had a cruising range of about 500 miles. There wasn't an ounce of armor on the boats; they were eggshells that—theoretically, at this point—would roar in close to a target, loose their torpedoes, then race off at full throttle (about forty-five miles per hour), zigzagging violently to dodge enemy return fire.

As the war progressed, these mighty midgets—with the impudence and wallop of Jack the Giant Killer—would multiply until there would be 212 PT boats operating in the Pacific. They would be known as the Mosquito Fleet, and to the Japanese, who had come to both hate and fear them, the "Devil Boats of the Night" or the "Green Dragons."

The PT boats themselves were but the means for coming to grips with the enemy at close range. It was their bright, eager young skippers and crewmen—twentieth century buccaneers—who would write a glorious chapter in American history with a relentless series of slashing attacks. These were a new breed of American fighting men, a combination of seagoing cavalry, commando-type raiders, and Indian scouts out of the Old West. They had more than their share of courage, venturesome spirit, endurance, and resourcefulness. The harried Japanese never knew when, where, or from what direction these Americans in Devil Boats would strike.

Except for a tiny hard core of professionals, the PT boat skippers were recent graduates from colleges across the nation. Their ranks were heavy with famed and less-famed sports figures whose imaginations had been fired by this swashbuckling branch of the Navy. Each skipper had volunteered for PT boat duty, fully aware that in the savagery of the Pacific there would be no grandstands, no cheering, no glamour. The only "fan" reaction would be in the form of hisses from Tokyo, where the bronzed, dashing young Americans in the lethal Devil Boats would soon be proclaimed Public Enemies and ordered to be smashed at all costs.

What follows is not a military history. It is the story of people: the men of the American PT boats and the enemy they fought during the struggle in the Pacific in World War II.

CHAPTER 1 "We're Under Attack!"

It was just past 7:00 A.M. on Sunday, December 7, 1941. A brilliant sun, rising majestically over Mount Tantalus, began drenching Pearl Harbor, Hawaii, in its first warming rays. Even for the island of Oahu, this was an uncommonly glorious and peaceful morning. Old Sol's magnificence enhanced the green of the sugarcane fields that stretched up the slopes of the purple-hued heights behind the harbor and deepened the azure shades of the lochs reaching inland from the shoreline.

Except for its handful of aircraft carriers, the United States Pacific Fleet was roosting drowsily in Pearl Harbor: the venerable battleships *Arizona, Tennessee, Maryland, Pennsylvania, West Virginia, California, Nevada* and *Oklahoma;* cruisers; destroyers; submarines; and assorted other vessels. The seventy combat ships and twenty-four auxiliaries all had one boiler lighted, but few had enough steam generated to make a quick sortie for the open sea in case of an emergency. But no emergency was contemplated. The U.S. Fleet was, in effect, a sitting duck on a small pond.

Those on duty aboard the ships were routinely performing appointed chores: cleaning brass, swabbing decks, wiping the dew from machine guns and 5-inch dual-purpose guns. Only one in four of these guns was manned. The main batteries had no crews on duty. Nor were the plotting rooms, the antiaircraft director facilities, and the ammunition storage chambers manned. The ammunition was locked up, and the keys were in the possession of the officer of the deck on each vessel. Most of the officers and crewmen were deep in slumber following a typical Saturday shore leave. As a result, Sunday morning found the United States Pacific Fleet suffering its full share of hangovers.

Earlier that Sunday morning—at 5:30 A.M.—Capt. Mitsuo Fuchido, an experienced pilot of the Japanese Imperial Navy, climbed into the cockpit of his red and yellow warplane aboard the aircraft carrier *Agaki*, several hundred miles north of Oahu. The captain was in a euphoric mood: he had been chosen to lead a powerful winged carrier force on an historic mission to wipe out the American Pacific Fleet and to destroy American air power on nearby fields, where the planes were parked like rows of bowling pins waiting to be knocked over. In his sky armada were forty "Kate" torpedo bombers, fifty-one "Val" dive bombers, fifty-one "Zeke" and "Zero" fighter planes, and forty-nine high-level bombers.

Surprise, Captain Fuchido knew, would be crucial. Through their intelligence channels, the Imperial Navy knew the precise location of each major American warship. As his flight neared the Oahu coastline at about 7:00 A.M., the strike leader issued a sigh of relief; his force had apparently arrived undetected. He had no way of knowing that an American outpost had sighted and reported the oncoming hostile flight: a report that was ignored at higher levels.

At 7:50 A.M., the sound of pealing church bells in Honolulu, summoning the faithful to eight o'clock Mass, wafted on the gentle breezes over Pearl Harbor. Over the mighty American naval base the tranquility was shattered by the sounds of powerful airplane engines. Below, on scores of ships and boats hundreds of sleeping sailors partially opened their eyes, roundly cursed the brass hats for disturbing their Sunday morning slumber with aircraft exercises, and rolled back over. Up in the cloudless blue sky over Battleship Row, Mitsuo Fuchido threw back the canopy of his cockpit and fired a smoke flare: the signal to launch the sneak attack. Fuchido could not believe his good luck; not a shot had been fired at his armada.

A short distance away, six of the craft from Motor Torpedo Boat Squadron 1, led by Lt. Comdr. William C. Specht, were moored at the Pearl Harbor submarine base. Ens. N. E. Ball, squadron duty officer, was gazing idly across Kuhua Island, puzzled by the swarms of airplanes circling like birds of prey over Battleship Row and Ford Island, just beyond. Suddenly Ensign Ball tensed; he had spotted "meatballs" (Japan's red Rising Sun insignia) on the wingtips. At his elbow, a chief petty officer called out excitedly, "They look like Japs!" Moments later the first bomb exploded, sending a towering plume of black, oily smoke into the clear sky. Then all hell broke loose.

Ensign Ball dashed into the nearby mess hall where some PT boat crewmen were eating a leisurely breakfast. He shouted, "We're under attack! Man the guns!"

For a few seconds, the men sat in stunned silence. Under attack? By whom? Then there was a mad scramble as the sailors raced for their machine guns. Even before the men reached their PTs, two of the squadron's .50-caliber automatic weapons were chattering angrily. GM1 Joy Van Zell de Jong and TM1 George B. Huffman, who had been lounging on the deck of PT 23, vaulted into the turrets and began blasting away at the unlimited targets darting through the sky over Pearl Harbor. Streams of their tracers riddled a low-flying Nipponese torpedo plane, and de Jong and Huffman howled with delight when they saw the Kate crash into the water. They may have been the first American gunners to draw blood in World War II.

At the first sound of the excited voices around the PT boat mooring, Ens. Edward I. Farley, of New York City, rushed out from below deck. His eyelids were heavy from lack of sleep, and he was clad only in undershorts. He had attended a Saturday night dance at the Royal Hawaiian Hotel, and it had been 4:30 A.M. before he returned to PT 23 and fell into a bunk.

Now Ed Farley was wide awake. He was horrified to see a torpedo bomber swoop in low and send its lethal "fish" crashing into the battleship *California*. Then, one after the other, in drill-like precision, Kates sent torpedoes racing for other battleships. Explosion followed explosion, rocking the harbor and its shoreline.

Farley scrambled into a gun turret and shouted at engineers to start the auxiliary generator that operated the hydraulic system for the turret. The ensign had forgotten it was broken. He pointed to targets in the sky, and the perspiring crewmen manipulated the turret into line by hand. After Farley had fired a few hundred rounds, the heat from the two machine-gun barrels caused the plexiglass dome to fog over.

"Chop it away!" the ensign shouted. Grabbing axes, crewmen

began hacking away at the tough fiber. Then Farley jumped back behind the automatic weapons and blasted away once more. Both guns, their barrels red hot, suddenly jammed. By the time the weapons were cleared, the targets were out of range.

Two miles across Pearl Harbor from the submarine base, the other six PT boats of Commander Specht's squadron had been caught in limbo. The 78-foot boats were in the process of being loaded aboard the oiler *Ramapo* for shipment to the Philippines and were resting in cradles on the adjacent dock and on the ship's deck. To make matters worse, the gasoline tanks of all six PTs had been covered with carbon dioxide (dry ice) in order to reduce fire hazard during the sea journey. As a result, crews could not start the engines to compress the air that in turn forced oil through cylinders to traverse the power-gun turrets.

Resourceful by nature and through training, the PT crews hurriedly cut the hydraulic lines, freeing the turrets. Then, four-man crews manned each of the pair of .50-caliber machine guns, with one man firing the weapon, two men maneuvering the turret back and forth by hand, and an officer directing the adjustment of the turret and the firing. For the crews firing from their PT boats in the cradles on the *Ramapo*'s deck, it was an especially trying ordeal, for the larger ship's guns were now in action and streams of bullets were hissing past just over their heads.

The commander of the *Ramapo* was on the bridge futilely banging away at the planes with a pistol. Tears of anger and frustration were streaming down his cheeks. Japanese pilots, emboldened by the lack of lead being thrown in their direction, flew so low that the Americans could see their toothy grins. A bosun's mate on the *Ramapo* threw wrenches at two Zekes racing over his ship at masthead level. From the magazine below came a call asking what he needed. "*Ammunition*, goddam it!" the bosun's mate roared over the earsplitting din. "I can't keep throwing *things* at 'em!"

In the meantime, Pearl Harbor had been turned into an inferno of exploding bombs, thick clouds of black smoke, machine-gun fire and sounding through it all the shrill, hoarse signal of general quarters. The veteran Japanese pilots, who had honed their skills in China and elsewhere, knew their business—as well as the precise location of targets. By 7:58 A.M.—three minutes after the attack began—the battleships *Arizona* and *California* were doomed, and over twelve hundred American sailors were dead.

Many senior American officers were on shore leave, but the junior

officers and bluejackets fought back with every means at their dis-
posal. Sailors pounded the locks off ammunition rooms with axes and
sledgehammers. Water swirled into the fatally stricken *California,*
where, in the forward air compressor station, MM Robert Scott was
trying to feed air to the 5-inch guns. His comrades dashed off, shouting at Scott to get out in a hurry. He yelled back: "This is my station.
I'll stay here and give them air as long as our guns are going." The
departing men shut the watertight door and left Scott at his post.

Twenty-two-year-old SN Joseph Hydruska scrambled aboard the
battleship *Oklahoma,* which had been struck by six torpedoes below
the waterline and was about to capsize. He was shaking from fear but
cut through a thick bulkhead to try to rescue trapped comrades. He
found six naked men waist deep in water. They were incoherent and
did not know low long they had been down there. All were badly
wounded.

Joe Hydruska continued to cut away frantically. He could hear
tapping all over the ship: SOS pleas for help, but no voices. There
was nothing anyone could do for them.

On the cruiser *New Orleans,* the chaplain, Howell Forgy, went
from gun crew to gun crew, telling them he was sorry he would be
unable to hold religious services on deck but to "praise the Lord and
pass the ammunition."

On one destroyer, sailors were hurriedly issued machine-gun ammunition so old (dated 1918) the belts fell apart in the loading apparatus. On an unarmed auxiliary vessel, crewmen grabbed their only
weapons, ancient 1904 Springfield rifles. The relics wouldn't shoot.
Gunners on the destroyer *Argonne* shot down their own antenna.

The sudden onslaught, planned for ten years, had been devastating. Within thirty minutes Captain Fuchido and his pilots had achieved
their primary goal: the destruction of the United States Pacific Fleet's
battle line.

During this half-hour time frame, other Nipponese aircraft had
been pounding Army and Marine Corps air bases on Oahu. Within a
few minutes, thirty-three aircraft had been destroyed on Ford Island,
and at the Marine field at Ewa nearly all of the fifty parked planes
were wiped out. Twenty-seven of the thirty-three Navy Catalina patrol planes based at Kaneohe were wrecked and six more damaged.
The three Army airfields on Oahu—Hickham, Wheeler and Bel-
lows—were nearly blasted off the map, and their planes, neatly lined

up wingtip-to-wingtip, were blown to smithereens. American airpower on Oahu had been virtually destroyed.

At 9:45 A.M., only four-and-a-half hours after he had lifted off, Captain Fuchido returned to his carrier north of Oahu. In steady streams, all but twenty-nine of his pilots landed. The elated airmen were greeted with frenzied shouts of "banzai!"

Back at Pearl Harbor, Lt. Comdr. Bill Specht made a hasty assessment of his twelve PT boats. He breathed a sigh of relief. In spite of the utter destruction and the smoking, blackened hulks of ships on all sides, the PTs had emerged unscathed. No doubt the tiny boats had been passed up by the attackers in favor of the multitude of major targets available to them.

The six PTs at the submarine base got under way by late morning and cruised the debris-laden harbor. Several dozen wounded Americans were fished from the harbor's waters and taken to the hospital landing. Nearing Battleship Row, Ens. Ed Farley, skipper of PT 23, was sickened by the sight that greeted his eyes. The *Arizona* was sunk in place with only the tip of her superstructure visible. Later Farley would learn that 1,103 of her officers and men (of a crew of 1,400) were entombed in the battleship. Altogether, seven battleships were but charred, twisted wreckage, as were three cruisers, three destroyers, and five or six auxiliary vessels.

Wild rumors abounded: a powerful Japanese invasion force was on the way; much of the Nipponese fleet could be expected on the horizon at any minute. Ed Farley had a curious feeling based on what he had seen and endured that morning: the twelve PT boats of Squadron 1 were about all that remained at Pearl Harbor to engage the enemy when he came. Farley had no way of knowing—nor did any other American—that Adm. Chuichi Nagumo, commander of the Japanese carrier task force, had given the order to withdraw at full speed, even though the plan had called for follow-up strikes.

In the meantime, 5,123 miles and four time zones to the west of devastated Pearl Harbor, only the sounds of sleeping men disturbed the silence inside the officers' quarters at Cavite Navy Yard, eight miles southeast of Manila. It was early morning on December 8.*

---

* The Philippines are on East longitude. At 8:00 A.M., December 7 in Hawaii, it was 3:00 A.M., December 8 in Manila.

Suddenly, a telephone jangled impatiently in a dark room. Lt. John D. "Buck" Bulkeley sleepily picked up the instrument and placed it to his ear.

"We're at war," a voice straining to remain calm blurted out. "The Japs have just bombed Pearl Harbor!" The solemn voice added that "the Old Man wants you to get down here right away." The Old Man was Rear Adm. Francis W. Rockwell, commandant of Cavite Navy Yard.

Now Bulkeley, commander of the six-craft Motor Torpedo Boat Squadron 3, was wide awake. He glanced at his watch; it was a few minutes past 3:00 A.M. The young skipper was not surprised at the grim news. For several weeks he and other fighting men in the Philippines had been aware that war clouds were gathering over the Pacific. Bulkeley's surprise was that the Japanese war machine had struck first at Hawaii, not at the much closer Philippines.

Bulkeley shook awake one of his officers, Ens. Anthony Akers, a lanky, soft-spoken Texan, and told him the news. Akers thought his commanding officer was playing a joke on him. With his eyes still half-closed, Akers mumbled, "It's a hell of a time to be declaring war!"

Dressing rapidly, Lieutenant Bulkeley hopped into a jeep, and the driver roared off for the Commandantia, the thick-walled old Spanish structure that served as Admiral Rockwell's headquarters. When Bulkeley arrived, Rockwell and his chief of staff, Capt. Herbert J. Ray, were dressed and waiting. Dawn was just starting to break. A grim Admiral Rockwell gazed into the graying sky and remarked that "they" should be here any minute. "They" was the powerful Japanese air force.

The Cavite commander then issued Bulkeley his orders: he was to take his PT boats across Manila Bay to Mariveles Harbor at the tip of the Bataan Peninsula, opposite the rugged, two-and-one-half-mile-long fortress of Corregidor, a huge rock perched in the mouth of the bay.

Buck Bulkeley, rushing back to his boat mooring, was unaware that he, a lowly naval lieutenant, had learned that the United States was at war before Gen. Douglas MacArthur, the Army commander in the Philippines, had been advised of that fact. Just before 3:00 A.M., Adm. Thomas C. Hart, the diminutive, irascible naval commander and MacArthur's opposite number in the Philippines, had received a radio signal from Vice Adm. Husband E. Kimmel in Honolulu:

AIR RAID ON PEARL HARBOR. THIS IS NO DRILL.

Hart and nearly all other admirals had been feuding with MacArthur for years, and relations between the two services had become so strained that Hart did not pass the startling information on to MacArthur. About thirty minutes later, an Army private on duty in Manila heard the first flash over a San Francisco, California, radio station. He quickly passed on the news to his commanding officer.

At 3:40 A.M., about the time that Lieutenant Bulkeley had reached the Commandantia at Cavite Navy Yard, General MacArthur replaced the telephone on the table next to his bed in his family penthouse in the Manila Hotel. "Pearl Harbor!" he muttered in amazement. "That should be our strongest point!" MacArthur dressed, read his Bible for ten minutes, then set out for his office. There his top commanders had congregated, along with Admiral Hart. The situation was chaotic. No one knew what was going on in the Pacific. Rumors abounded.

Following his orders, at about 5:00 P.M., three of Bulkeley's PT boats under his second-in-command, Lt. Robert B. Kelly, set out from Cavite for Mariveles Harbor. Bulkeley's orders to Kelly were simple: "Remain on the alert and ready to attack *anything* I order you to attack."

As the motor torpedo boats set off for their Bataan destination, both Lieutenants Bulkeley and Kelly were aware that they were being sent to war but would have to operate on a trial-and-error basis. They and their men were truly pioneers. PT boats were so new to the United States Navy that no operational doctrine for their combat deployment had yet been established.

Lieutenant Kelly had several military passengers to deliver to Corregidor and, by the time his three PTs neared the mine fields guarding Mariveles Harbor, it was pitch black. Kelly had anticipated no difficulty in snaking through the mines, for he had done it many times, even at night. But now he was confronted with a different situation. The mine field lights were off, and he could not turn on his boat lights. The three PTs edged into the harbor, their tense occupants expecting to be blown to pieces at any moment.

Inland, nervous soldiers heard the roar of PT engines echoing across Mariveles Harbor and thought Japanese planes were approaching. Chaos erupted. Searchlights all over Bataan winked on and began sending long fingers of white into the dark sky. Every antiaircraft battery and artillery post for miles around went on the alert, ready to open fire at any moment. The unexpected turmoil made the PT men anxious; they conjectured in hoarse whispers about whether more likely they would be blown up by a mine or by American shore batteries.

Somehow, Kelly's little boats reached the submarine tender that was their goal and tied up alongside it. A PT boat had to have a tender or mother ship to furnish it with needed supplies: food, gasoline, spare parts, torpedoes, and ammunition. Now Bob Kelly received a jolt, the tender's skipper told him that he had orders to pull out to sea to an unknown destination far to the south. Kelly's three PTs would be left behind to manage the best they could.

Dawn found the mother ship gone, and Lieutenant Kelly received another shock. What little amount of gasoline and oil he had available had been sabotaged, the oil with sand, the gas with a wax that clogged the carburetors.

Shortly after daybreak in Hawaii, Lt. Bill Specht's handful of Squadron 1 PTs launched a round-the-clock patrol of Pearl Harbor. The skippers were cautioned particularly to be on the lookout for submarines, so they had to improvise. The depth charges taken aboard would be rolled off the fantail on two long wooden slats. Scores of depth charges were dropped as periscopes were sighted regularly. These proved to be mops from sunken ships that were floating handle up.

CHAPTER 2 A Sneak Into Enemy-Held Manila Harbor

For two days after the massive Japanese blow against Pearl Harbor, an ominous quiet had fallen across the Pacific. In and around Manila, American fighting men of all ranks waited for the proverbial second shoe to fall. It fell just before noon on December 10.

At Mariveles Harbor, Lt. Bob Kelly received an urgent signal. A large formation of Japanese warplanes was headed for the Manila Bay area from the direction of Formosa, to the north. Not wanting to be caught like sitting ducks moored to the docks, Kelly rapidly pulled his three PT boats out into open water (he had since scrounged a limited quantity of fuel). Out in the large bay, Kelly's PTs would be able to dodge and weave to avoid bombs, much like a boxer ducking the sledgehammer blows of an able opponent.

Some twenty minutes after leaving the docks, Kelly and the other PT men squinted skyward and saw several flights of twin-engine bombers—perhaps 125 or so—winging majestically through the bright blue sky at an estimated twenty-five thousand feet. The enemy formations were in precise alignment but, Lieutenant Kelly mused to his men, "they'll get their hair messed up a little when our fighters show up."

But where *were* the American fighter planes? The Japanese bombers disappeared over the mountains. There was no doubt in the skipper's mind where they were headed: Cavite Navy Yard, the only

American sea base in the Far East, and Nichols Field, the U.S. Army
Air Corps's major base, a short distance from Cavite.

At the Navy base at Cavite, Lt. Buck Bulkeley had also received
ample warning of the approaching enemy bombers and had hurried
his three PTs out into the bay. He and his men gazed up into the sky as
the planes with the meatballs on their wings drew closer, and eagerly
anticipated the imminent arrival of swarms of American fighters,

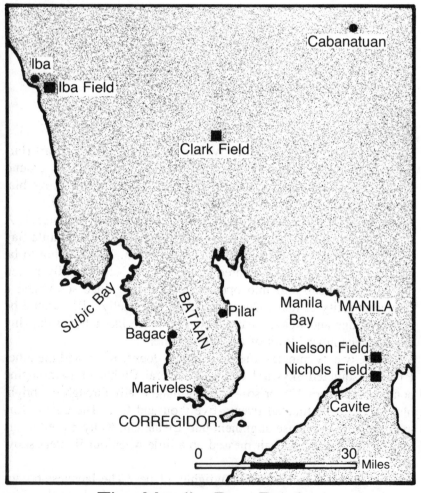

The Manila Bay Region

which, no doubt, would cut the Japanese formations to pieces. The minutes ticked past. "Where in the goddamned hell is our Air Corps?" the men called to each other in mixed puzzlement and anger.

The Japanese bomber flights began circling impudently over Manila Bay as though they were passing in review for Emperor Hirohito back in Tokyo. They hovered over Fortress Corregidor—The Rock. Now they'll catch hell, Bob Kelly and his crewmen told each other. Corregidor bristled with antiaircraft guns. But the Japanese planners had known what they were doing. When the two score 3-inch guns on The Rock opened fire, the shells exploded 7,000 to 10,000 feet below the enemy bombers.

The Japanese flight commanders had been getting their bearings, making one last reconnaissance. Now they struck with fury and accuracy. At 12:47 P.M., the first bombs exploded on Nichols Field. The Nipponese pilots could hardly believe their good luck: down below lay their prey, huddled wingtip to wingtip. Coming in waves, the attackers hit with heavy bombers, dive bombers, and fighters. Zooming in low, Zeros and Zekes poured tracer bullets onto the sprawling air base, setting fire to one fuel tank after the other. In less than thirty minutes, Nichols Field and its aircraft had been demolished. The hangars and headquarters building were twisted wreckage; the once sleek warplanes were charred skeletons.

In the meantime, enemy dive bombers had pounced on shipping in Manila Bay, but only a few vessels were hit. The Japanese flights next turned their attention to Cavite Navy Yard. Out from the shore, Bulkeley and his men watched in anger as bombs exploding on their home base sent fiery orange balls skyward. Soon the three PT boats had an even more personal problem. Five dive bombers with the Rising Sun insignia peeled off and headed for them. The speeding boats twisted and dodged, and the lethal missiles, dropped from about twelve hundred feet, exploded harmlessly in the water.

The dive bombers returned to strafe the pesky PTs. But Bulkeley's gunners went into action, and with their .50-caliber machine guns began spewing tracer bullets toward the oncoming planes. Bulkeley's men relished the clash. After three days of frustrating idleness, they were finally getting a crack at their tormentors. MM2 Joseph C. Chalker, a "good ol' Texas boy" from Texarkana, fired until his gun barrels were red hot. His jaw was set; he was as cool as though he had been doing this all his life. And he was mad.* TM1 John L. Houlihan, Jr., of Chicopee Falls, Massachusetts, was blasting away with the other pair of fifties. He too was cool and angry.

Chalker and Houlihan concentrated their fire on one plane, and moments later the men saw the attacker begin to smoke, then wobble, before plunging into Manila Bay about two miles away. A shout of triumph rose from Buck Bulkeley's craft. The gunners on the three boats continued to fire at the darting bombers, and two more were seen to splash into the water.

Shooting down three Japanese dive bombers hardly avenged Pearl Harbor, Bulkeley and his men agreed; "But it's sure as hell a step in the right direction!" one crewman declared.

While the PT boat dive-bomber vendetta had been raging off-shore, the nearby Cavite Navy Yard had been transformed into a Dantesque inferno of fierce conflagrations and towering plumes of black smoke. Aware that the antiquated American antiaircraft guns could not reach them, Japanese bombers had swept over the Navy base for almost an hour dropping their lethal cargos at will. Direct hits were scored on nearly all buildings, and vessels along the shore had been set on fire. Cavite Navy Yard had been wiped off the map. So had Lieutenant Bulkeley's crucial spare parts, extra engines, equipment, and thousands of drums of high-octane gasoline desperately needed by his thirsty boats.

Across twenty-mile-wide Manila Bay, Lt. Bob Kelly and his three boats had been cruising offshore. Crewmen had been hoping that a few Japanese planes would attack them to give their gunners a crack at the enemy. But nothing had happened. Then Kelly received his third big jolt in the three-day-old war. High in the sky after dropping their loads on Cavite and Nichols, the Japanese bomber formations flew over on their return home, still in the same tight, parade-ground formation—and apparently without a plane missing. The PT warriors turned the azure sky a deeper shade of blue with their curses. Where in the hell *was* the United States Air Corps? How could our flyers let the Japs get by with this? Kelly now realized the magnitude of the disaster.

---

* Later in the war, Joseph C. Chalker was killed in action.

What skipper Bob Kelly and his little knot of men had no way of knowing was that, for all practical purposes, the United States Air Corps in the Philippines no longer existed. It had been wiped out in one fell swoop. The Japanese had bombed and strafed key American targets all over Luzon: Nichols Field, Clark Field, Nielson Field, Vigan, Rosales, San Fernando, and La Union.

Shortly after 3:00 P.M., the last bomber droned off into the distance. Again a curious hush fell over Manila Bay. Buck Bulkeley took his PTs into Cavite. No longer was there time to ponder over the to him mysterious and maddening absence of American fighter planes. Amid the shambles and chaos Bulkeley and his officers and men began loading grievously wounded survivors to take them to the Cañacao hospital. Reaching the landing at Cañacao, Bulkeley's group had a difficult time keeping their footing—the unloading platform was slick with fresh blood.

Once the wounded were unloaded, Lieutenant Bulkeley took his three craft back to Cavite, most of which was still engulfed in flames. He saw the base commander, Adm. Francis Rockwell, personally engaged in the perilous task of directing the fire apparatus in an effort to extinguish the blaze at the ammunition depot. "Better get out; it could blow at any moment," Rockwell told the PT skipper. Bulkeley offered the admiral a lift to the relative security of Bataan. No, Rockwell responded, his job was to remain at his post and try to save the ammunition depot.

At Imperial General Headquarters outside Tokyo that afternoon, Gen. Hideki Tojo and his commanders rejoiced. At the negligible cost of seven to ten fighter planes, the mighty Japanese war machine had eliminated Cavite Navy Yard and Nichols Field—two of the great obstacles to Tojo's massive drive into the South Pacific.

Two days after Cavite Navy Yard had been blasted to rubble, one of Bulkeley's men, Ens. George Cox, of Watertown, New York, returned to that base. The tall, blond ensign had volunteered as an ambulance driver for the French army in 1940 and had been awarded the croix de guerre for gallantry. Yet even he was horrified by the damage that Japanese bombs had inflicted at the yard. He estimated that over a thousand men had been killed, most of them Filipino workers. On this day they were burying the dead. It was such a gruesome task American officers had difficulty rounding up men for the job. Only after they had consumed large amounts of grain alcohol, gladly furnished by the Americans, did enough Filipinos come forward.

Ensign Cox saw that the burying procedure consisted of collecting heads, arms, legs, and torsos, pitching them into bomb craters, and shoving rubble over them. Cox saw one staggering Filipino rolling a bloody head along with a stick as though it were a hoop. The young ensign struggled to keep from vomiting.

That same day, twelve miles to the northwest, a nervous aide approached Gen. Douglas MacArthur and suggested that the American flag in front of his headquarters building in Manila be taken down permanently. It was highly conspicuous and could identify the structure for the Mitsubishi bombers regularly flying unmolested over the city. MacArthur bristled. "The flag stays," he declared. "Take every normal precaution, but keep Old Glory flying."

Meanwhile, with the destruction of the Cavite Navy Yard, Lt. Buck Bulkeley established a base—of sorts—for his six PT boats at Sisiman Bay, a small cove just east of Mariveles Harbor. The craft tied up to a rickety old fishing dock, and the men lived in nearby nipa huts, ramshackle straw structures on stilts. During the following week, the boats made daily patrols but did not spot a single Japanese vessel. Bulkeley and his men were both puzzled and frustrated. Where was the enemy?

Shortly before midnight on December 17, the SS *Corregidor*, a converted interisland steamship, was cutting through the dark waters of Manila Bay and heading for the exit. She was bound for the island of Cebu, crammed with some thousand men, women, and children, most of whom were Filipino civilians fleeing the capital. The *Corregidor* had a proud heritage. She had been an aircraft carrier during World War I, had fought at the battle of Jutland (the largest sea fight in history), and was said to have been the first ship to have launched an airplane in a combat situation.

Among the refugees on board were Americans Jack Fee, manager of the Cebu office of Standard-Vacuum Oil Company, and his wife, Dode, who was three months pregnant. The couple had a fourteen-month-old daughter back home in Cebu. Suddenly the old vessel's engines stopped, and the Fees felt the ship drifting. There was a total blackout. Then came an enormous explosion that echoed for miles across the dark seascape. The *Corregidor* had struck an American mine guarding the entrance to Manila Bay and was sinking rapidly. Jack and Dode Fee were knocked down. They struggled to their feet, donned life jackets, and worked their way out to the deck. Chaos reigned. Masses of milling humanity were trying desperately to climb into lifeboats. Shouts and screams pierced the dark. The Fees tried and failed to get into a lifeboat. Fee led his wife to an open deck under the captain's bridge. "Oh, my," Dode exclaimed. "I've forgotten my purse." Just then the *Corregidor* gave a final shudder and went under.

Fee's last conscious act was to give his wife a strong push and shout, "Start swimming!" Water engulfed her as she was dragged under. Finally an air bubble caught her, and she bounced to the surface like a bobbing cork. She screamed, "Jack! Jack!" several times. There was no answer. All around her in the water were oil drums and oil and screaming people. Hysteria took over. Dode's slacks had been ripped down to her ankles, so she kicked them off, along with her shoes. Now it was her time to panic; she had started swimming and found herself floundering alone in the black, cold water.

In the meantime, Jack Fee, after having given his wife a shove to clear her from the sinking ship, had caught his foot in a guy wire and was literally about to go down with the *Corregidor*.

The tremendous explosion when the vessel hit the mine woke John Bulkeley's men who were asleep at their nearby camp. They dashed out of the nipa huts to the shoreline and could see tiny lights flickering on the water. Three of the PT boats hurried to the scene. Scores of heads were bobbing about. Crews rigged ladders and pitched out lines to haul aboard the oily survivors. The refugees were so thick that when a line was tossed into the water ten or twelve frantic Filipinos would grasp it.

The PT men had pulled aboard so many passengers that their arms had grown weak. After an hour, all survivors had apparently been rescued; Bulkeley gave the order to head for shore. The engines had not yet been restarted and it was deathly still, quite ghostlike. Then, from out of the ominous dark, whistling was heard—a popular song. The men were dumbfounded.

One craft headed in the direction of the whistler and soon located him. He was an American pilot who had been blown far out into the water and away from the other passengers. Luck had smiled on him, for she had also blown three life preservers out with him. He had put one under his head, one under his posterior, and one under his feet and was floating with his hands folded over his stomach. Hauled aboard, the pilot said he couldn't swim. When asked why he had been whistling, the airman replied it was just to idle away the time until someone rescued him. Who did he think might happen along in the middle of black Manila Bay? He didn't know.

Oil-drenched Filipinos were sitting, lying, and standing on every inch of the relatively small PT boats. Not until the survivors were put ashore on Corregidor, at Mariveles, and then onto the SS *Si-Kiang* could they be counted; 296 had been rescued. Among them was the pregnant Dode Fee and her husband, Jack, who had finally wrenched free from the guy wire. Bulkeley's boat, a 77-footer built for two officers and nine men, itself had taken aboard 197 refugees. "The miracle of the loaves and fishes has been repeated," Bulkeley quipped.

Motor Torpedo Boat Squadron 1's "reward" for its rescue effort was to be notified the next morning that, due to an extreme food shortage, Navy personnel in the region would be put on two meals daily. Typically, the free-spirited Buck Bulkeley would respond: "Effective immediately, we will have breakfast, supper, and a stomach-ache for lunch."

These were nerve-racking days and nights for General MacArthur and Adm. Tommy Hart. MacArthur's "air force" consisted of four obsolete P-40 fighter planes. Japanese bombers and fighters roamed the Philippine sky at will. The enemy also controlled the ocean on all sides of Luzon. The American chiefs could only sit and wait for the certain amphibious invasion of Luzon. MacArthur was convinced that the Japanese would strike in the Lingayen Gulf, some 125 miles north of Manila, and drive southward over the central plain of Luzon to the capital.

Four days before Christmas the blow fell—right where Mac-Arthur said it would. At dawn, China veterans under Lt. Gen. Masaharu Homma stormed ashore unopposed. Untrained, undisciplined, confused Filipino soldiers threw away their ancient Enfield rifles and fled. By afternoon, General Homma's crack troops were pushing along Route 3, the old cobblestoned military highway that leads to Manila.

At this crucial point, General MacArthur and Admiral Hart, who hated each other intensely, got into a bitter dispute. Hart told the general that he was going to pull out his Asian Fleet and move his headquarters far south to the Dutch East Indies. MacArthur was livid. He accused the Navy of being "fearmongers" as a result of the Pearl Harbor catastrophe and declared that Hart's warships would have to remain behind and keep the sea lanes open if he, MacArthur, was to save the Philippines. Can't do it, Hart retorted caustically, the Japanese have too strong a blockade around the Philippines. It's only a "paper" blockade, MacArthur snapped.

The heated dispute took place at Tommy Hart's headquarters in Manila's two-story Marsman Building on Calle Santa Lucia. Three times the argument was interrupted when the Japanese bombed the structure.

After General MacArthur departed, Admiral Hart held his final conference with flag officers. All of them except for Adm. Francis Rockwell would sail for Java, Hart told them, taking with them nearly every naval vessel. Rockwell, who had established headquarters on Corregidor, would command the remaining "fleet": a few leaking old gunboats, a handful of ancient tugs, and Buck Bulkeley's six PT boats. When even this pitiful collection of vessels had been expended, junior officers and bluejackets were to fight as infantrymen under MacArthur.

Yet the Americans on Luzon remained defiant, confident that help was on the way. That same day Francis B. Sayre, American high commissioner in the Philippines, flashed an upbeat broadcast to the United States: "Out here on the firing line we have come to grips with reality. We are in the fight to stay. War enjoins upon us all for action, action, action. Time is of the essence. *Come on, America!*"

But America would not be "coming on." She had nothing to come on with. And unknown to anyone in the Pacific, based on a recommendation by an obscure brigadier general named Dwight D. Eisenhower in Washington, President Roosevelt and the Joint Chiefs of Staff had reached a fateful decision: the Philippines would be abandoned, written off.

Meanwhile, General Homma's tough veteran fighting men were flooding down Luzon's central plain, hell-bent for Manila, and by December 24 were on the outskirts of the capital. In order to spare Manila massive destruction and to save civilian lives, MacArthur declared it an open city, a notice to the enemy commander that no effort would be made to defend Manila. Less than an hour later a flight of

Mitsubishis heavily bombed the city, destroying the San Juan de La-trán college, the old Santo Domingo church, the Philippine *Herald* building and killing some two hundred civilians.

That night, Christmas Eve, MacArthur and other high ranking officers, like thieves in the night, slunk out of ghostlike Manila to Corregidor, the only locale in the Philippines that had communications with Washington. With the general were his young wife, Jean, and four-year-old son, Arthur.

One week later, on the night of December 31, a PT boat running on only one engine to muffle the noise slipped into dark and eerie Manila Bay. In the cockpit, Lt. Buck Bulkeley peered intently ahead as the craft neared the docks. The skipper and his men expected to be raked with fire at any moment.

Manila was burning. An orange glow and a death pall of smoke hovered over the doomed city once known as the Pearl of the Orient. The sight made the PT warriors both sick and angry. Bulkeley and his men had been sent on a mission to destroy what was left of harbor shipping to keep it out of the hands of the conquering Japanese. The skipper peeked at his luminous watch face. It was a few minutes before 9:00 P.M.

Bulkeley's venturesome spirit caused him to toy briefly with the idea of going ashore to see what mischief he and his men could cause the new landlords of Manila. But he quickly abandoned the suicidal notion. Far down a street, against a background of burning buildings, the Americans could spot the silhouettes of dome-helmeted Nipponese soldiers plodding along in columns.

Off to one side, near the wharf, Lieutenant Bulkeley discerned the outline of the large Army and Navy Club where he and other officers had spent many a happy social hour. It flashed through his mind that had it not been for the ambitions of the warlords in Tokyo, at this precise moment he would be in the club, drinking in the New Year with pals.

Now the Army and Navy Club stood dark and silent. Moments later Bulkeley's reverie was shattered. Lights flashed on inside the building. The Japanese were taking it over as a headquarters. Watching the lights come on made Bulkeley even angrier. At his elbow, Ens. Anthony Akers was furious also. "Goddamn them!" Akers exclaimed in a stage whisper. "I had to leave my spare uniforms in a locker there. I hope none of them fit the bastards!"

But there was much work—hazardous work—to be done. With enemy troops prowling about, the slightest noise could give away the fact that an American craft was in the harbor. The raiding party climbed into the smaller boats and sank them by bashing in their bottoms with axes. Each blow seemed to echo for miles. On larger craft, the men set explosives timed to detonate later. Six hours after arriving, at 3:00 A.M. on the first day of 1942, the Americans completed their sabotage mission. Powered by one motor, the PT slipped out of the dark harbor and headed across Manila Bay for Sisiman Cove on Bataan.

There, in the following days, the torpedo boat crews would have plenty of company, in General MacArthur's ground troops who were pulling back into the peninsula from all over Luzon to make their last stand.

Three miles from Bataan, deep in the tunnels of Fortress Corregidor, Admiral Rockwell, the tall, gray-haired commander of the Philippine "fleet," scrawled in his war diary: "Motor torpedo boats are rapidly deteriorating due to lack of spare parts and bad gasoline . . . Because of [constant] emergency trips and patrol duties their crews are becoming exhausted."

A gloomy assessment. But it would soon get even worse.

CHAPTER 3   The Wild Man of the Philippines

When Lt. John Bulkeley reported to his Corregidor headquarters—still designated grandly as the 16th Naval District—on January 18 he was handed a tersely written order by Capt. Herbert Ray, Admiral Rockwell's chief of staff: "Army reports four enemy ships in or lying off Port Binanga. Force may include one destroyer, one large transport. Send two boats, attack between dusk and dawn."

Returning to his base at Sisiman Cove, Bulkeley began preparing for the night's mission. By now, his daring, courage, seemingly unlimited supply of nervous energy, and his swashbuckling exploits had gained him a widely known nickname: Wild Man of the Philippines. A striking physical appearance strengthened that label; he looked like a cross between a bloodthirsty buccaneer and a shipwrecked survivor just rescued from months spent marooned on a desolate island. His shirt and trousers were soiled, wrinkled, and torn. He wore a long, black, unruly beard, and his green eyes were bloodshot and red rimmed from endless nights without sleep while out prowling the coasts. On each hip he carried a menacing pistol, and he clutched a tommy gun in a manner that caused others to believe he was itching to locate a Japanese to use it on. Bulkeley indeed was a wild man.

For that night's raid Bulkeley selected PT 31, skippered by Lt. Edward G. DeLong, of Santa Cruz, California, and PT 34, whose temporary captain was Ens. Barron W. Chandler. He would be pinch-hitting for Lt. Bob Kelly, who was hospitalized in a Corregidor tunnel with a serious infection. The Wild Man decided to go along "just for the hell of it."

The PT boats would be poking their noses into a hornets' nest. Port Binanga was located at the top of Subic Bay, which borders the northwest portion of Bataan. Both the bay and the port were infested with Japanese.

It was a very black midnight when the pair of PTs reached the entrance to Subic Bay. According to plan, the boats split up: Chandler and Bulkeley in 34 were to prowl up the western shore of the bay, and DeLong's 31 would sweep up the eastern side. The two boats would rendezvous outside Port Binanga, at the top of the bay. If they failed to join up there, each was to proceed on its own to attack the Japanese ships, then rendezvous just outside the Corregidor minefield at dawn.

No American vessels, including PT boats, had ventured into Subic Bay since the enemy had taken over there. On Bulkeley's and Chandler's boat, all hands were tense. They began to perspire despite the cooling ocean breeze. It was deathly still except for the purring of the muffled engines. Suddenly, the blackness was split by the beam of a powerful searchlight on shore. The PT was caught in its unyielding gaze. Men froze in place, faces were ghostlike in the glare, but the boat kept moving.

The PT quickly altered course and headed out into the bay. Now the dreaded *boom! boom! boom!* was heard, a coastal battery had opened fire. But its aim was faulty, and the shells splashed far from the boats.

Bulkeley's craft plowed onward. Minutes later a blinking light on a ship in the bay challenged the 34 boat. But the Americans could see she was a small craft, one not worth wasting a torpedo on. So they ignored the challenge and continued ahead.

Then all hell broke loose. Searchlights flashed on along the shoreline, and many big guns began blasting away. The Japanese apparently believed that the bay was being invaded by a task force of American warships. Bulkeley's men ducked instinctively as shells whistled overhead, but the speeding boat, skittering like a waterbug on a farmer's pond, escaped being hit.

Bulkeley eventually reached the rendezvous point outside Port Binanga at 1:00 A.M. DeLong never appeared. Bulkeley decided to go into the harbor on his own. Speed was cut to eight knots, and only two engines were running.* The harbor was tomblike. Bulkeley suddenly tensed. There she was! Less than five hundred yards away: the silhouette of the Japanese cruiser.

Like the keenly trained team that they were, PT 34's men quickly began arming two fish as the boat crept closer to the quarry. And closer. *Wham!* With the effect of a powerful blow to the face, a searchlight on the cruiser erupted in a blinding mass of brilliance. The 34 boat, only three hundred yards from the warship, was caught and held by the light; from it rang out the order "Fire!" and two torpedoes leapt forward.

At the wheel, Ensign Chandler gave a hard rudder right, and the boat roared off into the night. Glancing back, the men saw an enormous explosion at the cruiser's waterline, and a fireball shot into the night sky. Then in rapid order, two more blasts (probably ammunition magazines) rocked the enemy ship. But there was no time for elation over the first major "kill" of the war by a PT boat. Number 34 was in big trouble.

One of the torpedoes had malfunctioned and failed to clear its tube. It stuck there, half in and half out, propellers whirling madly, compressed air hissing with an earsplitting din. Crew members hardly dared to exhale. All knew that a torpedo was designed not to fire until its propellers had made a specified number of revolutions. After that, the torpedo was cocked, much like a rifle, and a blow on its nose, such as a slap by a wave, could cause it to explode, blowing PT and crew to smithereens.

Every man knew that the propeller had to be stopped, and stopped quickly. But what to do? TMC John Martino, of Waterbury, Connecticut, dashed to the head and grabbed a handful of toilet paper, then jumped astride the hissing, quivering torpedo as though it were a horse. He began cramming toilet paper into the vanes of the propeller, and with a groan of protest, the blades stopped spinning.

PT 34 had stopped dead in the water for this ticklish operation, but now Ensign Chandler threw the throttle forward and the boat roared

---

* A knot, or nautical mile, is the equivalent of 1.1516 statute miles per hour. One knot is 6076.115 feet (1852 meters).

off toward the mouth of Subic Bay. Despite her mortal wounds, the Japanese cruiser opened fire with her big guns, and other artillery pieces on shore joined in. None of the shells could find the zigzagging waterbug, and the PT returned safely to the dawn rendezvous point outside the Corregidor minefield where Bulkeley and Chandler were to meet Lieutenant DeLong's PT 31. Dawn arrived; DeLong did not.

After Bulkeley and DeLong had parted company at the entrance to Subic Bay just before midnight, DeLong almost immediately ran into trouble. His craft developed engine trouble—saboteur's soluble wax in the gasoline had clogged the strainers of his engines. The crew, working by muted lights, quickly cleaned them. Minutes after getting underway again, the cooling system conked out. As the crew was making frantic repairs, the boat drifted aimlessly. Then there was an alarming crunching sound. They had run aground on a reef.

The crew rocked the boat and raced the engines in a desperate effort to back off. For three hours they labored, until the reverse gears were burned out. They were still aground. On shore, the Japanese finally heard the racket and a gun of perhaps 3-inch caliber opened fire from Ilinin Point. The shells splashed closer and closer. Lieutenant DeLong gave the order all skippers dread: abandon ship!

There was no panic. The crew hastily wrapped mattresses in a tarpaulin to make a raft, and all but DeLong scrambled onto it. He remained behind to rip up the gas tanks and blow a hole in the boat's bottom with a hand grenade before setting it afire. All the while, Japanese shells were seeking out the stranded Devil Boat. His work done and the boat ablaze, DeLong tried to spot the raft in the darkness, but when ammunition on the PT began to explode, he had to give up and clamber across the reef onto the beach. Meanwhile, the raft had been drifting out into the bay. On it were Ens. William H. Plant, of Long Beach, California; the second officer; and eleven bluejackets.

Just before dawn, Ensign Plant and the others on the raft held a hurried council of war. They feared that first light would expose them to the Japanese, so nine men decided to swim for shore, where they could hide. Remaining behind on the raft were three men who could not swim: Ensign Plant, MM1 Rudolph Ballough, of Norwood, Massachusetts, and QM3 William R. Dean, of Ogden, Utah. The three would never be heard from again.

At daylight, Lieutenant DeLong began stealing southward along the shoreline. A half-mile later he spotted fresh tracks in the sand, followed them, and found nine crewmen hiding in a clump of bushes. All through the day the men had to remain motionless and carefully concealed. Just to the south a fierce battle was raging for the village of Moron, and Japanese warplanes were overhead. Between them, DeLong and his men had only one rifle and six pistols. So the skipper told his men that, unless they were rushed by far superior numbers, they should allow Japanese scouts to come into the clump of bushes and then "club their brains out" with the butts of the rifle and pistols.

It soon became clear that Japanese were on all sides. A lookout in a tree scrambled down to report excitedly that two Nipponese armored cars or light tanks about a mile to the north were headed toward the hiding Americans. There was no time to lose. DeLong spotted two *banca*s (native boats) a few hundred yards down the beach and sent four men to investigate. They reported that the *banca*s appeared seaworthy, so at dusk, in a column with wide intervals between each man, the ten marooned warriors crawled silently through the thick underbrush behind the beach to the *banca*s. They had found a board and two shovels to use as paddles. It was pitch black when they shoved off, at about 10:00 P.M. Enemy voices could be heard all around them from less than two hundred yards away.

Motivated by dim, flickering lights that indicated Japanese were all along the shoreline, the Americans paddled furiously. Thirty minutes after shoving off, heavy winds came up lashing the water, and both *banca*s capsized. By superhuman effort, the little craft were righted and the men climbed back in. One shovel had been lost, so now there was but one board and one shovel to paddle the two *banca*s.

For five hours the men battled the headwinds, taking turns with the improvised paddles. By 3:00 A.M., they were exhausted. A crucial decision was made; not knowing if there would be Americans or Japanese to greet them, they made for shore. There, after crossing a barbed-wire entanglement, they found themselves confronted by a steep cliff. DeLong told his men to wait right there until daylight.

With the first faint tinges of gray in the dark sky, Ed DeLong and the others spotted a helmeted figure holding a rifle with fixed bayonet a short distance up the beach. Friend or enemy? As the sky lightened, the sentry approached the exhausted, hungry little group. "Hey, Joe, got a cig-ret and match?" the Filipino sentinel asked in broken English.

Lieutenant DeLong and the others issued a collective sigh of relief; they had landed in friendly territory. That night the escapees were back at the Squadron 3 base at Sisiman Cove. But the loss of PT 31 had cut the squadron's unit strength by one-third, from six PTs when war broke out to four. One craft had run aground on Christmas Eve, could not be dislodged, and had to be destroyed.

For more than two weeks now, Lt. Bob Kelly had been a royal pain in the neck to harried doctors in the hospital in Corregidor's tunnels. At the insistance of Bulkeley, Kelly had gone there for treatment of an infected finger, an infection that had grown so serious Kelly had lost nearly thirty-five pounds. Despite the heavy drain on his strength, the lanky young skipper had been badgering doctors nearly every day to let him return to combat duty with his squadron.

On the morning following the raid into the hornets' nest in Subic Bay, Lieutenant Kelly once more collared his military physician. "Now you've got to let me go!" he exclaimed in a tone that sounded much like an order. "We've lost a third officer in our squadron [Ensign Plant]. There's a war on and I've spent all the time I intend to nursing a sore finger!"

The doctor threw up his hands in surrender. Kelly scrambled off his cot and returned to Sisiman Cove. Two nights later he took PT 34 up the coast of Bataan toward the hotbed of Subic Bay. John Bulkeley, as usual, went along—"just for the hell of it." It was a calm, quiet night, even monotonous. Then the monotony was broken. Guns on shore began firing at them. Bulkeley burst out with a series of colorful oaths. He could tell by the tracers that these were American guns blasting away at the craft and he calmly altered course.

"The main problem these nights," Bulkeley complained to Kelly, "is trying to keep from being sunk by our own side on shore. Half the time those dumb bastards don't know friend from foe."

Only minutes later the dim outline of a vessel was spotted, and the PT headed toward it. Lieutenant Bulkeley warned the men to hold their fire; the craft might have been stolen by Ens. Bill Plant and the other two men missing in Lieutenant DeLong's misadventure in Subic Bay a few nights earlier. General quarters (each man at his battle station) was sounded, and gunners crouched tensely as PT 34 slowed only seventy-five feet from the craft. Bulkeley raised a megaphone and called out: "Boat ahoy!"

Br-r-r-r-r. Machine-gun bullets hissed past the Wild Man's head.

Now a full-scale shoot-out erupted. All on board boat 34 joined in. The four .50-caliber machine guns were chattering raucously. Bulkeley grabbed a tommy gun and riddled the enemy vessel. Men below reached for their rifles, scrambled topside, and opened fire. Plenty of lead was coming back in answer.

As the heavy fusillades lit up the seascape, the Americans could see that their adversary was a motorized barge, about fifty feet long, crammed with helmeted soldiers. The PT, at full speed, began circling the barge. Bulkeley was inserting a new tommy-gun clip when he heard a yelp of pain behind him. He turned to see Ensign Chandler slumped in the cockpit, writhing in agony and bleeding profusely from both legs. A bullet had gone through both of his ankles.

Bob Kelly and Bulkeley dragged Chandler from the cockpit and stretched him out on a canopy. As a pharmacist's mate injected the ensign with morphine, 34 continued to circle and pump lead into the barge, which gave one last gurgle and went under. About thirty minutes later, as PT 34 was stalking the coast in search of more victims, the boat was raked by heavy machine-gun fire from the shore. The weapons were manned by itchy-fingered American soldiers. A chorus of curses rang out on the boat as chains of tracer bullets zipped past overhead. "Oh, what the hell," John Bulkeley exclaimed, shrugging his shoulders. "Our Army seems to enjoy shooting at us—and the bastards can't hit anything, anyhow!"

It was now nearly dawn, and 34 set a course for home. In the growing light, Bulkeley spotted a flat, low-slung vessel and was eager to go after it. But the "squad dog" (as the Navy called squadron commanders) knew that his crew had had a rough night, so he put the question to them. Let's go after the bastard, they chorused. Revenge for Ensign Chandler!

They raced toward the vessel, and at three hundred yards the PT's fifties opened fire. The barge was heavily plated. Bullets ricocheted off her, shooting sparks a hundred feet in the air. She kept moving, even as the PT closed to within fifty feet and continued to riddle her with bullets. Suddenly an American bullet hit her fuel tank, and fire mushroomed upward. The barge's engines halted, and she drifted aimlessly.

"Pull up alongside her," the Wild Man of the Philippines called out to Bob Kelly at the wheel. "I'm going to board the bastard."

The enemy vessel was still full of fight. As Kelly eased the 34 next to her, the Japanese on board gave a hard rudder and tried to ram the PT. Now the Wild Man was furious. He grabbed several hand grenades and pitched them into the enemy craft. Then, clutching a tommy gun, he leapt onto the other vessel. He landed in several inches of liquid: a mixture of water, oil, and blood.

Lieutenant Bulkeley rapidly glanced around. Dead Japanese marines, perhaps twenty-seven of them, were sprawled grotesquely on the slimy deck. Three on board were still alive but badly wounded. One was a captain, and he pleaded with Bulkeley: "Me surrender! Me surrender!" Bulkeley put a line around the enemy officer's shoulders and hoisted him aboard. Then he repeated the process with the other pair.

Hastily, for the barge was sinking, Bulkeley began rummaging around in the sludge for papers, briefcases, and knapsacks. He collected enough to fill both arms, then was pulled into the boat as the barge went under. PT 34 began racing back to its mooring in Sisiman Cove.

A crewman with a .45 Colt was standing guard over the wounded captain, who was kneeling with eyes closed, waiting for a bullet through his head. John Bulkeley, who minutes before had been blasting away at the Japanese marines, now gently wiped the oil from the captain's eyes and examined his head wound. This act convinced the Japanese officer that the Americans were not going to shoot him, so he became surly. One prisoner, a dying private no more than five feet tall and looking about eighteen years old, asked feebly for a cigarette. A blue-jacket lit one and held it in the boy's mouth as he took a few puffs.

"What a crazy world," Lieutenant Kelly exclaimed to Bulkeley. "A few minutes ago we had all been pumping steel, hating every Jap in the world. Now we aren't mad anymore. Now we're sorry for these two—the little half-pint guy, even that arrogant bastard captain!"

John Bulkeley nodded his head in agreement. He couldn't understand it, either.

Bulkeley, Kelly, and the crew watched impassively as the little Japanese private lay on deck taking drags from the cigarette. The boy had five bullet holes in him, but he never moaned or even grimaced. He would be dead in a few hours. Reaching the dock at Bataan, the

men carried Ensign Chandler and the wounded Japanese off the boat.*
The documents Lieutenant Bulkeley had scooped up from the sludge on the sinking Japanese vessel proved to be a bonanza for Intelligence officers. One was an operation order that revealed the Nipponese were landing a force (a few barge-loads at a time during darkness) of eight hundred to one thousand marines behind American lines on Bataan. They were to hide in caves until the entire force had been assembled, then attack American ground forces from the rear. The two vessels sunk by Bulkeley's and Kelly's PT 34 had been engaged in this landing operation, and already some four hundred Japanese were concealed in caves.

Later that day, Navy officers rounded up three old gunboats that lay to off the shoreline and peppered the caves with machine-gun and shell fire. The sneak attack against unsuspecting American ground forces on Bataan had been broken up.

Since pulling back into Bataan on January 6, Gen. Douglas MacArthur's soldiers had been fighting for their lives. Bataan, a wild and desolate peninsula that forms the western shore of Manila Bay, is a montage of rocky hills and jungles, a forbidding green wilderness infested with crocodiles, snakes, and the world's largest pythons.

On paper, MacArthur seemed to be in good shape. He had 80,000 troops on Bataan—15,000 Americans and 65,000 Filipinos. However, they were poorly equipped, armed with ancient weapons, and only 2,000 Americans and 1,500 Filipino Scouts were considered fully trained as skilled combat soldiers. MacArthur's men fought desperately, but obsolete weapons refused to fire, old equipment wouldn't work, ammunition was short, aged belts of machine-gun bullets fell apart while being loaded, four out of five grenades failed to explode, and two-thirds of the mortar shells fired were duds.

Bitter toward their country, bitter toward MacArthur, knowing that they were doomed, the beseiged Battered Bastards of Bataan (as they now called themselves) fought on. They had been written off by the highest councils in Washington, sacrificed to buy precious time.

---

* Ens. Barron W. Chandler was taken to the hospital on Corregidor and was captured when The Rock fell on May 6, 1942. He was liberated when American forces returned to the Philippines more than two years later.

CHAPTER 4 MacArthur's "Impossible" Escape

As was his daily custom, on January 24 Lt. John Bulkeley took a PT boat from Sisiman Cove three miles across Manila Bay and tied up at a Corregidor dock. He was headed for Admiral Rockwell's tunnel headquarters to receive his orders for the night. Bulkeley had to take cover in a ditch before proceeding, as the Japanese were bombing The Rock heavily and pounding it with artillery, a daily occurrence.

It was 10:00 A.M. when the squadron skipper breezed into Rockwell's command post, just in time to hear the anxiously awaited newscast over shortwave radio station KGEI in San Francisco (6:00 P.M. California time). Bulkeley and the other eager listeners crowding around the old receiving set could hardly believe their ears. A harebrained announcer, safely perched eight thousand miles from the Philippines, after giving a news summary, exclaimed in a taunting tone: "This is for you, Tokyo. I *dare* you to bomb Corregidor!" In the dark tunnels of the battered Rock, curses, long and loud, rang out.

That night Bulkeley and DeLong were headed for Subic Bay once again. Due to rapidly dwindling supplies of gasoline, they took only one boat, Ens. George Cox's PT 41. No one aboard had any way of knowing that in another two months battle-worn PT 41 would become world famous—in the States, a household name. It was just before 10:00 P.M. as 41 neared the entrance to Subic Bay when, in a cove near Sampaloc Point, the men identified the shadowy outline of what appeared to be an anchored transport, 4,000 to 6,000 tons, of new construction. Crewmen sprang to their battle stations as the PT, running on one engine to reduce the noise, began creeping toward the juicy target. When the PT was within twenty-five hundred yards, all engines were opened up and the boat began racing toward the transport. It was heading into a Japanese trap designed to snare the PT boats as a spiderweb a fly.

Just in the nick of time, the crew spotted entanglements and wires floating in the water, and the boat swerved to avoid them. These obstacles were intended to foul propellers and leave PTs dead in the water, helpless targets for Japanese shore guns. With Cox at the wheel and DeLong at the torpedo director, number 41 closed to within eight hundred yards and fired one torpedo. Moments later gunners on the Nipponese vessel, which apparently had been the bait for the trap, opened with a heavy fusillade. Shells crashed and bullets hissed, but the PT roared onward, and at four hundred yards loosed a second fish.

Then Ensign Cox gave a hard turn on the rudder and raced alongside the transport; the four machine guns raked the enemy ship. It was a running gunfight; the Japanese were pouring lead back. Suddenly there was a shattering explosion that lit up the darkness. One torpedo had rammed into the transport, seeming to lift it right out of the water. Geyserlike bits and pieces of wreckage spurted into the sky and fell back all around the racing PT 41.

"Let's get the hell out of here!" the squadron skipper called out. Now a shore battery of 3-inch guns opened up and sent shells splashing into the water on all sides of the speeding boat. As the PT neared the open sea, George Cox, at the wheel, missed the floating wire entanglements by only twenty yards.

By the end of January, both the Battling Bastards of Bataan and the warriors of Motor Torpedo Boat Squadron 3 were desperately fighting not one, but two enemies: the determined Japanese and the pangs of extreme hunger. Foot soldiers were down to a cup or two of rice daily. Bulkeley's men had been luckier. They had discovered a cache of canned salmon, and for several weeks they had been eating this seafood morning, noon, and night.

Hungry as the men were, they soon grew nauseated over the very thought of canned salmon. So one man with a .45 plugged a tomcat, which had been roaming the premises. The feline was thoroughly boiled, and that night it was eaten. Buck Bulkeley, always upbeat, thought it tasted great. A lot like roast duck, he remarked. The others didn't agree; they thought it tasted like boiled tomcat.

In early February, Lieutenant Bulkeley was in his squadron headquarters, a concrete building for goat slaughtering, when he was called on by an artillery major. Gaunt and weary, the hollow-eyed Army officer explained that a large-caliber Japanese gun battery up the Bataan coast had been pounding his own artillery positions, and that observers were unable to spot the enemy weapons. Could the lieutenant help? He'd try.

Bulkeley sent for Ensign Cox and briefed him on a mission—a daylight mission. Cox was to take the artillery major up the western Bataan shoreline and, when he reached the suspected locale of the big guns, he was to cruise slowly back and forth. Cox's PT boat would serve as a decoy to unmask the enemy guns by tempting them to fire. When the battery opened up, the major was to chart positions. Later, his own artillery would pound the Japanese guns.

Neither George Cox nor his crew were enthused over their new role as the Army's bait. But at 5:00 P.M. that day their PT shoved off and headed up the western Luzon coast. As planned, Cox's boat loitered near the shoreline, its crew members expecting to be blasted out of the water at any moment. But the Japanese refused to bite.

On the way home, the crewmen were watching intently for a likely target. They soon spotted it. Along a beach, perhaps 150 Japanese soldiers, stripped down to their white underdrawers, were frolicking happily in the surf. Cox knew that they were Japanese, not natives, because some of them were wearing glasses. Apparently the enemy soldiers thought the PT was Nipponese, for they pointed tauntingly at it and laughed. It was the last thing some of them would ever do.

Suddenly there was grating br-r-r-r from the PT boat as all four fifties began firing into the midst of the frolickers. There were screams and loud shouts as bullets found their marks. The panicked soldiers scrambled to get out of the surf and off the beaches. Those who were able to ran frantically into underbrush above the shoreline. Floating facedown in the surf and lying crumpled on the sand were some fifteen Japanese, victims of the unexpected attack.

On into February, Squadron 3 continued its nightly patrols, stalking up and down the dark shorelines in search of Nipponese vessels or other targets of opportunity. It was on the night of the seventeenth that two PTs led by Lieutenants Bulkeley and Kelly once more stuck their necks into the Japanese noose at Subic Bay, shot up the shoreline with streams of tracers while racing by at full speed, fired their torpedoes at a large enemy vessel tied up at a dock at Olongapo, and executed the classic naval maneuver known technically as "hauling ass."

Back at Sisiman Cove, the Squadron 3 officers held a council of war. They concluded that the time was nearly at hand when their four battered PT boats should make a dash for the China coast, some thousand miles to the northwest, where they would continue the fight against the Rising Sun. Torpedoes were gone, except for four to take to China, and gasoline containers were nearly empty. Even the most optimistic fighting man knew that Bataan was doomed, that no help was on the way.

A week later, in his cramped, dank office in the Malinta Hill tunnel on Corregidor, General MacArthur received a signal from President Roosevelt, dated February 23, ordering him to Australia to "assume command of all U.S. troops [there]." MacArthur, who had already made a pledge to die fighting with his men on Corregidor, was plunged into gloom. He was skewered on the horns of a dilemma, he told his staff. If he disobeyed President Roosevelt, he could be court-martialed. If he followed the order, he would be deserting his trapped Battered Bastards of Bataan.

MacArthur could not bring himself to leave. His staff pleaded with him to go, pointing out that his taking charge of the Army in Australia was the best hope for salvaging the situation in the Philippines. Ten days later Roosevelt prodded the reluctant general: "Situation in Australia indicates desirability of your early arrival."

Three more days went by before MacArthur made up his mind to go. On March 9 he sent for the skipper of Motor Torpedo Boat Squadron 3, who the general called "Johnny Bulkeley, the buckaroo with the cold green eyes." Ten days earlier, MacArthur had confided to Bulkeley that he had been ordered out of the Philippines by the president and that the PT boats would play the key role in his escape. Now MacArthur gave Bulkeley the specific time of departure: sunset Wednesday, March 11.

Four decrepit motor torpedo boats, all barely gasping after numerous transfusions of cannibalized parts, would carry General

MacArthur and his party on the first six-hundred-mile leg of the long trek to Australia. Operating in total darkness, largely through uncharted waters, the PTs would have to infiltrate the Japanese naval blockade and slip undetected past enemy-held islands in order to reach Mindanao, the southernmost large island of the Philippines. There, heavy bombers sent from Australia were to pick up the refugees from Corregidor.

The men of Squadron 3, let in on the secret for the first time, took the startling news with grim resignation. The dash to China had vanished, and with it went their hopes of seeing America again and escaping death or a Japanese prison camp.

On returning to Sisiman Cove, Buck Bulkeley sent for his officers: Bob Kelly, Anthony Akers, George Cox, and Vincent Schumacher. The squadron leader, solemn for once, outlined the escape plan. He stressed that the four PTs should keep together, but if one broke down, the others were to continue and let the stalled craft manage for itself. The enemy was to be avoided if at all possible, but if swift Japanese vessels were to give chase and were overtaking the American craft, Bob Kelly was to lead three of the PTs in an attack on the pursuers. Bulkeley's PT 41, carrying General MacArthur, the man who would lead America back to the Philippines and on to Tokyo, would race off and try to escape.

Bulkeley shifted uneasily, fidgeted with pencils, and turned his gaze downward. This fleeing while his men fought was not to Bulkeley's liking. He had always been the one in the forefront of the action. But all present knew that the primary objective of the mission was to get General MacArthur to Australia, so this contingency plan was solid.

Meanwhile, in the gloomy tunnels of Corregidor, Navy officers were whispering to each other about the imminent escape. Knowing the enormous obstacles, they were giving one in five odds that it would succeed.

In Tokyo, and in Washington eleven thousand miles away, the impending effort had become something of an open secret. Reporters at presidential press conferences in the White House were asking such questions as: "When is General MacArthur going to leave Corregidor? Where is he going to go?" In the Japanese capital, Tokyo Rose was beaming it gleefully over the airwaves that the American general was going to be captured and put on public display in a cage in the large square fronting the emperor's palace.*

Typically, Buckaroo Bulkeley approached the daring escape mission as though it were just another day at the office. Yet, deep inside he knew that it would take little short of a miracle for the operation to succeed. If by some chance the four PTs were to evade the Nipponese dragnet, it was doubtful if the craft themselves could withstand the pounding. Engines were meant to be changed every few hundred hours, but after three months of heavy use on combat missions, without spare parts or adequate maintenance, Squadron 3 had already quadrupled the engines' normal life span. Due to their being clogged with rust, the once powerful engines could attain a top speed of perhaps twenty-seven miles per hour, a pace that would allow many Japanese vessels to overtake the PTs.

None of the PTs were equipped with a pelorus (a navigational instrument having two sight vanes), so a course would be followed using ancient methods: a simple compass and dead reckoning.

As time approached for departure, ominous danger signals emerged. Filipino coast watchers radioed Corregidor that a Japanese destroyer flotilla was steaming north from the southern Philippines at full throttle. Other lookouts reported a considerable increase in Nipponese activity in Subic Bay, north of Corregidor. Enemy reconnaissance planes in recent days had tripled their sweeps over The Rock.

The sun was just dipping into the western horizon when Lieutenant Bulkeley's war-weary PT 41 slipped up to Corregidor's North Dock along what was known as Bottomside. Over him, looming like a huge bulbous head, was the rugged, 550-foot-high Topside, with its once immaculate parade ground now littered with debris and its rows of troop barracks smashed by bombs and shells. On all sides, Bulkeley saw utter destruction: every shed and building was a twisted wreckage, charred and grotesque.

As PT 41's Packards idled, General MacArthur and his party arrived. His wife Jean's valise contained a dress and a pantsuit, and

---

* Later in the war when the tide began to turn against the Japanese, Tokyo Rose's line became more vicious. Instead of being put on public display in the square, she declared, MacArthur would be hanged as a war criminal at that location.

little Arthur's nurse Ah Cheu's belongings were in a folded handerchief. Arthur carried a stuffed toy, and the general, clad in worn khaki, did not have an ounce of luggage, not even a razor (he had slipped a toothbrush into his pocket). A tiny mattress was brought aboard for Arthur.*

The four-star general was the last to board. For several moments he stood alone on the shell-torn dock, a forlorn figure—even a dejected one. He looked up at rugged Topside towering majestically over Manila Bay and lifted his gold-braided Philippine marshal's cap in a final salute. MacArthur's face was drawn and ashen; his emotional torment palpable. Not only was a proud Douglas MacArthur being forced to slink away like a sneak thief in the night, but he was taking with him the honor of an unprepared America.

MacArthur replaced his cap, stepped aboard, and remarked evenly to Lieutenant Bulkeley, "You may cast off when ready, Johnny." PT 41 edged out into Manila Bay. It was now pitch black, for there was no moon. At 7:00 P.M., precisely on schedule, 41 linked up with PTs 32, 34, and 35 outside the Corregidor mine field. In order to attract the least attention possible, the others had picked up their passengers in obscure coves and inlets on Bataan. Already crewmen had grown anxious. A last-minute reconnaissance by a patched-up P-40 fighter plane had disclosed that a Japanese cruiser and a destroyer were charging in the direction of these precise waters.

On the torpedo boats were sixteen passengers—fourteen Army, two Navy—who MacArthur had carefully selected to join him in the dash for Australia. They were key personnel the general would need when he reached his Down Under destination. Rank made no difference; all were specialists. There was even a staff sergeant, a technician. Left behind on Bataan were more than twenty of MacArthur's generals.

---

* Although only a handful of Americans witnessed the top-secret departure, long after the war thousands of servicemen swore they had been present and had seen all of the MacArthur's household furniture being loaded aboard the PT boat. This would have been quite a trick; virtually every foot of the tiny craft was occupied by gasoline barrels, and prior permission would have had to have been obtained from the enemy commander to remove the family furniture from the Manila Hotel penthouse in the Japanese-held capital.

The escapees and crew members were perched on powder kegs. Each craft had on its deck twenty steel drums, each filled with fifty gallons of high-octane gasoline. An enemy bullet igniting fuel fumes could quickly turn the plywood boats into raging torches. In single file, with Bulkeley's 41 out in front, the PTs slipped out of Manila Bay. Behind them roared Corregidor's big guns, being fired at Japanese positions on Bataan to mask MacArthur's departure. Bulkeley set a straight course out to sea. Presently, the Americans spotted huge bonfires on the shores of the Apo islands, the historic signal that a night escape through a blockade is being attempted. Clearly enemy coast watchers were signaling Japanese leaders on Luzon that the MacArthur flotilla had passed. Enemy warplanes could be expected overhead at dawn.

Back in Lt. Bob Kelly's boat, Admiral Rockwell was beginning to show concern. The boat was dropping steadily farther behind the others—fifty yards, one hundred yards, then two hundred yards. The young skipper, not wanting to alarm the commander of the Philippine's "fleet" unduly, had not advised the admiral that his was the only boat of the four that had not been overhauled, and that the engines were so filled with carbon that they could not gain much speed until the carbon had burned out.

Eventually, Kelly's 34 was so far behind the others that they were out of sight. Rockwell snapped, "Goddamn it, let's close up!" Bulkeley now noticed that Kelly was lagging, so he slowed and permitted PT 34 to catch up.

At this point, the lieutenant thought he had better tell the admiral the true reason for his boat's sluggish performance. "My God," Rockwell muttered softly. Knowing that 34 might go dead in the water at any moment, Admiral Rockwell suggested that Kelly take a bearing to determine how far they were from shore. Kelly said he couldn't. Why not? Because he had no pelorus. Does Bulkeley have one? No. Then how did the PT flotilla intend to navigate? "By guess and by God," Kelly replied nonchalantly. This time Rockwell thundered: *"My God!"*

The inevitable happened. At 3:00 A.M. Kelly's engines went dead. PT 34 drifted aimlessly. As crewmen began frantically cleaning wax and rust from the strainers, the other PTs pulled out of sight. That was the plan; no boats were to halt for any that had become disabled. In thirty-five minutes the engines coughed, then turned over, and the

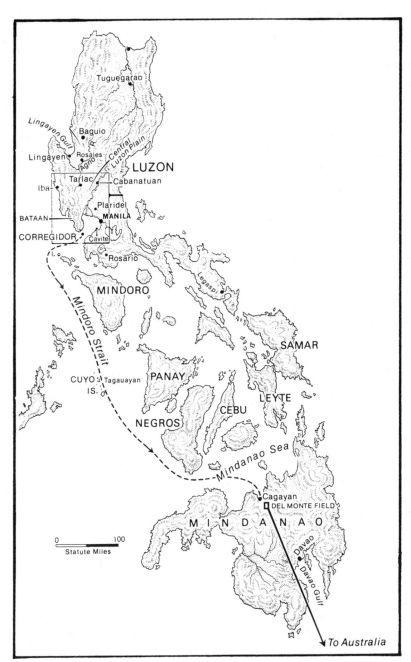

MacArthur's Escape from Corregidor (U.S. Navy)

boat continued onward. Dawn was approaching, so Kelly headed for a cove in the Cuyo Islands that had been designated as an emergency rendezvous in the event the PT boats became scattered in the darkness. He could only hope that the other PTs had picked out the same rendezvous.

PT 32, skippered by Lt. Vincent S. Schumacher of Kalamazoo, Michigan, had also gone astray. At dawn, Schumacher spotted a Japanese destroyer racing toward him. The enemy vessel appeared to be gaining, so the drums of gasoline—crucial if 32 was going to reach Mindanao—were pitched overboard. Even with the PT's heavy load jettisoned, the destroyer continued to close the gap. Schumacher ordered torpedoes to be fired at the pursuing vessel, but just before the fish were sent plunging into the water, an Army officer on board shouted, "Hold your fire!" He had recognized the other craft as Bulkeley's 41, with General MacArthur and his family as passengers. The early morning mists had played strange tricks with the contours of PT 41 and nearly caused disaster.

In the meantime, Lt. Bob Kelly's 34 had reached the designated cove and was later joined by Schumacher's and Bulkeley's boats. As the pair of late arrivals tied up, Kelly caught a glimpse of MacArthur sitting calmly in a wicker chair on deck, soaking wet. Next to him was his wife, Jean, smiling and also drenched to the skin. Four-year-old Arthur was happily chasing Tojo, a pet monkey belonging to the 41's cook.

All that day the trio of PTs hid from the Japanese aircraft and warships that were searching the region. Crews worked feverishly on engines, inspected hulls and sides for damage (the boats had taken a beating), and waited for Ens. Anthony Akers's PT 35 to arrive. Akers would never show up. Only later would Bulkeley learn that the 35 boat had broken down, its passengers and crew had made their own way to Mindanao.

At noon, General MacArthur, Admiral Rockwell, and Lieutenant Bulkeley huddled to ponder a critical question: in order to reach Mindanao on schedule (they were already behind), should they continue in daylight, thereby adding enormously to the hazards? Or should they wait for dawn the next day when the submarine *Permit* was to arrive at the Cuyo island cove to provide General MacArthur with an option for the remainder of the trek to Mindanao?

The general was leaning toward taking the submarine, but

Rockwell pointed out that the *Permit* might never show up. The admiral declared: "We'd better get out of here—fast!" Self-assured as always, John Bulkeley was in no way awed by powwowing with a famed four-star general and the Navy commander in the Philippines. Bulkeley warned that the sea would probably become even more turbulent, but recommended that MacArthur and his party continue to Mindanao on the PT boats.

MacArthur was faced with a difficult decision. Despite the added perils of traveling in daylight, the schedule was the primary consideration. He and his party were to arrive at the port of Cagayan on Mindanao at sunrise the next day, Friday. If they did not show up, they could be given up as lost, and the heavy bombers sent from Australia might be ordered to return without them. Finally, MacArthur turned to Bulkeley and said evenly, "Well, Johnny, let's go."

At 4:30 P.M., PTs 41 and 34 cast off. Schumacher's boat 32 was left behind, its passengers divided between the 41 and 34.

Twenty minutes after they pulled out of the cove, a lookout on Bulkeley's boat called out: "Sail-ho! Looks like a Jap cruiser!" The PT squadron leader grabbed his high-power binoculars. Sure enough, she was a cruiser: a large, heavily armed, thickly plated warship capable of making thirty-eight knots. The PTs were moving at only twenty knots, and on their present course would cut directly across the cruiser's bow. Bulkeley shouted orders to alter the course and take evasive action, and as those on board held their breaths, the boats raced off with open throttles. Passengers and crew members alike sighed with relief as the enemy warship eventually disappeared from view. Apparently, the froth whitened waves had masked the PT boats from lookouts on the cruiser.

Later in the day a Japanese destroyer was spotted directly ahead, and again the PT boats took evasive action and escaped detection. Just after sundown, as the tiny flotilla was passing Negros Island, a coastal battery's searchlights suddenly flipped on to pierce the night sky. The enemy had apparently heard the sound of the PT's engines and thought American warplanes were overhead. As silently as possible, Bulkeley's boats slipped past, almost under the muzzles of the Japanese guns.

Throughout much of the trek, General MacArthur had been violently ill and lying on a bunk in 41's lower cockpit. The general was in such torment that he constantly ground his teeth. Jean MacArthur was crouched on the floor next to her husband, constantly chafing his hands to improve circulation. She too was ill, having vomited several times. Although she had heard the periodic outbreaks of excitement above, knew that the PTs had been in extreme danger several times, she had never shown any sign of fear or even concern.*

Landlubbers on Bob Kelly's 34 were also deathly ill from the ceaseless jolting. One general, draped over a torpedo tube on deck, refused the offer of a young sailor to help him below, away from the unremitting stream of salt spray that was deluging him. "No, no," the general moaned. "Let me die here!"

After sunset that Thursday, the fleeing little boats were struck by a violent storm. Heaving angry waves, perhaps fifteen feet high, thundered over the bows, drenching everyone topside. Lightning flashed in the distance. Knifing through the turbulent swells in pitch blackness, the PTs shook violently from the thrust of the powerful engines. With bows lifted out of the water, the boats were smacked brutally on the exposed hulls by waves several times each minute. Each smack gave those aboard the sensation of being struck a hard blow to the stomach. One of MacArthur's party moaned between vomiting sessions, "This is like riding a bucking bronco." Another compared it to "being inside a revolving concrete mixer."

Helmsmen, trying to steer on a compass course, were nearly blinded by constant blasts of stinging salt spray. Due to the heavy winds, water, and speed, it got extremely cold; the men's teeth were chattering uncontrollably. But the pair of PTs plowed onward, even though they were in dark, uncharted waters, with scores of tiny islands and hundreds of treacherous reefs all around.

On deck next to Bob Kelly, Admiral Rockwell shouted above the roar of the wind and the engines, "I've sailed every type of ship in the Navy except one of these PTs, and this is the worst bridge I've ever been on." Pausing briefly to wipe a sheet of saltwater off his

---

* Admiral John Bulkeley told the author in late 1985 that, forty-three years after the event, the one thing that stands out in his mind is Jean MacArthur's courage and calmness in the face of looming death or capture. In early 1986, Mrs. MacArthur was living in New York City's Waldorf Astoria Towers, her home since 1952.

face, the fifty-four-year-old veteran sailor added: "I wouldn't do duty on one of these goddamned PTs for anything in the world!"

Cutting eastward through the heavy swells of the Mindanao Sea in the gathering dawn of Friday, the pair of PT boats seemed to be huffing and gasping. How much longer could these decrepit craft last? Suddenly, those on board were electrified when, at about 6:30 A.M., a lookout spotted the light on Cagayan Point—the destination. After thirty-five gruelling hours, having steered through 580 miles of Japanese-controlled sea and past enemy-held islands, without sleep for three days and two nights, navigating with what amounted to a Boy Scout's compass, John Bulkeley had hit the target right on the nose and precisely on schedule.

As the two boats limped up to the dock, MacArthur was standing elegantly in the prow, looking for all the world like the famous painting of George Washington crossing the Delaware to get after the British. Col. William Morse and a ragtag honor guard of American soldiers were on hand to greet the new arrivals. MacArthur helped his wife step up from the PT boat to the dock. She had lost her handbag and was carrying comb, compact and lipstick in a red bandana. Turning back toward the 41 where the bearded, exhausted Bulkeley was standing, the general said, "Johnny, I'm giving every officer and man here the Silver Star for gallantry. You've taken me out of the jaws of death, and I won't forget it."

Bulkeley, seldom at a loss for words, was taken aback slightly by the profuse praise from the commander in chief. "Well, thank you, sir," he finally stammered. The two men shook hands warmly.

As MacArthur turned to leave, Bulkeley called out, "One more thing, general. What are my orders?"

MacArthur pondered the question momentarily, then replied: "You will conduct offensive operations against the Empire of Japan in waters north of Mindanao. Good luck."

Typical of John Buckeley's fighting heart, the directive from General MacArthur caused his adrenalin to surge. In his mind at least, MacArthur had just placed him, a thirty-year-old junior lieutenant, in charge of United States naval operations in the South Pacific. But the Wild Man's elation was tempered by a sobering thought: "That's a hell of a lot of water, an area larger than the United States, for my 'fleet' of two battered PT boats to cover!"

Brig. Gen. William F. Sharp, commander of the twenty-five thousand partially trained, poorly equipped troops on the island of Mindanao, rushed up to Douglas MacArthur, saluted, and said that the guest lodges and clubhouses at Del Monte plantation had been readied for the general's party. He added that the entire five miles of road between the dock and the pineapple plantation had been lined with soldiers. MacArthur winced. These men could be much better used fighting the Japanese. Besides, MacArthur's stopover was to have been ultra-secret. Now the entire island would know he was there.

CHAPTER 5　Kidnapping a President

Only three hours after General MacArthur reached the Del Monte plantation, where an air strip had been bulldozed, he received an alarming report. Manuel Quezon, the diminutive president of the Philippine Commonwealth who was thought to be an ardent friend of the United States, was wavering in his loyalty and on the verge of going over to the Japanese. Quezon had fled Corregidor on February 20 in the submarine USS *Swordfish* with his wife, son, and two daughters, and a few key members of his staff. Two days later Quezon's party landed on the island of Panay, and from there the president moved on to the large island of Negros, about a hundred miles from Mindanao's port of Cagayan.

Now MacArthur received a second report: seven Japanese destroyers were maneuvering off the coast of Negros. The implication was plain. Either the enemy flotilla was preparing to land men to capture President Quezon, or the Philippine chief executive voluntarily was going to board one of the Nipponese warships. Either eventuality would have been both a propaganda and a military disaster for the United States in the Pacific.*

* This true account of the "Quezon affair" is told here publicly for the first time. It contradicts history books that have portrayed the Philippine president as an unyielding supporter of the United States in the war against Japan. Adm. John D. Bulkeley has broken a self-enforced silence of more than four decades to reveal to the author what actually took place.

Manuel Quezon, fiesty, acid tongued, racked with tuberculosis, had altered his viewpoint drastically since the Japanese invaded the Philippines three months earlier. At that point, Quezon had been convinced that President Roosevelt would rush massive reinforcements to the embattled islands and that MacArthur would soon drive the Nipponese from the land. But when not one American soldier, airplane, or warship arrived, Quezon suspected the truth: his "friend" Franklin Roosevelt had written off the Philippines to concentrate on defeating Adolf Hitler's legions.

Quezon grew bitter. When he and MacArthur had been virtual prisoners of the Japanese on encircled Bataan, Quezon was listening to Japanese-controlled Radio Manila and was shocked to hear the voice of a longtime comrade, old Gen. Emilio Aguinaldo, urging Douglas MacArthur to surrender. Then a Japanese official came on the air and announced in both English and Tagalog that "General Hideki Tojo has decided to grant independence to the Philippines in the near future."

Quezon was thunderstruck. The Tojo "promise" made a deep impression on the bewildered man who considered himself first and foremost a Philippine patriot. His bitterness grew. His loyalty to the United States began to waver. In his cubbyhole of an office in the Malinta Hill tunnel on Corregidor, he heatedly exclaimed to Carlos P. Romulo, a confidant: "We must try to save ourselves, and to hell with America. The Philippines are being destroyed . . . The fight between the United States and Japan is not our fight."*

Now, weeks later on Mindanao General MacArthur dispatched an aide to find PT skipper John Bulkeley and bring him back to the Del Monte plantation. The aide had no trouble locating the squad dog. Even though Bulkeley had had no sleep or rest in forty hours, he was at the Cagayan dock patching up his boat.

Bulkeley grabbed his tommy gun, leapt into a jeep with the aide, and sped off for Del Monte. There he found everyone but Douglas and Jean MacArthur in a state of jitters. Word had indeed traveled fast that the famed American general was at Del Monte, and a report had just arrived that the Japanese were rushing up from Davao, in

---

* Carlos P. Romulo, *I See the Philippines Rise,* Doubleday, Garden City, N.Y. 1946.

southern Mindanao, to kill or seize him. General Sharp doubled the guard around the premises. Then he doubled it again. MacArthur and Bulkeley met on the veranda of the old clubhouse. The PT skipper masked his shock over the general's appearance. Normally a portrait of sartorial elegance, MacArthur was unshaven and his eyes were bloodshot from the lack of sleep and illness on his long trek in Bulkeley's "concrete mixer." His customary immaculate and sharply pressed khaki shirt and trousers were threadbare, wrinkled, and streaked with salt from sprays of Sulu Sea.

Bulkeley had never seen the customarily placid general so agitated. His face was flushed and his jaws were clenched as he told the PT skipper: "Johnny, I've got another crucial job for you, and I know you won't let me down." MacArthur paused briefly for effect (as was his wont), then said, "I want you to hop over to Negros, find Quezon, and bring him and his whole tribe back here. I don't care how you do it, just get them back."

Again, a few moments of silence ensued before MacArthur added, "We're sending Quezon to Australia to form a Philippine government-in-exile—whether he likes it or not!"

Bulkeley, a junior officer not privy to high-level machinations, was puzzled by MacArthur's hostile tone toward President Quezon. Hadn't the Commonwealth's president always been a staunch ally of the United States? MacArthur had even been injecting swearwords into his remarks, and Bulkeley had never heard the general swear before.

Now MacArthur began briefing the young lieutenant on the "Quezon affair." If the Philippine president were to go over to the enemy, or be captured by them, the general predicted that the Japanese would imprison Quezon in Malacañan Palace in Manila, make him their puppet, and forge his name on orders and proclamations. This could force Filipinos still resisting to lay down their arms, and all civilians could be ordered, as a patriotic duty, to report the location of American soldiers, sailors, and airmen fighting as guerrillas in the jungles and mountains.

What's more, General MacArthur told the intent Bulkeley, President Quezon's getting in bed with the conquerors of his country would be a propaganda bonanza for the Japanese. Tojo and his fellow warlords in Tokyo had insinuated a race factor into the war. Their battle cry had been and was: drive the white devils out of the Pacific. As long as millions of brown-skinned Filipinos and their president were resisting, the cry had a hollow ring to it. So it was critical to America's interests and the future of the war in the Pacific that President Quezon head a free Philippine government-in-exile.

His briefing concluded, MacArthur introduced Bulkeley to Don Andres Soriano, a Philippine national. "He will serve as your guide and interpreter in the rescue operation," the general said. *Rescue operation?* To John Bulkeley it was looking more and more like a kidnapping.

Bulkeley instinctively took an immediate dislike to Soriano, about whom he knew nothing and whose loyalty was unknown. Nothing tangible. Just a gut reaction. He made a mental note to keep a watchful eye on his guide. If Bulkeley didn't make it back because of treachery, then Soriano sure as hell wouldn't survive, either. The skipper would see to that.

Drawn and near exhaustion, General MacArthur shook hands warmly with the man he called Buckaroo and gave a parting reminder: "Don't forget, bring him back—by whatever means necessary."

John Bulkeley rushed back to the Cagayan dock. The old adrenalin was pumping hard once again. By now, only two boats remained in his South Pacific "fleet": his own PT 41, with George Cox serving as captain, and Anthony Akers's PT 31. The two boats cast off for Negros Island after sundown and plunged into the blackest of nights. An hour later, the PT crews spotted the dim outline of a Japanese destroyer. If lookouts on the enemy warship saw them, a chase and fight would follow, and the crucial Quezon mission, one that could affect the war in the Pacific, would go down the drain. The two boats hid behind a small island, and as those aboard held their breath, the destroyer continued on its way.

Bulkeley's PTs resumed the trek to Negros, and just before 1:00 A.M., reached the port of Dumaguete. It was dark and uncannily quiet. On muffled engines, the boats slipped into the harbor. The skippers had no maps or channel charts, but the water was found to be extremely shallow, and Bulkeley concluded that conditions were ripe for an ambush. Nonetheless he had to get ashore, for President Quezon was supposed to be at a house in Dumaguete. He decided to wade in rather than to risk getting his boats shot up.

Clutching his tommy gun and taking along the interpreter Soriano and two heavily armed crewmen, Bulkeley began striding through the surf. Before leaving the boat, he had whispered explicit instructions to the pair of bodyguards: "Any monkey business and Soriano goes down first!"

Reaching the unlit dock, Bulkeley and his party headed rapidly for Quezon's house. They were met by a local constable who declared that the president had left Dumaguete that day for an undisclosed locale and had stressed to the constable that any Americans who might show up should be informed that he had no intention of leaving Negros with them.

"Where did President Quezon go?" Bulkeley demanded in a menacing tone.

"I can't tell you that," the constable replied.

"The hell you can't!" the PT officer roared, cocking his tommy gun.

Now the Filipino was visibly frightened. He blurted out that Quezon had gone to the village of Bais, about twenty-five miles up the coast. Bulkeley, Soriano (who was said to have been an aide to Quezon), and the two bodyguards returned rapidly to the PTs, and both vessels raced on to Bais. There Bulkeley directed Akers in boat 31 to patrol the shoreline while the squadron skipper searched for the elusive Manuel Quezon.

Lieutenant Bulkeley promptly "borrowed" two handy automobiles, and in a manner befitting the Wild Man of the Philippines, drove off at breakneck speed, hell-bent for the house where, a local had informed him, President Quezon had taken up residence. Arriving at the nipa hut perched on the side of a hill, Soriano called to Quezon. Two minutes ticked past. Soriano shouted again. Moments later a light flashed on inside, and the president of the Philippine Commonwealth appeared in the doorway, a small, lonely figure clad in nightclothes. Bulkeley, Soriano, and the two bodyguards entered the house. Quezon, coughing periodically, was ill at ease. Bulkeley noticed that the president's hands were shaking.

Part of Quezon's discomfiture may have resulted from his first good look at John Bulkeley, who resembled a reincarnated pirate. Bulkeley wore no uniform, only an old oilskin. His boots were mud caked, and his unruly beard and longish hair gave him a menacing appearance. (There had been no barbers or razor blades available.) The tightly clutched tommy gun, the pair of ominous pistols, the nasty-looking trench knife in the belt, all contributed to the PT squadron skipper's look.

It was now 2:30 A.M. There was no time to lose. If the "rescue" party was to cover the perilous hundred miles back to Mindanao before daylight exposed the boats to Japanese warships and aircraft, President Quezon, with his family and entourage, would have to be hustled aboard very soon. But almost at once, Manuel Quezon dug in his heels. He wasn't going with his "rescuers," he declared emphatically.

Buccaneer Bulkeley pierced the nervous, spare figure before him with what MacArthur called "those cold green eyes." He minced no words. In his stacatto delivery, Bulkeley reminded Quezon of the Japanese track record for treachery in Hong Kong, Mongolia, Singapore, and elsewhere. The president listened impassively. Bulkeley continued his verbal onslaught. He described the Japanese "Co–Prosperity Sphere" for the Pacific and the "Asia for Asians" theme as "a lot of goddamned hogwash." General Tojo's promise to grant the Philippines free and total independence was categorized in even more earthy terms.

Lieutenant Bulkeley glanced at his watch. Fifteen precious minutes had slipped past. Rising from his chair, the American glared at the Filipino and asked in a stern voice, "Well, Mr. President, are you ready to come with us?" Quezon, expressionless, pondered the question (or was it an order?) several moments, then replied softly, "Yes, I am."

Quickly, family and staff members in the house were rounded up and herded into the pair of "borrowed" automobiles. The old vehicles were straining at the seams. Into them, besides Bulkeley and Soriano (the bodyguards rode on the fenders) squeezed President Quezon and his wife; their two daughters; Vice President Sergio Osmeña; Quezon's chief of staff, Maj. Gen. Basilio Valdes; and two cabinet members.

With a raucous revving of motors and thick clouds of exhaust smoke, the antiquated cars roared into the night in another wild dash across the dark countryside. Shortly after reaching the old Bais dock, Lieutenant Bulkeley learned that his "fleet" had been cut in half. While patrolling the shoreline, Akers's boat had struck a submerged object and was so damaged that it could not make the return trip to Mindanao. It was sunk.

Meanwhile, as if by magic, seven more of Quezon's cabinet appeared at the dock, as did huge amounts of assorted baggage belonging to members of Quezon's family and entourage. Among the cargo were seven bulging mail sacks filled with United States currency.

Depending upon the denominations of the bills, there must have been twelve or fifteen million American greenbacks going along to Mindanao.

Now it was past 3:00 A.M. The dock was in chaos. There was much milling about, constant chatter, heavy debates on who would sit where, rows over what luggage would have favored positions. Bulkeley was growing angrier by the minute. Considering the number of persons (including Akers's crew from the 31 boat) going along, there was far more luggage than could be carried safely. The squad dog had seen enough. "All right," he shouted above the uproar, "that's it! Everyone get aboard and forget the goddamned suitcases!"

Bulkeley's angry outburst did the job. One by one, the Filipinos began scrambling onto the 41 boat. All but Manuel Quezon. He approached Bulkeley and stated matter of factly, "I've changed my mind. I'm not going to go." The skipper, who had now gone more than fifty hours without sleep or even rest, was nearly apoplectic. A shouting match erupted, and when it concluded President Quezon got onto the boat. But Bulkeley had to make a concession in order to avoid the necessity of physically wrestling the reluctant president aboard: he agreed to Quezon's wish to head for the tiny port of Oroquieta located on Iligan Bay opposite Cagayan de Oro on Mindanao.

Shortly after the crowded PT headed out to sea, storm demons began shrieking. The sea turned vicious, pitching 41 about as though it were a canoe; within minutes nearly all of the passengers were violently ill. Pieces of luggage were swept into the angry waters. John Bulkeley, however, had more pressing concerns: the seven Japanese destroyers reportedly prowling between Negros and Cagayan, directly in his boat's path.

Now a new specter reared its ugly head. There was a good chance that the pitching boat would be blown to smithereens at any moment. A heavy wave had snapped the shear pins of two after-torpedoes, causing the engine of one fish to start while still in the tube. In short order, the torpedo was knocked half out of its tube with its nose in the water. This activated the firing mechanism. A sharp slap by a wave could detonate it.

Bulkeley, TMC James D. Light, and TM1 John L. Houlihan began working feverishly at the delicate task of forcing the armed torpedo out of the tube. The bucking of the boat threatened to wash the three men overboard, but they finally succeeded in releasing the fish.

As if as reward for their efforts, the winds ceased howling and the waters calmed. PT 41 and its cargo of packed humanity was half-way to Mindanao. President Quezon, who had been anxiously watching the torpedo-releasing project, came up to Bulkeley and said, "I want to go back to Negros."

"Well, if you want to go back to Negros, help yourself," Bulkeley exclaimed in exasperation. "But you'll sure as hell have to walk on water to get there!"

PT 41 burrowed on through the black waters, and at 6:00 A.M., just as the sky was becoming streaked with light, the boat tied up at the Oroquieta dock. Notified by radio that Bulkeley would bring the "rescued" President Quezon to Oroquieta, General Sharp had an honor guard of American soldiers on hand to greet the staunch ally.

Debarking from the boat, Manuel Quezon launched into a short speech, telling how delighted he was to be back among his American friends. When Quezon began speaking, John Bulkeley stalked off. He was exhausted. Besides, he couldn't care less what the President of the Philippine Commonwealth had to say.*

---

* Later, Lieutenant Bulkeley admitted that his "gut reaction" concerning the loyalty of his guide, Don Andres Soriano, had been faulty. "Soriano's loyalty was exceeded only by his intense desire to make the mission successful," Bulkeley declared.

CHAPTER 6 Taps for the South Pacific "Fleet"

Shortly after midnight of March 16 at the Del Monte pineapple plantation, two Flying Fortresses, after a 2,275-mile, seven-hour flight from Australia, touched down on the bulldozed air strip, which was illuminated only by a flare at each end. A third B-17 had developed engine trouble and had had to turn back.

General Douglas MacArthur and his party had spent three tense days at the plantation, as a Japanese force tried repeatedly to seize Del Monte and kill or capture America's number one soldier in the Pacific. Now, in the darkness of the air strip, Lt. Frank P. Bostrom, the lead pilot, was telling MacArthur that the pair of four-engine bombers could carry the entire party of Corregidor refugees—if all baggage was left behind.

Minutes later, Lieutenant Bostrom lifted off with passengers crammed into every nook and cranny of the airplane. The other B-17 followed. One of Bostrom's engines began to sputter, but eventually righted itself. A course was set for Darwin, Australia, 1,579 miles away. On the way, the planes had to take constant evasive action. Below them lay the lands that General Tojo had already conquered—the Indies, Timor, and northern New Guinea. Tojo's thrust toward Australia had already made remarkable progress.

Shortly after dawn, Zero fighter planes rose from captured airfields to search for the B-17s which had been reported by Nipponese coast watchers. On nearing the Australian coast, pilot Bostrom received an alarming radio message. Darwin was being bombed and strafed. Were the Japanese warplanes after MacArthur? The B-17s headed for Batchelor Field, a tiny emergency strip fifty miles from Darwin.

Hardly had General MacArthur landed than he received the most shocking jolt of his military career: the "army" that he was to lead in a swift return to the Philippines to rescue the Battling Bastards of Bataan did not exist. Counting Australians, there were only thirty-two thousand Allied troops in the entire land, and nearly all of them were noncombat types. There were less than a hundred serviceable aircraft, most of them worn and obsolete, and not a single tank existed in all of Australia.

For one of the few times in his life, Douglas MacArthur was nearly plunged into despair. With a grim face, he muttered to an aide: "God have mercy on us!"

As General MacArthur set off by rail across a thousand miles of wasteland for his new headquarters at Brisbane, American commanders in the southern Philippines were considerably more optimistic. On the afternoon of April 8, Lt. John Bulkeley was summoned by the general in command on the island of Cebu, where the battered PT boats had been taken for repairs. The general was in an expansive mood. He told the lieutenant that, sure, those myopic little monkeys had scored some initial successes due to their sneak attack at Pearl, but now the bleepers were going to get the hell kicked out of them.

A big American offensive was to be launched in the morning, the general stated. At least twelve four-engine bombers were coming up from Australia to Mindanao, to be joined by "swarms" of fighter planes. But there would be no "big offensive" nor were there any airplanes available to fight in the Philippines. The general had been deceived by the false rumors of impending reinforcements, rumors that had been rampant on the island.

A recon plane had spotted two Japanese destroyers heading southward to Cebu, the Army officer stated. Would Bulkeley like to take a crack at those two warships? An enemy cruiser carrying four seaplanes had also been sighted steaming toward Cebu, the general said. "But don't worry about that," he added breezily. "Our planes coming up from Australia will take care of that cruiser."

Shortly after sundown, Bulkeley in PT 41 (skippered by George Cox), followed by Bob Kelly in the 34 boat, which had just undergone extensive repair work, headed out of Cebu City to intercept the pair of Japanese destroyers. Two hours later QMC DeWitt L. Glover, of Stockton, California, a lookout on PT 41, discerned the dim outline of a ship. "There she is!" he shouted. Moments later, Glover added: "Jumping Jesus! There she is!"

What Glover had seen, five thousand yards ahead, was not one of the expected destroyers, but a much larger Japanese cruiser, heavily plated and armed with 5.5- and 3-inch guns, and bristling with automatic weapons. This would be another David and Goliath encounter-to-the-death.

Bulkeley gave orders to attack. Like a giant jungle cat, PT 41 began creeping toward the big warship. Closer. And closer. Hearts beat fast; only the sound of muffled engines marred the stillness of the night. At five hundred yards, Ensign Cox fired two torpedoes. The fish straddled the cruiser. On the other side of the Japanese ship, Kelly's 34 had sneaked in close and also fired two torpedoes. Both missed. Despite the flurry of activity, the cruiser gave no indication of being aware that she was under attack.

Boat 41 made a wide circle, then returned to fire the last two torpedoes. Crew members felt a surge of exultation as the fish crashed into the warship. But there was no explosion, no fiery flash, only a plume of water gushed upward. However, the cruiser was rocked, for she came angrily to life moments later.

All hell broke loose. Japanese gunners began sending torrents of lead into the sea. The blinding searchlight caught boat 34 in its grip. "Shoot out that goddamned light!" Lieutenant Kelly called out. Shells were whistling over, and other splashed into the water nearby. One shell clipped off the 34's mast. Commissary Steward Willard J. Reynolds, of Brooklyn, New York, was firing at the searchlight with a pair of fifties when he suddenly felt an enormous surge of pain, as though white-hot pokers had been jabbed into his neck and shoulders. His agony had been caused by shrapnel ripping into him. He collapsed to the deck. Another man leapt to the machine guns and resumed the firing.

Still bathed in the beam of the searchlight, Kelly's 34 continued to bore in on the cruiser. At three hundred yards, Kelly fired his last two fish, then gave a hard rudder to race away. Moments later, an unseen destroyer some two thousand yards to starboard sent shells whistling toward the speeding little craft. Shrapnel tore into 34's topside, already riddled with machine-gun holes.

As the lead hissed past and into 34, TMC John Martino glanced back and saw two spouts of water shoot skyward amidships at the Japanese cruiser's waterline. Lieutenant Kelly had seen the geysers too, through binoculars. Apparently 34's final two fish had scored bull's-eyes. At once the cruiser's searchlight began to fade.

From the time Kelly had fired the two torpedoes, only a minute had elapsed. On PT 41, which had been blasting away at the cruiser with machine guns, John Bulkeley saw the water spouts, but no explosions. He saw the searchlight flicker off and the cruiser (he thought it was of the 5,100-ton *Kuma* class) enveloped in a cloud of brown smoke.

Its torpedoes and machine-gun ammunition exhausted, the 34 boat, zigzagging violently, headed for its base at Cebu City. Suddenly, from out of the darkness dead ahead loomed the outline of another Japanese destroyer. She was charging directly toward the PT at high speed, clearly bent on ramming the pesky little hornet. Kelly avoided a head-on collision by swerving sharply to the left, and his boat passed along the length of the enemy warship and raced onward.

Meanwhile, Bulkeley's 41 was catching hell. It was hemmed in by several destroyers. A searchlight held the boat in its blinding beam, then guns on all the warships opened fire. Trying to get out of the trap, Bulkeley raced east, bumped into a destroyer, altered course to the north and ran into another destroyer, then darted east once more where he was confronted by two more warships. There was only one possible escape route—to the south. Bulkeley roared off in that direction, and after running a gauntlet of fire from destroyers on three sides, PT 41 reached port on the coast of Mindanao. There, like a hunted beast, it holed up in an inlet that was too shallow for destroyers.

At the same time Bulkeley's 41 reached port, Bob Kelly's shot-up 34 was limping into Cebu City harbor. It was daylight, ordinarily a dangerous time for a PT boat to be cruising slowly in the open, but Kelly was not worried. The American air umbrella the general had told Bulkeley about the previous day should be appearing at any minute. Willard Reynolds, shot in the throat and shoulder, seemed to be displaying astonishing resiliency. He was sitting topside soaking in the rays of the early morning sun. Reynolds, the 34's cook and bow gunner, was ravaged by thirst. But each time he tried to take a drink, the water poured out of the bullet hole in his throat.

Suddenly, crewmen heard a roar in the sky, and looked up to see four Japanese float planes diving at them from out of the sun. The first bomb landed ten feet away, blew a large hole in the washroom and shattered a .30-caliber machine gun. For thirty minutes, the planes dropped bombs at their leisure; all the while Kelly was desperately zigzagging. Each bomb exploded less than thirty feet from his craft.

Now the Nipponese pilots pounced on the 34 with machine guns blazing, and machine gunners on the PT boat returned the fire. The first enemy shots ripped open the throat of TM2 David W. Harris, of Richmond, Virginia, who fell to the deck, his weapon also knocked out.

QM1 Albert P. Ross, of Topsfield, Maine, saw his tracers tear into one aircraft, which flew off smoking heavily. Moments later a strafer's bullet plowed into Ross's leg, and other slugs disabled his machine gun.

The 34 was full of countless holes; the engine room was full of water; all the guns had been destroyed; and the craft was sinking. Kelly had only one course of action: he beached the PT in an effort to save the wounded. As the enemy planes continued to strafe the helpless craft, the skipper went below to the engine room. A ghastly sight greeted him. MMC Velt F. Hunter, of Piedmont, California, was covered with blood. His arm had been virtually blown off by a bullet and was dangling from shreds of skin. But he was still manning his post.

Now Kelly gave the inevitable order: abandon ship. Only three on board had not been hit. The skipper came upon Willard Reynolds, now lying in a pool of blood. His face was ashen, his breathing labored. "Mr. Kelly," he gasped, "leave me here." Kelly saw that Reynolds was clutching his stomach with one hand in an effort to keep his intestines in. He had been hit again during the strafing.

"I'm done for, sir," Reynolds gasped. "I'll be all right. Get the others out."

"Well, to hell with that," Kelly responded. Despite the dying youth's protests, the skipper and Martino carried Reynolds out onto solid ground. Meanwhile, David Harris, who bled to death, and the other wounded also were lugged laboriously ashore. Willard Reynolds died a short time later.

At 12:30 P.M., Japanese warplanes returned to finish their job. They set the 34 on fire, and for over an hour the war-worn little vessel burned and exploded.

Lieutenant Kelly was both anguished and angry over the killing and wounding of his men and the destruction of his beloved 34. It was a familiar phenomenon among skippers and crews alike that they developed an affection, bordering on love, for their PT boats. Kelly went to the American Club in Cebu City where he understood the general could be found. The young skipper wanted to know what in the hell had become of the big American offensive and the "swarms" of American bombers and fighter planes. The general was drinking with friends and did not have time to discuss the matter with Kelly. Furious, Kelly stomped off.

Squadron 3 had but two boats left. On April 12, with Japanese troops pouring into Cebu City, the skipper of PT 35, Lt. Henry J. Brantingham, of Fayetteville, Arkansas, burned his vessel to keep it out of enemy hands.

Then there was only one.

In the meantime, John Bulkeley had embarked on a new venture as guerrilla chief. Before departing for Australia, General MacArthur had asked the PT officer to "take a hard look at the Cotabato River area" on Mindanao. Believing at the time that there was a strong army waiting for him in Australia, MacArthur planned on his return to the Philippines in a few weeks to land on the beaches where the Cotabato River flows into the sea.

The Wild Man dashed about the Cotabato River region with customary gusto. In a short period of time he organized a network of native guerrillas, dressed them like fishermen, and had them paddle about the area in *bancas*. The "fishermen" took soundings in bays and inlets by the primitive means of lowering a string with a rock tied to the end of it; they recorded their findings on crude maps and charts. Bulkeley collected this data and sent it on to General MacArthur in Brisbane along with a terse note: "Cotabato River beaches no goddamned good for large-scale landings."

His brief career as a guerrilla chief concluded, Bulkeley rushed back to Cagayan de Oro and reported to the island commander, Gen.

Bill Sharp.* He told him he planned on taking the battle-scarred 41 to Cebu City to pick up torpedoes and go back into action. Too late, Sharp replied, the enemy was already there. And there were no more torpedoes on Mindanao.

Then General Sharp sprung a shocker on Bulkeley: General MacArthur had ordered the squadron skipper to be flown to Australia—that same day. Bulkeley protested vigorously. But orders were orders. Vowing to return to the Philippines and wreak vengeance upon the Japanese, Lieutenant Bulkeley flew away.

The Army planned to take PT 41 to Lake Lanao, fifteen miles inland, and use it to prevent Nipponese float planes from landing on the water there. A strenuous effort was made to haul the boat over a steep, twisting mountain road to Lake Lanao. But up in the heights, a Japanese force was closing in, and the PT boat had to be destroyed.

Now there were none.

By this time, the final curtain had been lowered on the epic drama in the Philippines. Each day the Battling Bastards of Bataan had become weaker and their power to resist had dwindled. They were racked by disease—malaria, dysentery, scurvy and beriberi—and for several weeks had existed by eating mule, dog, cat, lizard, monkey, and iguana, and by gnawing on tree bark and eating leaves.

By early April, Maj. Gen. Jonathan M. Wainwright, a gaunt, leathery faced, fifty-eight-year-old cavalryman who had been left in command of Luzon forces when MacArthur departed, was faced with an agonizing decision. Knowing that his exhausted men on Bataan were virtually out of food and ammunition, on April 10 General Wainwright surrendered.

On May 4, the Japanese saturated Fortress Corregidor with sixteen thousand artillery shells, and their troops stormed ashore at Bottomside. Heavy fighting raged, but the American situation was hopeless. A white flag of surrender was hoisted on May 6, and fifteen

---

* Actually, in 1956 John Bulkeley got back into the guerrilla business. The Joint Chiefs of Staff assigned him to the "Zulu Team," a cloak-and-dagger outfit working with the CIA on covert operations. His Zulu activities are still supersecret. In late 1985, he would tell the author only that they were "sneaky and successful."

thousand Americans (only thirteen hundred of whom were combat soldiers) marched into captivity.

As American forces in the Philippines disintegrated, the eighty-three officers and men of Squadron 3 became widely dispersed. Many grabbed rifles and joined guerrilla forces. Thirty-eight of Bulkeley's men, including most of those in the Manila Bay region, were taken prisoner.* On direct orders of General MacArthur, Lieutenant Kelly, Ensign Cox, and Ensign Akers were evacuated by air joining John Bulkeley in Australia. A handful of other officers and men managed to get to Australia by submarine.

By spring 1942, Japan's war machine, ten years in the building, had carried out a blitzkrieg that dwarfed German warlord Adolf Hitler's blitzkriegs in Europe. General Tojo had conquered the Philippines, Singapore, Hong Kong, Dutch East Indies, Malaya, Borneo, the Bismarck Islands, Siam, Sumatra, the Gilberts, the Celebes, Timor, Wake, Guam, most of the Solomons, and northern New Guinea.

Emperor Hirohito, whom most Nipponese regarded as a god, now reigned over one-seventh of the globe. His empire radiated for five thousand miles in several directions.

The power and speed of the Japanese juggernaut had stunned the free world. In gloom-ridden Washington, grim admirals and generals reached a sobering conclusion: even if the Nipponese could be halted now, which seemed unlikely, with full mobilization of manpower and resources and at a frightful cost in bloodshed, it would take another ten years to reconquer the Pacific.

Japanese bombers had pulverized the Australian port of Darwin, and citizens of Brisbane, Melbourne, and Sydney were terrified over the prospect of an invasion. Zeros were roaming at will up and down the rugged northern coast of Australia, strafing and bombing. Dead Japanese soldiers in New Guinea were found to have their pockets stuffed with paper money, printed in Japan, bearing the English inscription, "One Pound Note." This invasion currency was to have been used in the shops of Melbourne and Sydney.

---

* After enduring long months of brutal captivity, most of the Squadron 3 men taken prisoner were removed in mid-1944 to prison camps in Japan and Manchuria. Nine died in camps; twenty-nine were liberated at the war's end.

In Tokyo, General Tojo's sharp eye was focused on Australia. Unless it were conquered, Douglas MacArthur would use it as a base for air, naval and ground offensives to recapture the southwest Pacific. Over Radio Tokyo, Tojo's translated remarks were aimed at the people from Down Under:

> The Australians themselves must be fully aware of the fact that it is utterly impossible for Australia to defend herself against the might of our invincible forces . . . Therefore, let the Australians be sensible and perceive that Japan is their best friend.

Until the mighty Rising Sun of Japan had burst southward a few months earlier, Aussies thought they had a protective screen in the wild, desolate islands that lie off Australia's northern and eastern shores: the Solomons, the New Hebrides, New Britain, New Georgia, New Caledonia, New Guinea. Now a haunting new prospect emerged: in Japanese hands, this protective wall of islands could turn into a stepping-stone for a bayonet-tipped leap into Australia.

For weeks now, Lieutenant Bulkeley had been pacing about Brisbane like a caged tiger, itching to get back into action. Unbeknownst to him, the PT squadron skipper had become the center of a high-level controversy. One of General MacArthur's first acts on reaching Brisbane had been to recommend Bulkeley for the Medal of Honor, the nation's highest award for gallantry, for the Navy officer's feats in the Philippines. Hearing of MacArthur's recommendation, Adm. Ernest J. King was furious. The Big Bear (as Roosevelt called King for both his size and sometimes grumpy disposition) fumed to aides, "No way is MacArthur going to dictate a Medal of Honor for one of my men. *I* will make the recommendation for the Navy."

In Brisbane, Lieutenant Bulkeley was invited to lunch with General MacArthur and president of the Philippines, Manuel Quezon. Bulkeley's appearance had changed drastically from his Wild Man days. He was clean shaven, his hair was trimmed to regulation length, and he was wearing an official Navy uniform. During the meal, President Quezon was in an expansive mood. He related in fine detail how he had been rescued from Negros by a gallant "American sea wolf." Bulkeley was puzzled. Who in the hell is this "sea wolf" Quezon is talking about?

Nearly finished with his tale, President Quezon turned to the youthful looking Bulkeley and said, "I want to express my sincere appreciation to your father, the sea wolf, and commend him on his great courage."

The normally imperturbable John Bulkeley was taken aback. "*My father?*" General MacArthur and other guests roared with laughter. Quezon had been confused, mistaking the clean shaven, neatly dressed Lieutenant Bulkeley for the son of the grizzled Wild Man of the Philippines who had "rescued" the president from Negros. When Quezon realized his error, he too broke out in laughter.

A short time later, General MacArthur sent for Bulkeley. The Wild Man had been awarded the Medal of Honor and was to return to the States to receive it from President Roosevelt personally. "When you get there," the general said, "I want you to stress to the president the vital need to retake the Philippines." Cautioning Bulkeley to put nothing on paper, for more than a half-hour MacArthur briefed the PT skipper on what he wanted him to say. With a grin, knowing the aggressive Bulkeley as he did, the general added, "And, Johnny, don't add or subtract anything."

Bulkeley was especially elated over one part of MacArthur's message:

> I want a hundred or more motor torpedo boats here . . . two hundred boats, if possible, within eight months . . . With enough of this type of craft, hostile Japanese shipping could be kept from invading an island or a continent [Australia].

A short time later, newly promoted Lt. Cmdr. John Bulkeley walked alone to the gate at 1600 Pennsylvania Avenue in Washington, D.C., and told the guard that he had an appointment with President Roosevelt. Bulkeley was wearing his wartime washable khaki uniform and had neither identification papers nor an invitation. The guard was immediately suspicious. The President of the United States seldom conferred with Navy officers of modest rank. A flurry of phone calls ensued before word reached the gate to send Lieutenant Commander Bulkeley right in. Outside the White House three officials came out to greet the Pacific war hero and escort him to the Oval Office.

There John Bulkeley, composed as always, leaned forward and President Roosevelt, crippled by polio at age thirty-nine, flashed his famous lopsided smile and placed the Medal of Honor around the PT squadron skipper's neck. As he did so, he invited Bulkeley to "come back this evening for a chat."

After the ceremony, anxious presidential aides cautioned Bulkeley not to upset the chief executive that night. Bulkeley knew exactly what they meant: keep mum on the fact that General MacArthur and every fighting man on Corregidor and Bataan had thought massive relief would arrive.

A glittering galaxy of generals and admirals was present in the Oval Office that night, and Bulkeley proceeded to the best of his knowledge to brief the president on each detail of the debacle in the Philippines. Then, without missing a beat, he glided right into General MacArthur's message—including the vital need for two hundred PT boats within eight months.

An hour later, Franklin Roosevelt warmly thanked Bulkeley, who then departed, leaving in his wake a collection of sober-faced military brass. The situation in the Pacific was even blacker than they had thought it to be.

CHAPTER 7   Collision With the Tokyo Express

Geneal Hideki Tojo's stunning blitzkrieg that engulfed all before it in the vast Pacific had left Japan's 36,000,000 citizens in a state of euphoria. *Hakkō-ichiu* (bring the eight corners of the world under one roof) had become the national slogan. There was nothing to halt the rampaging war machine but the decimated American fleet.

Nine thousand miles from the islands of Japan, the American home front had also been stunned. Angry citizens were writing President Roosevelt demanding that he "do something." In the hallowed halls of Congress, lawmakers were rising to inquire with anger, "Where is our Army, our Navy, our Air Corps, our Marines?" Many legislators who protested the loudest were those who had voted repeatedly against even paltry sums to adequately arm, equip, and train America's peacetime armed forces.

America's anger and confusion in mid-1942 was partly due to public ignorance of the Pacific Ocean area. Newspaper polls had revealed that 90 percent of the people had never heard of Pearl Harbor, some were not sure if the Philippines was a group of islands or canned goods.

America, like Rip Van Winkle, had slept for twenty years while Japan and Nazi Germany built the two most powerful military juggernauts the world had ever known. But now the sleeping giant had slowly but steadily awakened. The United States had launched a crash program to rearm; hopefully it would not be too late. Congress legislated an all-out shipbuilding program, but it takes years to construct a battleship or carrier—and America did not have those years. The answer to this perplexing problem would be a vessel that could be built quickly and still pack a lethal punch. The motor torpedo boat would be part of the response to *hakkō-ichiu*.

Work started immediately on the construction of hundreds of PT boats, models that incorporated scores of improvements over the 70-foot types that had snatched General MacArthur "from the jaws of death" and had tormented the Japanese in the Philippines. Elco Boat Company of New Jersey and Higgins Industries of Louisiana were building the hulls; Packard Motor Company of Michigan was producing the powerful engines. Work proceeded at a frantic round-the-clock pace.

The speedy torpedo boats were just so much hardware unless manned by skilled skippers and dedicated, highly trained crews. A crash program to produce these Navy cavalrymen had begun not long after the smoke had cleared at Pearl Harbor. Lt. Bill Specht, one of the PT men caught in the sneak punch at the American naval base, was rushed to Melville, Rhode Island, to organize a high-priority training program.

When Lieutenant Specht arrived at the Motor Torpedo Boat Squadrons' Training Center at Melville shortly after the first of the year, the base was a quiet, sleepy naval station. In a short period of time, it mushroomed into a bustling military community, with a few hundred Quonset huts for living quarters, classrooms, headquarters, mess halls, and machine shops. It was not long after the new commanding officer had reached Specht Tech, as it became known, before he was joined by several experienced PT skippers who had seen action at Pearl Harbor and in the Philippines.

Soon eager ensigns and blue jackets were flocking to Specht Tech, located ten miles up Narragansett Bay. Each new group was greeted by the commanding officer: "There are vast numbers of young men throughout the country who would give a great deal to have the opportunity which is now yours—that of qualifying to operate and fight the finest motor torpedo boats the world has ever produced."

Lieutenant Specht stressed that standards were high, for each officer and man on board these tiny swift craft not only had to have a thorough knowledge of his own duties but also those of every other

78' HIGGINS MTB
PT 791 - 808

SCALE $\frac{1}{8}$" = 1'-0"
DRAWN BY FERRELL
DRAWING NO. 48

BUSHIPS PLAN NO. S-0101-601103

1. LIFE RAFT BOX
2. SMOKE GENERATOR
3. EMERGENCY STEERING
4. LAZARETTE VENT
5. TORPEDO RACK
6. HATCH
7. 20 M.M. SPARE BARREL
8. 40 M.M. READY BOX
9. FUEL COMPT. VENT
10. 20 M.M. READY BOX
11. DEPRESSION FIRING STEP
12. ENG. ROOM INLET
13. COWL VENT OVER C.G. OF ENGINE
14. PLATE OVER C.G. OF ENGINE
15. LIFE RAFT
16. RADAR
17. ENGINE HATCH
18. CHOCK
19. SIREN
20. 37 M.M. READY BOX
21. ARMOR

W.L.
BASE LINE
WT. BHD.

(Courtesy PT Boats, Inc.)

man on board. The implication was not lost on the bright young PT candidates: some would be killed or wounded and boat mates would have to take over the duties of these casualties.

The commanding officer compared the PT boat crew to a well-coached football team. "But there is one important difference with that eleven-man football team," he stressed to new arrivals: "When the whistle blows and the game starts, there are no substitutes [on the PT team], and there's no coach sitting on the bench. If a PT player goes out, a teammate must take over the missing man's job as well as his own."

"Another thing, this game is being played against professionals—and they're plenty tough. They make up their own rules, and they change rules without warning. One slip on your part and they'll kick hell out of you!"*

PT boat candidates were not only put through stiff mental calisthenics to learn their jobs. Gruelling physical training matched that of America's elite ground troops—paratroopers, Marines, and Rangers. For the Navy's cavalrymen would not only fight on the water, but would find themselves in hand-to-hand combat in shore raids and while boarding enemy vessels.

As, day after day, the candidates huffed and puffed through the most rigorous physical training exercises that human minds could devise, whole new sets of muscles were brought into play. Most of the ensign trainees had been athletes—football players, swimmers, boxers, rowers, basketball players, runners, hockey players. They sweated and groaned and cursed like everyone else in the program.

Skipper candidates reserved their choicest epithets for a burly, menacing-looking physical fitness instructor, an expert at judo and karate, known only as "Butch" Smith. Right after Pearl Harbor, Butch had decided he could serve his country best by giving up professional wrestling and teaching the art of self-defense—which featured dirty fighting.

Mercilessly, Butch Smith drove small groups of men through arduous training in the fine points of murder and mayhem, demonstrating the techniques on each trainee. "Never give the other bastard an

---

* During the course of the war, about twenty-five hundred officers and fifteen thousand enlisted men would be trained at Melville.

even break; he won't give you one," Smith roared repeatedly. "Kick him in the balls, gouge his eyes out, break his goddamned arm!"

Ens. Robert Reed, who had been a collegiate heavyweight boxing champion, was watching his first session, during which his classmates were thumped, pummeled and pounded by the husky instructor. Reed was smugly confident when it came his turn. Crouching low, he tried to draw Smith out of position by feinting with his left. Then he unleashed the haymaker that had knocked out many collegiate opponents and won him his boxing title.

As Reed swung, Butch rolled with the punch, sprang in like a cat, and clamped an iron grip on an arm and a leg. Before the trainee knew what was happening, he was whirled around and around in the air by Smith. Then—wham! As though he were a rag doll, two-hundred-pound Bob Reed was slammed against the ground. Brightly colored stars danced crazily before the boxing champ's eyes.

Butch Smith leaned over the dazed ensign. "You okay?" he asked.

"Yeah," the candidate replied, shaking his head to clear the cobwebs. "What happened?"

"The trouble with you guys," Smith rasped, "you keep forgetting that anything goes! There ain't any referees where you're going!"

Now Smith handled a nasty-looking, razor-sharp trench knife, a type every PT man would wear in his belt. "There will be times," he explained to his bug-eyed trainees, "when this little beauty will turn out to be a mighty useful weapon. The Nips are first-rate fighters in hand-to-hand combat—but I'll show you a few good tricks to keep up your sleeves."

To a man, the candidates came to like and greatly admire Butch Smith.

As highly trained PT skippers and crewmen were being turned out steadily at Melville, and as vastly improved boats were moving off assembly lines at Bayonne, New Jersey, and New Orleans, Louisiana, the Joint Chiefs of Staff were planning offensive action in the Pacific. Cushioned by the eleven thousand miles between Washington and the grim realities of the Far East, and possibly under prodding by Roosevelt who was under pressure from anxious citizens to "do something, you're the president," the Joint Chiefs were optimistic to an absurd degree. On July 2, 1942, they ordered the recapture of the Solomons, New Ireland, and New Britain, major islands shielding Australia from the oncoming Japanese tidal wave. Considering the woefully weak military resources available to a reeling America in mid-1942, the Joint Chiefs might just as well have ordered the seizure of a Tokyo suburb.

At the same time, pessimistic Australian generals were drawing up a drastic plan born of desperation. They would abandon the vast reaches of northern and western Australia, scorch the earth in those regions, blow up military installations and power plants, then establish a last-ditch-defense line to protect the heavily populated east-coast cities—Melbourne, Sydney, Brisbane, and others.

On August 7, 1942, some ten thousand men of the U.S. 1st Marine Division, under Maj. Gen. Alexander Vandegrift, waded ashore on Guadalcanal and neighboring Tulagi and Florida, all islands in the Solomons, without a shot being fired. By sundown the next day, the Marines had secured their major objective, an air base the Japanese were building on Guadalcanal from which to strike at American convoys to Australia. The strip was renamed Henderson Field.

It looked as though the enemy had fled in panic. But on the night of August 8/9, the United States Navy took one of its worst whippings ever near Savo Island, just off Guadalcanal. Sunk were the heavy cruisers *Astoria, Quincy,* and *Vincennes,* and the Australian heavy cruiser *Canberra.* The following morning the bodies of hundreds of sailors were washed onto the beaches. In the weeks ahead, so many ships—American and Japanese—would be sunk in the sound between Florida Island and Guadalcanal that the area would become known as Iron Bottom Bay.

It would be in this region of the Solomons that the United States would make its first real stand against the southward-bound Nipponese juggernaut. Fighting, on land and sea, would be as fierce as any in the war.

General Vandegrift's Marine force was young (average age nineteen) and green. Among his hard-core professionals, few had ever heard a shot fired in anger. Hardly any Marines knew anything about ninety-two-mile-long Guadalcanal. But they learned rapidly. Guadalcanal was infested with fierce, giant rats, poisonous snakes, and nasty frogs as large as a football. It was an island of swamps and impenetrable jungles. The putrid soil bred fever and sickness. Many of the natives were headhunters.

Imperial General Headquarters in Tokyo was as determined to wipe out the Americans on Guadalcanal as Vandegrift's Leathernecks were to hang on. If the Nipponese could recapture Henderson Field, American forces in the Solomons, without land-based air cover, would be doomed to another Bataan. In was to this desperate situation that the spearhead of a growing Mosquito Fleet returned.

On the night of October 11/12, four PT boats of Squadron 3 were knifing through the swells headed for Government Wharf, on Tulagi Island, their new base in the Solomons. Tulagi is thirty miles north of the then hotbox of the southwest Pacific, Guadalcanal and, across Sealark Channel, its crucial Henderson Field. This squadron (more boats would follow) had been given the same numerical designation as that of John Bulkeley's flotilla, which had been wiped out in the Philippines six months earlier. But these were new-model, vastly improved PT boats, and they carried fresh officers and bluejackets.

The nervous men approaching Tulagi in the dark (most of the skippers and crew were in a combat zone for the first time) nearly stumbled into a major Japanese effort to regain control of the southern Solomons. At that precise time, only forty miles to their west off Cape Esperance, the cruisers *Boise, Helena, Salt Lake City,* and *San Francisco,* attempting to land a large body of troops on Guadalcanal, were slugging it out with a strong enemy naval force. In this fierce battle, one Japanese cruiser and three destroyers were sunk before the enemy broke off the engagement. But the U.S. Navy had paid dearly for blocking this all-out effort to reinforce Guadalcanal: the destroyer *Duncan* was sunk, the cruisers *Boise* and *Salt Lake City* were badly damaged, and hundreds of officers and sailors were killed or wounded.

All through September and on into October, night clashes, from small skirmishes to major engagements, had raged in the waters around Guadalcanal. Night after night a convoy of Japanese transports, escorted by battleships, cruisers, and destroyers, rumbled down The Slot, the passage between the islands of Santa Isabel and New Georgia, bringing troops and supplies to Guadalcanal. Treks through The Slot were so regular that they appeared to be on a timetable, so the Americans labeled these nightly excursions the Tokyo Express.

At 2:00 A.M. on October 14, the rumble of heavy shelling across Sealark Channel woke the PT men at Sesapi, on Tulagi. The Tokyo Express had returned and was pounding Henderson Field. Lt. Cmdr. Alan Montgomery, leader of Squadron 3, rapidly rousted all hands: "Prepare for action! All boats underway immediately!" Like well-trained firefighters responding to an emergency call, the men raced to their boats and roared off to do battle. Halfway to Guadalcanal, crew members could see the lightninglike flashes of Japanese guns shelling Henderson Field. Commander Montgomery gave the order to deploy and attack.

Montgomery was riding in PT 60, skippered by Lt. John M. Searles, a Princeton graduate from Leonia, New Jersey; directly behind was PT 39, commanded by Searles's brother, Lt. Robert L. Searles, four years junior to John and also a Princeton alumnus. Suddenly Bob Searles discovered that his boat had become separated and was alone. Minutes later, lookouts on Bob Searles's PT 39 spotted the shadowy outline of a light cruiser. Creeping up on the big warship at ten knots, Searles fired a pair of torpedoes at four hundred yards, then charged forward to let loose his other two fish at barely two hundred yards. As the PT boat turned to dash off, those on board saw a fiery explosion amidships on the cruiser and felt intense heat from the blast.

Meanwhile, boat 60 carrying Commander Montgomery and John Searles had been sneaking up on a warship (probably a cruiser) that was shelling Henderson Field. When almost ready to fire two torpedoes, the boat was caught in the bright beam of a destroyer's searchlight. Moments later another destroyer opened fire on PT 60. Undaunted, Montgomery and John Searles charged forward and at less than 300 yards loosed two fish. From the boat, MMC H. M. Ramsdell saw two explosions on the cruiser. Although damaged, the cruiser fired at PT 60, and a shell hit so close that it rocked the boat from fore to aft.

"Let's get the hell out of here!" Montgomery called out.

As 60 raced away, it was caught in two searchlights. From all sides, Nipponese destroyers were closing in on Montgomery's PT boat. Now more of them opened fire. Skipper John Searles zigzagged violently. One shell exploded twenty-five feet away nearly lifting PT 60 out of the water. Barrelling along at full throttle, the PT laid smoke to mask its getaway and dropped two depth charges to discourage the pursuing Japanese.

Eventually, PT 60 outdistanced its adversaries but soon sighted another enemy destroyer off Sandfly Passage, at the western end of Florida Island. Idling close to the beach to escape detection, PT 60 ran aground on a coral reef and became stuck. The crew held its breath as the patrolling Japanese warship sailed past.

The struggle for Guadalcanal grew more savage. The Tulagi-based

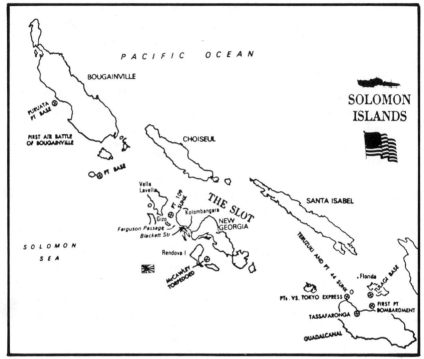

PT boat area of operations. (Courtesy PT Boats, Inc.)

PT boats ventured out night after night to prowl the coastlines in search of trouble. They usually found it. Iron Bottom Bay, between Florida Island and Guadalcanal, became the favorite hunting ground for the lethal motor torpedo boats.

Boat commanders quickly developed an operational technique similar to that once used by the U.S. Cavalry in the Old West fighting cunning bands of Indian warriors. Each night one or two PTs played the role of scouts. They would go forward to the entrance channels off Savo Island and, concealed by darkness, give warning that the Tokyo Express was on track and approaching (just as scouts on fast horses had ridden ahead, hiding behind terrain features, and had alerted the cavalry when an Indian band was headed its way). The PT commander in the rear then would deploy his boats, and as the cruisers, destroyers and transports drew closer, the PTs would pounce on the much stronger Japanese force in the dark waters of The Slot.

This almost constant action took a heavy toll on PT crews and craft. The climate was torrid, so the official "uniform" for all ranks became a tattered undershirt or no shirt; khaki pants torn off above the knees; scuffed and battered shoes with the toes cut off to permit air to enter. Most men were on the verge of exhaustion. Many were ill with tropical fevers, but they stayed on duty. Although the average age of the PT men was nineteen or twenty, the Atabrine tablets they were given to help ward off malaria had turned their skins yellow, and many looked like shriveled old men. Despite their condition, each night they sallied forth to engage in a lethal game with the Tokyo Express.

There was little time for sleep. All night the PTs would prowl and fight, returning to base shortly before or at dawn. Days were spent preparing boats and weapons for the night's action. Muscling onto the boats some three thousand gallons of high-octane gasoline was a gruelling task, and it consumed most of the day. It was not uncommon to see a crewman who had passed the peak of his endurance slumped on a scorching deck, baked by the rays of the hundred-plus-degree sun, and deep in slumber, undisturbed by the incessant racket a few feet away.

The boats became decrepit from constant use and lack of adequate maintenance facilities. The Packard engines should have been replaced every couple of hundred hours; but there were no replacements. So each day machinists worked arduously to whip engines into shape for that night's battle. Often parts had to be cannibalized from other PTs. Few of the boats were able to maintain the speed that was crucial to survival. Often their speed had been reduced below that of the Japanese destroyers chasing after them.

There would be no rest for the weary. Air reconnaissance disclosed on November 12 that a beefed-up Tokyo Express, under Vice Adm. Hiroaki Abe, was approaching at high speed. The force had two battleships, one cruiser, and fourteen destroyers. Its mission was to knock out Henderson Field and slaughter Marines.

At dusk, the only American force available, two heavy and three light cruisers and eight destroyers, under Rear Adm. Daniel J. Callaghan, headed out for a collision with the onrushing Tokyo Express. "Uncle Dan" Callaghan, deeply religious, beloved by those who served under him, knew that he had been dispatched on a suicide mission. He would be no match for the powerful Japanese force.

Admiral Callaghan's force was steaming across an eerily quiet Iron Bottom Bay. It was 1:50 A.M. Suddenly the tranquility was shattered. Callaghan had collided with the Tokyo Express. Guns on both sides roared. White, jagged flashes lit up the seascape. Greenish light from flares and starshells flooded the sky. Red and white streams of tracer bullets zipped through the night. Powder magazines exploded in blinding bouquets of white flame, and oil-fed blazes sent up spiraling columns of yellow fire and brown-tinged smoke. It was a gruesome panorama of death and destruction.

Hulks of abandoned ships glowed red. The dark waters were littered with oil, flotsam, and the bobbing heads of hundreds of sailors from both sides. Cries for help pierced the night. The thunderous crescendo of the violent clash echoed for nearly forty miles.

At 2:26 A.M., only thirty-six minutes from the first shot, Capt. G. C. Hoover on *Helena,* the senior undamaged cruiser, ordered all ships to retire. Only the cruisers *San Francisco* (with a dead Uncle Dan Callaghan aboard) and *Juneau* and three destroyers could comply. The destroyers *Atlanta, Barton, Cushing, Laffey,* and *Monssen* had gone to the graveyard in Iron Bottom Bay. The *Juneau,* badly damaged and limping, was struck by a torpedo and took with it to a watery grave some 700 sailors, including the five Sullivan brothers from the Midwest.

It had been one of the bloodiest American naval disasters of the war. But the Japanese had suffered also: two destroyers sunk, one battleship so badly damaged that Marine Wildcat fighters sent it to the bottom. Despite the heavy losses, including his own life, Uncle Dan Callaghan had carried out his mission: the all-out onslaught by the Tokyo Express had been sidetracked.

But that night the Express got back on the rails and headed once more for Guadalcanal. Only a handful of PT boats would be at the station to greet it.

Lt. John D. Bulkeley (Author's Collection)

PT boats moored at Pearl Harbor shortly before the Japanese struck. (U.S. Navy)

Lt. Robert B. Kelly (PT Boats, Inc.)

Ensign Barron W. Chandler (PT Boats, Inc.)

Lt. Cmdr. William C. Specht (Author's Collection)

David and Goliath. *A painting depicting Lt. John Bulkeley in PT-34 torpedoing a Japanese freighter in Bananga Bay, Bataan, January 19, 1942. (Naval Historical Foundation)*

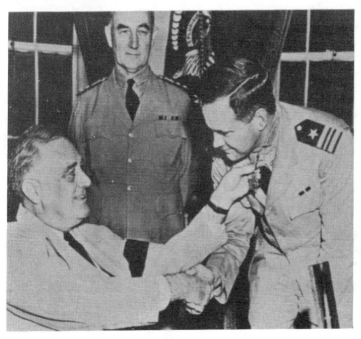

Lt. Cmdr. John D. Bulkeley receives the Medal of Honor from President Roosevelt. (U.S. Navy)

Lt. Charles E. Tilden
(U.S. Navy)

PT-66 moored at waterfront base. (National Archives)

Lt. Barry K. Atkins
(PT Boats, Inc.)

Lt. John F. Kennedy (U.S. Navy)

Lt. Rollin E. Westholm (PT Boats, Inc.)

Lt. William F. Liebenow, Jr. (PT Boats, Inc.)

Machinist's Mate 1st Class Eldon C. Jenter (PT Boats, Inc)

Aces & Eights' crew who rescued Lt. John F. Kennedy and his men. (PT Boats, Inc.)

PT boat crew went ashore on New Ireland to set fire to this Japanese warehouse full of supplies. (U.S. Navy)

Lt. Henry M. S. Swift (PT
Boats, Inc.)

Ensign Roger W. Berlin (PT
Boats, Inc.)

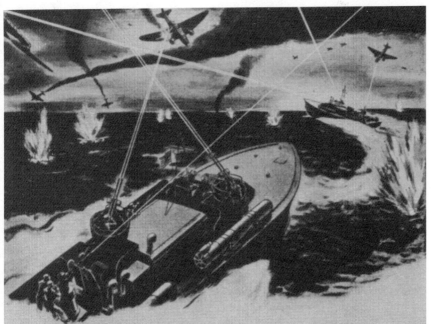

The epic fight by Bambi and Jack O'Diamonds was heralded at home in a
national advertising blitz.

At the wheel of a knocked-out Japanese barge, L to R: Lt. Edward I. Farley, Lt. Cmdr. John Harllee, Ensign Rumsey Ewing, and Ensign Robert F. Hunt. (Author's Collection)

Devil Boats leave their Morobe base on New Guinea to prowl for Japanese vessels. (U.S. Navy)

CHAPTER 8 Bloodbath on Iron Bottom Bay

As midnight of November 13 approached, the Tokyo Express was chugging back through The Slot and on into Iron Bottom Bay. Veiled by both an ink black night and the rain squalls that swept down from the jungle-covered mountains of Guadalcanal, two heavy cruisers and a few destroyers were headed for a spot offshore from Henderson Field.

At 12:45 A.M., Lt. Henry S. "Stilly" Taylor was at the helm of his PT 47 as it knifed through the dark waters of Iron Bottom not far from the course taken a short time earlier by the Express. Somewhere out there in the night, Taylor knew, was PT 60 skippered by Lt. Jack Searles. The two boats had started the patrol together, had become separated, and now were looking for each other as well as for the enemy.

Stilly Taylor and his crew, in their thin cotton clothing, were shivering from the rain and the brisk ocean breeze. In front of Taylor was nothing but blackness. He squinted constantly to read the dials that told him if engines were functioning properly, pausing only to wipe the salt spray from his burning eyes. At the same time, he was watching intently for unmarked coral reefs that could rip out the bottom of the boat, dumping all on board into the sea to drown or be eaten by the giant sharks that roamed the strait betwen Guadalcanal and Tulagi.

Suddenly, off in the distance, the sky was lit up by brilliant flares.

Taylor knew at once that these flares had been fired above Henderson Field, which meant that the Tokyo Express had reached the shoreline and was shelling the airstrip. Then came orange muzzle flashes, telltale signs that cruisers and possibly battleships were in action; flashes from the guns of Japanese destroyers were white, as the skipper had learned.

The radiant light from the flares over Henderson reached far out to sea and bathed PT 46 in a ghostly glow, making it plainly visible to the enemy. Undaunted, Taylor ordered full speed ahead and roared off toward the fiery orange bursts. When only nine hundred yards from the dim outline of a Japanese destroyer, the 46 loosed three torpedoes, and as Skipper Taylor gave a hard right rudder and sped away, crewmen looked back to see at least one fish plow into the dark enemy vessel.

Meanwhile, Lt. Jack Searles had also spotted the flares and the orange gunfire flashes and raced toward them. Minutes later, he saw the contours of a Japanese destroyer, neatly outlined against the backdrop of the flares' brilliance. PT 60 fired two torpedoes at the enemy warship, and the crew could barely restrain a jubilant shout as they saw the fish rip into the target. As Searles left the scene at full throttle, the destroyer was sinking into the sea.

Shelling of Henderson Field halted immediately. Apparently, the Japanese commander had not known of the disaster that Admiral Callaghan's force had suffered the night before and now was not certain what was attacking him and in what strength. The Nipponese warships began pulling out and heading back up The Slot.

By the time the two hornet-like PT boats had sent the Tokyo Express scampering toward its home station at Rabaul, eighteen American planes had been destroyed and thirty-two damaged by the heavy shelling. But Henderson Field had been spared more destruction and was still usable; shortly after dawn Marine Wildcats lifted off from the strip to pound Japanese warships in The Slot.

While nightly mayhem was raging in the waters around Guadalcanal, on the atoll of Funafuti in the Ellice Islands men of PT Squadron 1, Division 2, were electrified on November 12 when, near dusk, Lt. Frederick E. Woodward, pilot of a Navy Kingfisher scout plane, returned from a patrol and reported that he had seen a yellow raft ten miles south of the atoll. Could this be carrying famed World War I fighter-pilot ace Capt. Edward V. Rickenbacker and other survivors of a B-17 Flying Fortress that had been lost at sea on October 21? Captain Eddie, as Rickenbacker was known in nearly every American household, and seven companions had been winging across the Pacific on a secret mission for the War Department when the pilot reported he was lost and running low on gasoline.

Upon receipt of Woodward's news, Lt. Alvin P. Cluster and his crew leapt into PT 21 and raced to the reported raft site. There they found one man, Capt. William T. Cherry, pilot of the Rickenbacker plane. Bearded, gaunt, and near death, Cherry had been without food and water for many days. Speaking through lips parched and cracked by the merciless sun, the pilot said other survivors were on two rafts that had become separated from his a few days earlier.

The search continued after dawn, Friday, November 13. Four PT boats, the PT tender *Hilo,* under Lt. Cmdr. Frank A. Monroe, and four Navy patrol planes scoured hundreds of square miles of trackless ocean. Eyes burned and ached from constant, intense concentration on watching the dazzling water. The day dragged on, with no results. Then at sunset, the *Hilo* received a radio message that Lt. William F. Eadie, on patrol in a Kingfisher, had found another raft northwest of the atoll and was landing near it. The pilot gave the bearing.

Hilo relayed the news to the nearest boat, PT 26 skippered by Ens. John M. Weeks. The squadron division leader, Lt. Jonathan F. Rice, was aboard. Weeks and his executive officer, Ens. Edward Green, pushed up the throttles and raced toward the given bearing. At this crucial point, the engines threw a temper tantrum. Their water jackets started leaking and throwing out sprays of hot water. Three crewmen quickly formed a bucket brigade in the engine room to keep water in the Packards. PT 26 had nearly thirty-five miles to go, and darkness was approaching. The engines might hold up—or they might not.

As soon as the Kingfisher pilot, Bill Eadie, had landed near the raft he knew he was faced with a dilemma. There were three men on the raft, and he knew he could not fly with extra passengers in his two-seater. But if he did not pick up the survivors, the PTs might miss them after it grew dark.

So Eadie took the survivors aboard: Captain Eddie, Col. Hans C. Adamson, and Pvt. John F. Bartek, the flight engineer. Adamson was in excruciating pain with a back injury, so he was put in the back seat of the Kingfisher with the radioman, L. H. Boutte. The resourceful Bill Eadie lashed Rickenbacker to one wing and Bartek to the other, and began to taxi the forty miles to Funafuti. It was risky business: should a sudden storm strike—always a possibility—the Kingfisher would be swamped.

A short time later, Ensign Weeks's PT 26 raced up, just as it was getting dark. Captain Rickenbacker and Bartek were transferred to the PT boat, but a decision was made for Lieutenant Eadie to continue taxiing to the atoll due to Colonel Adamson's injury, which was thought to be a broken back. As Rickenbacker neared the fantail of the PT, there was a mad scramble as crewmen jockeyed for the honor of being the first to help the national idol aboard. These youngsters were calling him Mister Rickenbacker, and he exclaimed, "Just call me Eddie, boys, but get me on this damned boat!"

As the PT set a course for the forty-mile run to Funafuti atoll, Bartek stretched out on deck, was covered with blankets, and was soon in exhausted slumber. Captain Rickenbacker, the oldest of the survivors by a considerable margin, glanced around and said, "I've never seen a PT boat before, so I'd like to look it over." In spite of the fact that Rickenbacker had been on a raft for twenty-one days, most of the time without food or water, he insisted that Ensign Weeks take him on a tour of the PT.

Rickenbacker later was taken below to Ensign Green's bunk, but instead of resting he sat up and for two hours talked about his harrowing experiences during three weeks on a raft.

Awed in the presence of a noted celebrity who had just been snatched from the jaws of almost certain death, the young PT officers stared at the bearded, sunburned skeleton with the piercing blue eyes and hawk nose as though he had just arrived from another planet.

Reaching Funafuti lagoon in the early hours of November 14, Rickenbacker was rushed to a hospital, but not before noting that Friday, the thirteenth, was certainly his lucky day. More good news reached the atoll. A raft with three survivors had washed ashore on an island sixty miles to the northwest. The *Hilo* hurried there and brought back the gaunt, haggard men.

Back in the States, the rescue of Captain Eddie and his companions was proclaimed in banner headlines. But as war in the Pacific continued to rage, the dramatic event was soon forgotten. All through November, fierce naval clashes were a nightly routine in The Slot and on Iron Bottom Bay. The graveyard for American and Japanese vessels was becoming steadily more populous.

Feeling pressured by General Tojo, Japanese commanders in the Solomons had grown desperate. There were sixty thousand first-rate troops at Rabaul, the enemy bastion on New Britain, that were earmarked for Guadalcanal, and Rear Adm. Raizo Tanaka, naval commander in the Solomons, conceived an innovative technique for getting at least a portion of them to that destination. Tanaka planned to halt the Tokyo Express a mile off Guadalcanal, jettison rubber-wrapped drums of provisions, shove hundreds of soldiers overboard, and hope that all would be picked up by small craft operating from shore.

Led by Admiral Tanaka himself, the Express rolled again on the night of November 30. Crammed with soldiers and supplies, the six destroyers and several transports were waylaid off Tassafaronga, at the western tip of Guadalcanal, by a larger group of destroyers and cruisers under Rear Adm. Carleton H. Wright. After a brief, furious exchange of fire, Tanaka withdrew and hightailed it for home with the loss of one destroyer. The Express had been thwarted once again, but Wright's force had paid a heavy price: one American cruiser had been sunk and three cruisers were badly damaged.

On December 7—the first anniversary of Pearl Harbor—a Marine Corps reconnaissance plane flashed back word that a Tokyo Express of at least nine destroyers was heading down The Slot. Eight PT boats sallied forth from Tulagi to tangle with the oncoming force. Sent ahead to scout were PT 40, skippered by Stilly Taylor, and PT 48, commanded by Bob Searles. At 11:20 P.M., the boat captains spotted several ships heading directly toward them from the northwest. An alarm was radioed to the other six boats that had been patrolling the region in search of the enemy flotilla.

Taylor and Searles, not waiting for the other boats to arrive, started to deploy to attack the Tokyo Express. Moments later one of Searles's engines coughed, sputtered, and failed, and then a second one went dead. Now the Japanese were aware that they were under attack by the impudent plywood craft they had come to call Devil Boats of the Night, and destroyer guns began splashing shells around the disabled 48.

Despite the blackness and the confusion and the shellfire, Lieutenant Taylor quickly sized up the situation. Aware that Searles's boat was a sitting duck, Taylor swung his PT back across the oncoming destroyers' bows, laid a smoke screen to shield Searles's boat, then dashed off to the southwest.

Apparently unaware that Bob Searles's boat was crippled and indeed a sitting duck, the destroyers gave chase to Taylor's PT, which steadily outdistanced the pursuers. While the enemy warships were venting their wrath futilely on Stilly Taylor and his crew, Searles's PT slipped away on one engine into the lee of Savo Island and concealed itself close to shore.

The remaining six PT boats now reached the scene and quickly deployed to attack. It was 11:35 P.M. Minutes later searchlights pierced the darkness, and guns on the enemy destroyers barked. Lt. Jack Searles's PT 59 (aptly nicknamed Gun Boat) let go with two torpedoes, then raced along the length of a destroyer, a bare hundred yards away, and peppered her decks with automatic-weapons fire.

The destroyer returned with heavy fire and riddled Searles's Gun Boat in ten places. GM2 Cletus E. Osborne was blasting away at the Japanese warship with his pair of .50-caliber machine guns when an incendiary bullet set fire to his ammunition band. Osborne stuck to his guns as bullets hissed past his head like angry bees. Despite his excruciating pain, the young gunner reached out with bare hands, detached the blazing belt, pitched it overboard, reloaded, and resumed raking the Japanese ships.

Only three minutes after PT 50 had started its charge, PT 44, under Lt. Frank Freeland, and PT 36, skippered by Lt. M. G. Pettit, whipped in, fired four torpedoes each, and escaped unscathed. Rushing forward in PT 109 from the southeast, Lt. Rollin E. Westholm, commander of the newly arrived Squadron 2, heard an enormous explosion above the din just after Freeland had fired his four fish.

The Japanese commander had had enough. He turned his ships and hurried back up through The Slot. The Devil Boats, with little damage to themselves, had frustrated the reinforcement mission by a much heavier force. But the Tokyo Express would be back, that the young skippers knew.

In his desperate attempt to support the now nearly starving garrison on Guadalcanal, Admiral Tanaka began using submarines. These would surface close to shore, and barges would come out to unload them. On December 9, two nights after the PTs had hurled back the Express, the Japanese submarine I-3, a vessel 320 feet long, of 1,955 tons displacement, was surfaced just offshore in the blackness of

Kamimbo Bay. Several barges were trekking back and forth, unloading supplies and soldiers.

At the same time, Lt. Jack Searles, in PT 59, was cutting through the dark waters of that same bay. In the cockpit, Searles was peering ahead searching for some sign of the enemy. Suddenly he tensed. In front of him he saw the shadowy outline of submarine I-3. He ordered all hands to battle stations and prepared to attack. This indeed was a plum. PT 59 crept forward and then charged the submarine at full throttle. When a bare four hundred yards away, Searles fired two torpedoes.

Moments later a tremendous explosion echoed over the Guadalcanal area. The submarine seemed to leap out of the water. A 250-foot column of water spiraled into the sky. Mortally wounded, I-3 plunged under the waves and to the bottom, leaving only a large oil slick on the surface.

Two days later, on the afternoon of December 11, a recon plane sent back a chilling report: the heaviest Tokyo Express yet, at least twenty destroyers, was steaming hell-bent down The Slot. Every available PT was sent out to meet this latest threat. The first boats to encounter the enemy force were those of Lieutenants Lester H. Gamble, Stilly Taylor, and William E. Kreiner. The three PTs deployed, loosed torpedoes, and heard an enormous roar as the fish crashed into the destroyer *Terutsuki*. The doomed vessel was soon consumed by a sheet of flame and shortly afterward plunged to the bottom.

When the shooting had started, Lieutenant Freeland, in PT 44, and Lt. Charles E. Tilden, in PT 110, were several miles away; they immediately raced toward the scene of the action. QM1 Willard A. Crowe, who was at the wheel of Freeland's craft, suddenly called out, "Destroyer on starboard bow! There's your target, captain!"

Through his binoculars, Lt. Charles M. Melhorn could make out the destroyer, about six thousand yards away, and 44 began charging toward her to launch torpedoes. Sweeping the seascape with his glasses, Melhorn picked up two more destroyers, then a fourth. The little boat had stumbled into a trap. Japanese guns opened fire as 44 turned hard right, laid smoke, and sped back the way it had come. All the time, shells were splashing into the water all around the boat.

Finally out of range of both searchlights and guns, Lieutenant Freeland ordered Crowe to turn and head back. The craft had just come out of its turn when Lieutenant Melhorn spotted a gun flash on a destroyer. He shouted, "That's for us!" and jumped down from the transom between the machine-gun stops. Moments later there was a loud explosion; the boat rocked from bow to stern. The shell had plowed into the engine room.

Melhorn, Crowe, Freeland (who was at the throttle) and Ens. John D. Chester (who was in the cockpit behind Crowe) were all knocked down. Melhorn was dazed. For a period of time he felt nothing, could see nothing; then he looked back and saw a gaping hole in what had been the engine room canopy. The canopy was on fire.

A shout came from the bow: "Should we abandon ship?" Lieutenant Freeland picked himself up and gave the abandon ship order. Melhorn also got to his feet and instinctively glanced in the direction from where the shell had been fired. He saw another bright gun flash from the destroyer, knew another shell was on its way, and dived into the water. Two other men jumped in alongside. Melhorn went deep, but when the shell crashed into the PT, he was jolted by the concussion. Though he became aware that the explosion had paralyzed him from the waist down, he kept swimming underwater and fought off the twinges of panic that sought to overwhelm him.

He was aware that the water around him had turned red. It flashed through his mind that blood attracts sharks—and sharks were abundant in Iron Bottom Bay. Suddenly he found himself back on the surface, surrounded by burning debris from PT 44. He spotted an object edging slowly toward him. A shark? Again he had to fight off panic. It was a life preserver.

Melhorn tried to get away from the gasoline fire that was raging on the water barely fifteen yards behind him. As he turned, he spotted two heads bobbing in the water. From behind the fuel blaze came a faint cry. The lieutenant called out, "Head for shore. The Japs will be here any minute to machine-gun us!" There was no response.

Melhorn began swimming toward Savo Island, some two miles away. He could just make out its ridge line. He had a long way to go, but as the interminable minutes passed, Melhorn was surprised to see that he was making progress. Periodically he turned, tread water, and looked for other survivors. All he saw was the burning PT and, off to one side in the distance, a blazing Japanese cargo ship that had been torpedoed earlier.

Melhorn kept swimming. His strokes were growing steadily more feeble. His arms felt like lead weights. Always the thought of sharks was present. Just before dawn a PT boat passed, only twenty-five yards away. Melhorn waved frantically but was not seen. Finally, totally exhausted and gasping for breath, the lieutenant crawled onto a Savo Island beach. Dawn was just starting to break.

Later that day Lt. Stilly Taylor's boat, searching for survivors of the night's bloodbath, spotted Charlie Melhorn and took him off the beach. Only one other member of ill-fated PT 44 was rescued. Two officers and seven bluejackets had perished.

CHAPTER 9 Ambushed by Destroyers

At his headquarters at Port Moresby, New Guinea, General MacArthur had been keeping an eye on Adm. Bull Halsey's savage fight for Guadalcanal, six hundred miles to the east. By early December 1942, the four-star general felt the Guadalcanal issue was very much in doubt. He voiced his concerns only to a handful of confidants, but MacArthur believed that the Japanese navy, air and ground forces might soon overwhelm the Americans on Guadalcanal and that Marine Gen. Archie Vandegrift would become another "Skinny" Wainwright (of the Bataan disaster).

But Douglas MacArthur had his own hands full. When General Tojo launched his drive for Australia, it took the form of a double thrust; one through the Solomons and the other into New Guinea. In March 1942, Japanese forces landed on the north coast of New Guinea's Papuan peninsula, the large island's eastern tail and one of the world's most primitive, impenetrable regions. They advanced steadily toward Port Moresby, the only remaining Allied base north of Australia, on the south coast of the peninsula.

During September 1942, the Australian 7th Division, veterans of fighting in the North African desert, halted the Japanese tide only thirty miles from Port Moresby. Soon afterward MacArthur sent in elements of the U.S. 32d Infantry Division, even though he was aware that they were green and untrained for jungle fighting. Desperate times called for desperate actions. Now began the bloody, arduous task of driving the Japanese back through the crocodile- and snake-infested swamps and jungles of eastern New Guinea.

The setback at Port Moresby was a crushing blow to General Tojo, for he had been counting on that port as a stepping-stone for a leap into Australia, a bare three hundred miles across the Coral Sea. If the diminutive warlord's dream of "bringing the eight corners of the world under one roof" and driving the hated white devils out of the Pacific were to come true, he would have to conquer Australia. Tojo, however, had only begun to fight. His powerful forces had been barely committed, while America's meager resources were stretched almost to the breaking point in the effort to dam the Nipponese flood at Guadalcanal and New Guinea.

In mid-December, the first PT boats arrived on the tense and foreboding New Guinea scene. The six craft, designated Division 17, were commanded by Lt. Daniel S. Baughman. The PTs slipped into Tufi Inlet on the northern coast of Papua. Tufi resembled a fjord, with a narrow, deep channel, and abrupt cliffs on both sides. The PTs tied up along the shoreline of the inlet at places reasonably secure from Japanese air observation.*

Soon the newly arrived Devil Boats went out looking for trouble. On Christmas Eve, Ens. Robert F. Lynch in PT 122 was cruising along the black coast of New Guinea. With him was Lieutenant Baughman. Near the mouth of the Kumusi River, Lynch and Baughman spotted the dim outline of a surfaced submarine, and just beyond it was a dark hulk that the two men thought was a second underwater craft. The crew sprang to battle stations, and PT 122 began charging forward to launch torpedoes. At one thousand yards, two fish shot from the PT, and minutes later there was an explosion, a small flash of light, and a geyser of water spiraled skyward. But the Japanese vessel did not sink. The PT continued to race forward, and at five hundred yards Lynch fired his forward torpedoes. One hit home, and the Americans heard an explosion; moments later there was a second explosion. A long column of fiery orange shot upward, lighting the seascape for miles. Japanese Imperial Navy submarine I-22 shuddered

---

* Lt. Daniel S. Baughman later transferred to submarine duty and was killed in action when the *Swordfish* was lost in January 1945.

violently—a huge wounded beast—broke in half, and plunged to the bottom. Ten minutes after I-22 went under, lookouts on Lynch's PT spotted the wakes of four torpedoes heading toward their boat. Violent evasive action caused the lethal missiles to zip past. Apparently, the second submarine had submerged rapidly and shot the four torpedoes seeking vengeance for the death of its steel-plated companion.

A week later at Nouméa, New Caledonia, war correspondents were huddled around Adm. Bull Halsey. Pencils and pads were at the ready. The Bull was what newsmen call "good copy." Colorful, profane, and direct, Halsey could be counted on to come up with remarks that would make the headlines back home. It was New Year's Eve.

The admiral was asked to make a few predictions for 1943. He said that "we now have the initiative," and that New Year's Eve 1943 would find American forces in Tokyo. Several indelicate remarks were uttered concerning Tojo and Hirohito. Halsey puffed on his fiftieth or so cigarette of the day, as the newsmen scribbled furiously. He knew that Americans would not be in Tokyo at the end of 1943 or even at the conclusion of 1944. The admiral had made this startling prophecy to boost the sinking morale of his men, who had begun to believe they had been forgotten, their destiny being to suffer and die in the stinking swamps and jungles of Guadalcanal, to plunge to watery graves in Iron Bottom Bay or to be shot out of the tropical skies by Japanese warplanes.

In essence, Bull Halsey had said the Japanese, especially Tojo and Hirohito, were bastards. Even though his chief censor edited Halsey's comments, they caused a furor on the home front. Diplomats in the State Department fumed that it was unbecoming for a United States admiral to hurl such vile epithets at the Japanese Emperor and Premier. The Bull was accused of everything from tactlessness to drunkenness. But none of the State Department bigwigs had been present during the months of savagery on Guadalcanal when Marines had come across the bloody, sadistically multilated corpses of comrades.

In Japan, Tokyo Rose took to the airwaves to describe in vivid detail the tortures that would be inflicted on "war criminal" Halsey when he was captured. One of the more moderate horrors to be inflicted on the American admiral would be boiling him in oil in the sprawling square in front of the Imperial Palace in downtown Tokyo. Thus, Bull Halsey joined Douglas MacArthur as co–Public Enemy Number One in Japan.

In putrid foxholes on fever-ridden Guadalcanal, at the PT boat base at Tulagi, on bomb- and shell-pocked Henderson Field, on embattled ships at sea, American fighting men slapped their thighs in glee over the admiral's stinging remarks about their Japanese foe. And if Halsey said there was hope just over the horizon, then by God there was hope.

On the aircraft carrier *Enterprise*, two bluejackets engaged in a dispute over their chief. "I don't care what anyone says," exclaimed one, "the Bull is worth two battleships and three aircraft carriers to our side!" Snapped the other: "You're crazy as hell—he's worth two battleships and *four* aircraft carriers!"

Even as U.S. State Department bureaucrats, eleven thousand miles from the holocaust in the southwest Pacific, and Tokyo Rose were pouring invective on Bull Halsey's head, the PT boats at Tulagi were stalking the Tokyo Express nightly. Just after midnight on January 10, three boats under Lieutenant Westholm in PT 112 sighted four Japanese destroyers a mile off Savo Island. Westholm gave an order to his three-boat flotilla: "Deploy to the right—and make 'em good!"

Charlie Tilden in PT 43 bolted ahead and when a bare four hundred yards away from the first destroyer in line fired two torpedoes. The fish missed. But a bright red flash from one of 43's tubes, caused possibly by some defect, lit up the PT like a Christmas tree. The destroyer opened fire as Tilden tried to race away. Shells were splashing around the PT, and moments later the boat was rocked as a projectile tore into it and exploded. The PT went dead in the water.

"Abandon ship!" Tilden ordered. As the skipper and crewmen leapt overboard, they were raked by machine-gun bursts from the destroyer, which had moved in close for the kill. Tilden dove as deep as he could, but still he could see and hear bullets hissing into the water over his head. A few members of his crew were floundering around so close to the Japanese warship that they could hear her sailors chattering on deck.

While Charlie Tilden and his bluejackets were swimming for their lives, PT 40, skippered by Lt. Clark W. Faulkner, fired all four torpedoes at the second destroyer from five hundred yards. Faulkner and his men saw one fish strike home, sending a column of water skyward. Moments later a second torpedo struck the same destroyer.

At the same time, Rollin Westholm in PT 112 had roared in so close before loosing all four torpedoes that his crew thought fleetingly that he was going to ram the enemy warship. One fish hit the third destroyer amidships, sending the telltale plume of water reaching for the black sky. Westholm gave a hard left rudder, and, as skipper and crew held their breaths, the PT neatly zipped past the stern of the stricken Nipponese ship.

Torpedoes gone, Rollie Westholm began racing out of harm's way. But two Japanese vessels off in the distance opened fire on his boat with large-caliber guns, and another warship near Savo Island joined in. Typically, the PT found itself within a Japanese spiderweb. Suddenly a loud explosion jolted the boat; moments later another shell plowed into the craft. The PT's engine room caught fire. MM1 C. A. Craig fought the raging fire, burning his hands, arms, and face, in a desperate effort to save the boat. But Lieutenant Westholm had to give the order "Abandon ship!" and he and the painfully injured Craig were the last to leap overboard.

The entire crew scrambled onto a life raft. Iron Bottom Bay was calm and the raft hovered near the PT, which was still afloat despite two large shell holes near its waterline. At 1:30 A.M., Westholm decided to try to reboard the battered craft. Crewmen started paddling the raft toward the PT; when they were only one hundred feet from it, the little torpedo boat exploded and sank. Two minutes more and the raft would have been blown to smithereens along with the doomed craft.

After daylight, Lieutenant Westholm and his entire crew were rescued from the raft by other PT boats searching for survivors. Lieutenant Tilden and some of his men were also fished from the water, but two of Tilden's bluejackets were missing and one had been killed.

Later that morning, machine gunners on the other Devil Boats had a field day. Before pulling out hastily when the impudent PTs had disrupted their bombardment-and-resupply mission, the Japanese destroyers had pitched overboard about 250 drums of supplies, trusting that the tide would float them ashore to their beleaguered garrison. Now the PTs were scampering up and down the coastline, riddling the floating drums with bullets before the containers could reach the beach.

The Japanese on Guadalcanal were, in fact, beleaguered—even starving. The worm had slowly turned. Unbeknownst to American commanders, the bloody six-month struggle for primitive Guadalcanal was drawing to a close. At Imperial General Headquarters outside Tokyo on January 4, Hideki Tojo had reached an agonizing decision: the island would be abandoned. Only high-level generals and admirals were advised of the decision, for if Guadalcanal were to be successfully evacuated in the face of constant American PT boat, airplane and warship patrols, total secrecy would be crucial.

In mid-January, Admiral Halsey had been notified that Secretary of the Navy Frank Knox and Adm. Chester Nimitz would reach the island of Espiritu Santo, an American base 550 miles from Guadalcanal. Halsey left immediately to meet his two bosses. That night the vistors and Halsey had just settled into their beds aboard the aircraft tender *Curtiss* when the eerie whine of falling bombs pierced the night, followed by explosions around the vessel. No hits were scored.

As there had not been a raid on Espiritu in several weeks, Halsey and the others wondered if there had been an information leak. The following night the visiting party and Halsey were on Guadalcanal. Secretary Knox, Nimitz, Adm. John S. "Slew" McCain, and Halsey were in exhausted sleep in small huts at 10:30 P.M. when the ground around them was rocked by explosions. Japanese bombers, their engines sounding like washing machines in need of repair, were overhead.

With the first *wham!* Frank Knox (no spring chicken), McCain, and Halsey leapt out of bed, dashed outside, and barreled into foxholes to spend the remainder of the night, half-naked, in muddy holes as bombs continued to rain from the sky. All the while, Admiral Nimitz slept in his dry, comfortable bed, explaining after daybreak why he had not come out: he was afraid of mosquitoes.

Halsey and the traveling dignitaries were not the only ones convinced that a leak had disclosed their presence. When their plane lifted off from Henderson Field later that day, a communications officer in the previous night's heavily bombed area started to send out a routine departure signal when a shaken comrade quipped: "Do me a favor will you? Send the message in Japanese. I want 'em to know for sure that the high-priced hired help has left here!"

On January 23, Admiral Bill Halsey was reading top-secret dispatches on the disposition of the Japanese fleet. He had been privy to similar information almost since Pearl Harbor, data that had been of enormous assistance in allowing his far outnumbered ships to ambush and defeat the enemy fleet in several mighty sea clashes in the South Pacific. The reports Halsey was reading sounded as though they had come directly from Japanese naval headquarters—and indeed they had.

Early in 1942, one of America's most brilliant cryptanalysts, William F. Friedman, had broken the Japanese navy code, and since that time United States intelligence services had been intercepting, decoding, and passing top-secret enemy messages to a small, select group of leaders. This procedure was code-named Magic. Its existence was guarded so closely that only MacArthur, Nimitz, Halsey, and a few high officers in intelligence in the Pacific were aware of Magic.

Now, on the twenty-third, Magic was disclosing to Admiral Halsey that the Japanese were gathering a large number of destroyers, transports, and freighters at Rabaul, and aircraft carriers and battleships around Ontong, Java, north of Guadalcanal. Marine and Army scout planes confirmed the presence of the Nipponese armada. But Magic did not always reveal enemy intentions, and Halsey and his staff were convinced that the Japanese intended a massive reinforcement of troops on Guadalcanal. Actually, these ships had been collected to evacuate troops there.

All American naval and air forces around Guadalcanal were alerted to intercept the impending enemy strike from the north. It would not be long in coming. On the afternoon of February 1, reconnaissance planes reported that twenty Japanese destroyers, a sizeable force, were steaming down The Slot. Forty planes from Henderson Field pounced upon the enemy flotilla at dusk, badly damaging one ship. Overhead, a large swarm of Japanese Zeros closed in on the Americans and in a wild series of dogfights, three American and three Nipponese planes were shot down and plunged to watery graves.

Onward came the Tokyo Express. Every available PT boat was rushed out to blunt the threat. Eleven Devil Boats answered the bell. In the darkness of Iron Bottom Bay, two PTs, skippered by Lt. John H. Clagett and by Lt. Les Gamble, spotted the shadowy silhouettes of three destroyers. Gamble roared in to 700 yards and let go his four torpedoes, which apparently missed. As his PT 48 sped away, it was raked by fire from one destroyer, and while frantically dodging and twisting to avoid the shells, Gamble's craft ran aground on Savo Island.

In the meantime, Clagett's PT 111 had dashed forward and fired its fish, and moments later white flashes split the night as guns from all three destroyers began firing on Clagett's racing boat. Suddenly there was a mighty explosion on PT 111. It had been struck by a shell and burst into flames. Lieutenant Clagett was knocked violently to the deck, his face and arms horribly scorched. Despite the intense pain, the skipper slithered on his stomach across the burning deck and dropped into the water. Unable to muster the strength to swim, Clagett had started to go under when four hands grabbed him and kept him afloat. These hands belonged to TM2 Merle C. Elsass, and SN1 Walter L. Long, each of whom had also been painfully burned. Elsass and Long, their strength steadily ebbing, kept the now nearly unconscious skipper's head above water for nearly an hour until the three floundering men were fished from the water by another PT boat.

Nearby, three more wounded men were struggling for their lives. The shell blast had blown RM2 Russell J. Wackler into the water, where he floundered about in excruciating pain from compound fractures of both legs. Although they themselves were injured, Ens. A. E. White and FN2 Lamar H. Loggins stayed with the mortally wounded Wackler for over two hours; periodically they had to fight off hungry sharks attracted by the blood. Wackler died shortly before a rescue PT appeared. Lt. Philip A. Shribman was missing. But the remainder of John Clagett's badly battered crew was saved.

While the men of Gamble's and Clagett's boats were undergoing their ordeals, the other PTs had been catching hell. Even before they met up with the onrushing Tokyo Express, Lt. Jack Searles's PT 59, Lt. Bart Connolly's PT 115, and Ens. J. J. Kelly's PT 37 were bombed and strafed by Japanese warplanes but escaped damage by fighting off the attackers with heavy automatic-weapons fire. An hour later, after negotiating the Savo-Esperance channel, the three Devil Boats stumbled into a trap. As many as twelve destroyers were on three sides of them, and the Guadalcanal coastline was on the other.

There was only one course of action for the PTs: try to slug their way out of the trap. Bart Connolly charged to within five hundred yards of one destroyer, fired two torpedoes and saw the enemy ship lose speed then start to list. Suddenly, another warship loomed to his front. He fired his last two torpedoes at it, then reversed course to seek a way back to safety. The Japanese force was now fully alert— and angry. White flashes lit the sky and a series of roars echoed across the dark sea, as destroyers on all sides began pumping shells at the little American hornet. Then Providence took a hand—on Connolly's side. A heavy rain squall suddenly erupted, and under its protective veil PT 115 was able to race out of the trap. This same providential deluge also permitted Jack Searles, who had long been leading a charmed life, to slip out of the Nipponese noose.

Elsewhere on Iron Bottom waters, other Devil Boats were fighting for their lives. Ensign Kelly, in PT 37, had let go his four torpedoes when suddenly there was a blinding flash on his boat. A shell had struck the gasoline tanks. For a minute, pieces of kindling rained down from the sky. MM1 Eldon C. Jenter had been blasted into the air then dropped resoundingly into the water. Suffering intense pain from shrapnel wounds and burns over much of his body, Jenter wallowed in the water, only partially conscious, for an undetermined period of time—possibly three hours. Despite his groggy condition, he was aware on occasion that one or more sharks were circling him. Shortly before dawn, a PT boat pulled Jenter from the water. He was 37's only survivor.

Earlier, Lt. Clark Faulkner in PT 124 and Ens. R. L. Richards in 123 were bombed and strafed just south of Savo Island (they zig-zagged violently to escape hits). About an hour later, Faulkner sighted a destroyer barrelling through the Savo-Esperance channel, charged forward and let loose with three fish. Two crashed into the warship. Minutes later the destroyer was a solid sheet of flame, its orange glow visible for miles across the water. Nipponese sailors scrambled overboard to escape the raging blaze, which burned for three hours.

On the heels of Clark Faulkner's bull-like charge, Ensign Richards was ready to fire two fish at a second destroyer when, unseen and unheard by the crew, a Japanese float plane glided in and dropped a bomb on boat 123's fantail. The wooden craft was jolted and crew members were knocked down. Within moments the boat was a fiery torch; angry flames licked the black sky ninety feet overhead. Those aboard who survived the blast jumped into the water. Lighted by the brilliant blaze, the PT men splashed about as two Zekes zoomed in at wave level and raked them with machine-gun bullets. One American was killed, three sank beneath the water, never to be seen again, and three others suffered shrapnel or bullet wounds, burns, or broken bones. The trio of injured men was fished from the water by another PT boat just before going under.

All during the night, the fierce fight continued to rage. With the arrival of dawn, only eight of the eleven PTs that had gone forth to meet the Tokyo Express that night limped back to Tulagi. Sprawled on decks and the bunks below were many casualties. Once more the Express had been disrupted, and parts of it even turned back. Some of the destroyers succeeded in reaching the beaches of Guadalcanal, hastily loaded bedraggled troops, and beat a retreat back up The Slot. The Tokyo Express sneaked into Guadalcanal twice more, on the nights of February 4/5 and 5/6, and completed the evacuation of 11,000 troops. Now 2,500 square miles of fever-infected swamps and jungle-covered mountains were in the hands of the Americans. A ghostly silence had settled over Guadalcanal.

On February 7, precisely six months after the American invasion of Guadalcanal and Tulagi, Maj. Gen. Alexander M. "Sandy" Patch, commander of the America Infantry Division that had relieved the Marines a few weeks previously, radioed Admiral Halsey:

Total and complete defeat of Japanese
forces on Guadalcanal effected today. Tokyo
Express no longer has terminus on Guadalcanal.

CHAPTER 10 Disaster in Blackett Strait

G en. Hideki Tojo had not thrown in the towel in the Solomons. His forces began immediately to construct airfields and bases in the northwest islands of the group, points from where the struggle for the Solomons could resume. But in the meantime, the Japanese warlord's sharp eye turned toward New Guinea, where the second prong of his dual thrust toward Australia had run into unexpected trouble. After some 8,000 Japanese soldiers had been wiped out to a man as Australian and American troops seized Buna and Gona, the primitive villages on the north coast of Papua, Tojo began strengthening his garrisons at Lae and Salamaua on Huon Gulf, about 130 miles northwest of Buna.

Through Magic, General Douglas MacArthur learned that an armada of eight transports, crammed with 6,912 troops and escorted by eight destroyers, was ready to sail from Rabaul, on the northwest tip of New Britain. It was bound for Lae and Salamaua. On March 2, American scout planes spotted the Lae-bound convoy plowing through the Bismarck Sea and nearing New Guinea.

General MacArthur was still forced to run a shoestring operation (priority on manpower, aircraft and equipment had long before been given to the European war against Hitler), but he had managed to assemble a strong striking force of warplanes on the Papuan peninsula. Under the fifty-year-old, diminutive, crew-cut Maj. Gen. George

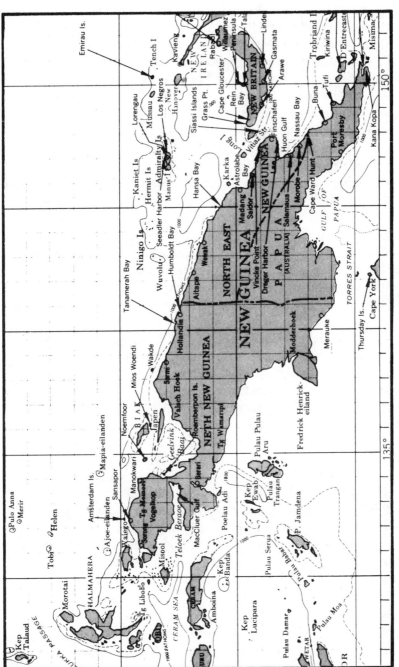

New Guinea and New Britain

C. Kenney, there were 207 bombers and 129 fighter planes of the U.S. Army Air Corps and Royal Australian Air Force. After daybreak on March 3, every warplane that could fly lifted off from strips around Port Moresby, flew over the inhospitable Owen Stanley Mountains, and at 10:00 A.M., the first wave pounded the Japanese convoy with devastating accuracy. Of thirty-seven bombs dropped, twenty-eight scored hits. By noon, more than two hundred bombs had fallen upon and around the writhing and squirming vessels. High in the clear blue sky, American and Japanese fighter pilots hooked up in a series of vicious dogfights. It was a great slaughter. Seven of the eight Nipponese transports and seven of the eight destroyers had been sent to the bottom; the Bismarck Sea was dotted with scores of Japanese life rafts and rubber boats and hundreds of swimmers.*

At dusk that day, March 3, ten motor torpedo boats set out from Tufi to attack any Japanese vessels remaining after the carnage. It was 11:10 P.M. when Lt. John S. Baylis in PT 43 and Lt. Russell E. Hamachek in 150 sighted a fire far to their front. They crept closer, and saw that it was the cargo ship *Oigawa Maru* (6,493 tons) dead in the water, burning fiercely, and apparently abandoned. The two Devil Boats sent torpedoes crashing into the enemy vessel, and with one enormous final explosion, she plunged to the bottom.

Lt. Comdr. Barry K. Atkins, leader of the ten PTs and with Baylis in the 43, ordered his boats to scour the area to the west of the sunken *Oigawa Maru*. He was puzzled when all boats reported no sign of the enemy ships. Later Atkins would learn that only two Japanese vessels had survived the onslaught from the sky: the burning transport and a destroyer that was polished off by Kenney's planes after daybreak.

Thousands of Japanese soldiers from the sunken transports were adrift in collapsible boats. American fighter planes raced up and down Huon Gulf, strafing and sinking everything in sight. For the next few days, the PTs were busy sinking these troop-filled rafts. To the Americans, it was a gut-wrenching task, but it had to be done. In the Pacific, the Japanese had set the ground rules months before: no quarter

---

* With the exception of the sneak attack on Pearl Harbor, the Battle of the Bismarck Sea was the most devastating air attack on ships of the Pacific war.

asked, none given. Besides, many Nipponese soldiers were armed with rifles and other weapons, and had their collapsible boats reached shore, Americans would have had to dig them out, one by one, in bloody encounters.

Capturing the floating Japanese soldiers was out of the question. They had been imbued with the Bushido philosophy that surrender was disgraceful, that they should resist unto death, thereby giving their lives for the emperor. If captured, Nipponese soldiers and sailors would frequently seek revenge on their captors. On Guadalcanal, a wounded Japanese had seized a scalpel and plunged it into the back of the American surgeon who was about to save his life. A Nipponese sailor, who had been rescued from certain death when pulled from the water by the crew of a PT, grabbed a gun and killed a bluejacket in the act of giving the enemy sailor a cup of warming coffee.

In an infrequent appearance at sea in daylight hours, two PTs, skippered by Lt. Jack Baylis and Lt. Russ Hamachek, shortly after dawn on March 5, spotted a large submarine idling on the surface twenty-five miles off Cape Ward Hunt. Near it were a large boat with perhaps a hundred Japanese soldiers in it and two smaller craft carrying twenty soldiers each. The submarine was taking aboard survivors of the Bismarck Sea sinkings. The PT men, pulling on helmets as they ran, dashed to battle stations, and each boat fired a torpedo. Both missed. Seeing that he was under attack by a pair of hated Green Dragons, the Nipponese skipper frantically ordered the submarine to crash dive, leaving the soldiers in the three boats to their fates.

Baylis and Hamachek threw their throttles forward and roared in; their machine gunners peppered the conning tower of the underwater craft with bullets as it disappeared beneath the waves. Now Baylis, Hamachek and their men were faced with an agonizing decision: what to do about the enemy soldiers drifting helplessly in the three boats. There was no alternative. The grating rattle of machine guns echoed across the sea and moments later the riddled boats plunged to the bottom, taking the ill-fated Japanese survivors with them.

In Tokyo on March 7, General Tojo and his top generals and admirals were holding a grim conference. "Razor Brain" and the others had been shaken by the Bismarck Sea disaster. For the first time since the Rising Sun had begun its overpowering surge toward Australia fifteen months earlier, a major defeat had been inflicted on

the Japanese juggernaut. Along with the eight transports and eight
destroyers lost, 3,500 to 4,000 veteran troops had drowned or been
killed—all within a space of a few hours. This called for new procedures. Never again would the Imperial Navy risk its transports in
New Guinea waters under the menacing shadow of growing American
and Australian air power. In the future, only Japanese coastal barges—
long, low-slung craft—would try to sneak troops and supplies into
New Guinea from Rabaul.

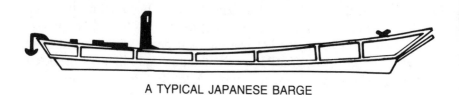

A TYPICAL JAPANESE BARGE

This switch in tactics was soon noticed by General MacArthur's
headquarters, and new countermeasures were quickly organized. General Kenney's airmen would prevent the 50- to 65-foot barges (some
would be much larger) from operating by day, and the Devil Boats
would seek out and attack them at night. The plan was to strangle
the Japanese water traffic, or reduce it to a thin trickle, and literally·
starve out the enemy on New Guinea. PTs would switch from being
torpedo boats to being gunboats.

The PTs would still lug along torpedoes (just in case a juicy target
were to pop up), but now each boat became a waterborne arsenal—
a high-speed one, at that. Crowded topside were two sets of twin-
mounted .50-caliber machine guns, a 37-mm cannon, two .30-caliber
machine guns, and a 40-mm cannon.

In addition to the heavy arsenal on the boats, officers and crews
had embellished their reputations as resourceful scroungers by begging, borrowing, or pilfering a wide assortment of personal weapons:
rifles, tommy guns, Browning automatic rifles, hand grenades. They
now went into battle armed to the teeth.

It was not long after the Japanese rapidly switched to barges that
the Devil Boatmen also adopted new tactics—the ambush. On the
night of March 15/16, Lt. Francis H. McAdoo, Jr., in PT 129, and
Frank H. "Skipper" Dean, Jr., in 114, were lurking in the shadows
of the shoreline in Mai-ama Bay, a suspected unloading point for

Japanese barges on the southern coast of Huon Gulf. Motors had been shut off. The current kept edging the boats out from their cover of overhanging trees, so Dean dropped anchor while McAdoo idled out on one engine to see if he could detect any unloading operations. It was a terrible night: windy and rainy, and visibility was poor.

Suddenly Skipper Dean's boat was jolted, and crew members were knocked off balance. They reacted tensely. They had heard the thump. But what had bumped them? Had McAdoo's PT returned from its recon and carelessly rammed Dean's anchored boat? Now Dean and his men could hear Nipponese voices. The sounds were so close the Americans felt they could reach out into the blackness and shake hands with their bitter foes. Two Japanese barges had collided with the PT, but those on the barges apparently thought they had run into one of their own vessels, for they showed no concern.

The barges nestled up under the spread of the PT's side, preventing her forward fifties from being depressed enough to blast the barges and their occupants. But moments later Dean's men opened a withering fusillade of tommy-gun fire at point-blank range. Screams and panic answered the torrent of bullets. The ensign quickly ordered his boat out, and when the anchor refused to budge, a crewman hacked the line in two. The riddled barge sank. There was a crunching sound as the other barge, caught under the bow of the PT, was literally run over and shoved beneath the surface.

As Dean's boat raced for the entrance to Mai-ama (Mamma Mia to the bluejackets) Bay, his machine-gunners poured bullets into two more barges that had slipped undetected into the shelter, sending both to the bottom. Outside the entrance, Dean linked up with McAdoo's PT, and the two boats charged back inside, where each sank one more barge, making the night's bag six barges.*

While the Devil Boatmen were battling the Japanese each night, they were confronted by another implacable foe each day: shortages and more shortages. There were not enough tools, spare parts, or

---

* Ens. Frank H. Dean was recognized as one of the outstanding PT skippers in the early days at New Guinea. But he became a Navy pilot, survived the war unscathed, only to be killed in a plane crash on September 7, 1945, a few days after hostilities ended.

gasoline. Generators, without which the boats could not operate, had to be taken from PTs returning from night patrol and put in those going out at dusk. When a boat was laid up for hull patching, it was quickly stripped of parts to keep other PTs in operation. When the hull repairing was finished, parts would be scavenged from other non-operative boats.

Fortified with "torpedo juice" (a potent mixture of alcohol and grapefruit juice) while off-duty, the PT crews harmonized their frustrations:

Some PTs go seventy-five
And some go sixty-nine.
If we get ours to run at all,
We think we're doing fine!

On March 8, General MacArthur, at Port Moresby, was still jubilant over the stunning Bismarck Sea victory. He held an upbeat news conference during which he declared, "The control of the sea no longer depends solely or even perhaps primarily upon naval power, but upon air power operating from land bases held by ground troops."

MacArthur's remarks set off a furor that reached all the way from forward naval bases in the Solomons and on New Guinea to the office of the Chief of Naval Operations in Washington, D.C. Adm. Ernest King, the sharp-tongued archenemy of General MacArthur, nearly had apoplexy. The general had intended to stress that the Bismarck Sea victory was scored through Army, Air Corps, and Navy teamwork. But the Navy, with PT boats playing a key role and suffering their share of casualties, had fought, and was still fighting, a series of bitter clashes in the waters of the Bismarck and east of the Papuan peninsula, so the supreme commander's comments were interpreted as a major slight. Throughout the U.S. Navy, Douglas MacArthur was verbally boiled in oil.

As with other fighting men in the U.S. Navy in the Pacific, the PT boaters soon forgot about the MacArthur hullabaloo. They were preoccupied with other urgent matters—such as staying alive to see another dawn.

At midsummer, the Joint Chiefs of Staff drew up Operation Elkton. It called for close cooperation between General MacArthur in the southwest Pacific and Admiral Halsey in the South Pacific to isolate the great Japanese navy and air bastion at Rabaul. Rabaul's magnificent harbor is surrounded by mountains. These were fortified and bristled with guns. Five airfields dotted the region. Some 60,000 first-rate troops were garrisoned at the citadel.

A major objective of Operation Elkton was to seize airfields close enough to Rabaul so that fighter planes could escort bombers to this Japanese fortress. Toward this end, Admiral Halsey's forces struck at Munda, New Georgia, on June 30. Munda is in the northwest Solomons some three hundred miles from Rabaul. Landing were troops of the U.S. 43d Infantry Division who were getting their baptism in jungle fighting. They drove rapidly inland for a mile and then ran into a buzzsaw: the Japanese main defense line. Bloody fighting ensued. Advance toward the objective of Munda airfield began to be measured in yards. Some 15,000 American troops had been allocated to wipe out the 9,000 Japanese on New Georgia, but soon 50,000 men from three divisions were hurled into the deadly struggle.

Shortly after the initial landings, twelve boats of PT Squadron 9 rushed to a new base at Rendova Harbor on the north side of Rendova Island, separated by only a few miles of water from New Georgia. There Lt. Robert Kelly, who had gone through the 1942 black days at Corregidor and in the Philippines with John Bulkeley and now led Squadron 9, was assigned an urgent mission. Intelligence had disclosed that the Japanese were sneaking barges up a narrow inlet to an inland lake to provide supplies and ammunition for the troops hotly defending the key Munda airfield. Kelly's task sounded simple: go up the inlet and shoot up the barges. Yet there was an ominous footnote to the Intelligence report—both sides of the inlet were lined with Japanese machine guns.

It was nearly midnight on July 6. PT 155 (Rapid Robert) and the 157 boat (Aces & Eights) were stealing up the inlet toward the lake. Engines were muffled. Crew members, muscles and nerves taut, manned weapons and kept intent watch on nearby banks. It was an especially black night. On Rapid Robert, BMC James M. "Boats" Newberry, of Finch, Arkansas, a veteran of many actions, reflected that this was "the scaredest I ever was." He had plenty of company on both boats in that respect.

Chief Newberry, who had fibbed that he had reached his seventeenth birthday when he joined the Navy, was at the wheel. Two lookouts on the bow were giving him steering instructions. Although deep in Japanese territory, Rapid Robert and Aces & Eights reached the lake without being shot at. There the Devil Boats opened fire, and sank twenty-one barges within minutes. Now the entire Japanese garrison in the region was aware that PTs had infiltrated their position. With flames from the destroyed vessels lighting the lake, the two boats raced back out the inlet. It seemed to Newberry and the others that every machine gun on New Georgia had the speeding pair in a cross fire. But Rapid Robert and Aces & Eights ran the gauntlet without crew members being killed or wounded.

Reaching the open sea, Chief Newberry saw that Rapid Robert had been pierced by scores of bullets, as had Aces & Eights. A miracle escape, crew members told each other. Newberry, sipping on a hot cup of coffee as the boats headed for their Rendova base, summed up the feelings of all: "I didn't have time to be scared coming out, but I sure was going in!"

On the afternoon of August 1, just before dusk, men at the PT base at Lombari Island in the Solomons heard the roar of approaching aircraft. Believing the flight to be friendly, they peered skyward and saw eighteen bombers headed toward them. Moments later came the eerie whine of falling bombs, followed by a staccato of sharp explosions that rocked the base. One bomb hit two PTs at the dock and killed a pair of bluejackets. Two torpedoes were blown off one boat by the explosion, somehow became activated, and began racing in circles around the bay. Finally the errant torpedoes skidded onto the beach and stuck. Their propellers were still revolving furiously, but the fish did not explode.

None of the warriors at the base had any way of knowing it at the time, but the heavy bombing was a prelude to a final effort by the Tokyo Express to land troops and supplies in the northern Solomons.

Scout planes soon flashed back the word: four or five Japanese destroyers were barrelling through Blackett Strait. Fifteen Devil Boats charged out of Lombari to meet the threat. One of these was skippered by twenty-five-year-old Lt. John F. "Jack" Kennedy, who was seeing his first action. Handsome, friendly, possessor of a keen sense of humor, Kennedy was well liked by his crew even though he talked "with that crazy Harvard accent." The bluejackets considered Kennedy "one of the boys" despite that fact that his Massachusetts family was extremely wealthy and his father, Joseph, had been President Roosevelt's ambassador to Great Britain. The skipper of PT 109, crewmen gossiped admiringly, had quite a reputation as a ladies' man at Harvard and could bend an elbow with the best of them.

Likeable or not, Jack Kennedy still had to prove himself where it counted: in the heat of violent combat where the stakes would be life or death. In the U.S. Navy's cavalry there was only one way for a new skipper to be accepted into the exclusive PT boat fraternity: by measuring up when the chips were down.

Now, just before midnight, Lt. Henry "Hank" Brantingham, in PT 159, leader of a five-boat group that included Kennedy's 109, made radar contact with vessels approaching from the north. Since they were hugging the coastline, Brantingham thought them to be barges. Along with Lt. William F. Liebenow's PT 157, Brantingham's boat charged forward to rake the barges with automatic-weapons fire. Moments later there were white flashes to the front: these were not barges, but enemy destroyers, and they were firing at the daring Green Dragons. Brantingham and Liebenow let go their torpedoes, then turned and roared away. Looking back, crewmen saw a fiery orange explosion on one of the destroyers.

Some fifteen minutes later, a second group of four PTs under Lt. Arthur H. Berndtson spotted the outlines of four destroyers heading down the coast. These were the same ships that Brantingham's boats had tangled with. Berndtson's PTs began creeping forward. Suddenly the water was bathed in iridescence: the destroyers had sent up starshells that gripped the PTs in an unworldly glow. Then white flashes blazed over the sea as the enemy vessels fired at the four craft.

Now a wild melee broke out. Berndtson's boat charged the belching guns, let go four fish, turned sharply, and dashed away. Berndtson's other three PTs had not been aware of the enemy's presence until the destroyers had begun shooting at Berndtson's craft. But now they dashed forward, started to loose their torpedoes, and held up just in the nick of time—Berndtson's boat was cutting directly across their path.

Meanwhile, the seascape had turned into a roaring crescendo of noise and light flashes. Streams of brightly colored machine gun tracers, looking like long strings of Christmas tree lights, crisscrossed just above the water. White searchlight fingers sought out the darting PTs. Starshells kept the stage aglow. Loud booms from the destroyers' guns echoed for miles and created a constant din. It was a grotesque scene. In the chaotic action, the Japanese warships, swift and highly maneuverable, were also dashing about, trying to swat the spunky devils that were buzzing around them.

To the north of this jumbled shootout, Lt. Jack Kennedy, in PT 109, was sweeping slowly southward. With him were Lt. John R. Lowrey, in 162, and Lt. Philip A. Porter, Jr., in 169. So far, the three craft had not seen or heard any indication of enemy vessels. In the cockpit of 109, Kennedy checked his luminous watch: it was 2:33 A.M. Suddenly a hulk loomed up darkly on PT 109's starboard bow. It was the destroyer *Amagiri*, and she was bearing down on PT 109 at full speed, perhaps forty miles per hour. Moments later an enormous crunching sound rent the night as the steel-plated warship rammed the largely plywood Devil Boat. Like a huge cleaver wielded by some mythical giant, the *Amagiri* neatly sliced 109 in half, leaving part of the PT on one side of her and part on the other. The destroyer sped onward, not having fired a shot or reduced speed.

Left floating behind were two large chunks of twisted wreckage. Clinging desperately to one mass, Jack Kennedy, Ens. Leonard J. Thom and Ens. George H. R. Ross heard cries for help from three crewmen, McMahon, Harris, and Starkey, who were in one group about a hundred yards away, and from Johnson and Zinser, who were in the water about the same distance in another direction. The three officers made a hurried decision. Kennedy swam toward the group of three officers while Thom and Ross went to the aid of the other two men. Kennedy found that McMahon was helpless due to serious burns so, leaving Harris and Starkey behind for the time being, he began the arduous task of towing the injured man back to the wreckage. The current was strong; McMahon was dead weight. It took over an hour to traverse the 100 yards. Then Kennedy swam back to the remaining two men and, with Harris's help, towed back Starkey, who also had received burns.

In the meantime, Ensigns Ross and Thom had reached Zinser and Johnson and saw that each was helpless after inhaling gas fumes. Only waterlogged life belts kept them from going under. Thom and Ross hauled the limp pair back to the wreckage. Three hours later, at dawn of August 2, eleven survivors were sprawled atop or clinging to the PT wreckage (two bluejackets, Marney and Kirksey, were never seen again after the collision).

It seemed certain that the wreckage would soon go under, or that Japanese vessels would discover the helpless survivors and machine-gun them. A crucial decision was reached: they would try to swim to a small island barely visible in the distance, some four miles away.

The badly burned McMahon was in terrible pain, but there was nothing that could be done for him. Jack Kennedy took him in tow and began swimming for the island. Johnson and Mauer, who could not swim, were tied to a makeshift floating apparatus of pieces of wreckage. Two or three of the stronger swimmers pushed or pulled the float. Late in the afternoon Lieutenant Kennedy, who had been a star swimmer on the Harvard varsity team, staggered out of the surf and onto the beach, pulling and half-carrying the nearly unconscious McMahon. Exhausted but thankful to be alive, Kennedy flopped on the ground. Perhaps an hour later, the remainder of the survivors reached the tiny, desolate island.

All day August 3, the men peered hopefully out to sea for some sign that comrades were searching for them. They saw nothing. Along with exhaustion, they were hungry; their main diet was coconut milk. Disdainfully, they labeled their place of refuge "Bird Island" (due to abundant droppings from the feathered gentry who seemed to take aim at these newcomers to their sanctuary).

Late that afternoon, Lieutenant Kennedy decided to swim out into Ferguson Passage, a route PTs were known to take, to try to flag down any passing boat. He had no luck and at about midnight started swimming back. He was caught in a strong current that carried him two miles in a circle and back to the middle of Ferguson Passage, where he had to start his homeward trek all over again.

Coconut milk was getting low, so the group, using the same methods as before, departed Bird Island at noon on August 4 and headed for a tiny islet west of Cross Island and near Ferguson Passage. They arrived in late afternoon; by the next morning, the survivors were racked by hunger pains. Jack Kennedy and George Ross decided to swim to Cross Island, about a mile away, in search of food. Two Australian P-40s had strafed Cross Island just after dawn, indicating that it was occupied by Japanese. But Kennedy and Ross set out anyway and reached their destination about 3:30 P.M.

Crawling up onto the hot, white sands of the beach, Kennedy and Ross ducked immediately into the brush. They saw or heard nothing. Sneaking through the vegetation to the other side of Cross Island, the two officers peeked cautiously at the beach through some brush, where they saw a box with Japanese writing on it. A trap? Kennedy and Ross, desperate for food, dashed toward it, snatched up the box, and scampered back into the brush. They had struck a bonanza: in the box were some fifty bags of crackers and candy—under the conditions, a feast worthy of a king.

When the two arrived back at their "home" island, at about 11:30 P.M. on August 5, they found that two natives in a canoe had joined the other survivors. Learning from the natives that there was an Australian coast watcher named Evans (one of hundreds of men strung out along the Solomons to inform MacArthur's headquarters of Japanese ship movements) on a nearby island, Jack Kennedy scribbled a message on a coconut husk, informing the coast watcher of the stranded refugees.

The next morning, two natives, Eroni and Biuku, paddled a canoe into a PT base at Rendova Island, a considerable distance from Cross Island. They were carrying a coconut husk, which was rushed to the senior officer, Comdr. Thomas G. Warfield. Scratched on the shell were the words:

> Native knows posit. Can pilot.
> 11 alive. Need small boat. Kennedy.

One week after PT 109 had been rammed, Lieutenant Brantingham, on PT 157, skippered by Lieutenant Liebenow, headed out to sea after nightfall to search for the survivors. In the cockpit were Eroni and Biuku, who seemed to be stupefied by suddenly being catapulted into the twentieth century in boats that moved swiftly without being paddled. Old Aces & Eights, PT 157, burrowed on through the night.

Earlier in the afternoon of August 7, eight natives had reached the islet holding the eleven survivors. They brought a message from coast watcher Evans (a civilian) instructing that the senior officer be brought to him. Lieutenant Kennedy, hidden under ferns in a native boat, was paddled to the Australian on Wana Wana. Evans, who had been in contact with the PT base, said that a boat would arrive that night to pick up the survivors.

At 11:15 P.M., when the night was at its blackest, Lieutenants Brantingham and Liebenow idled up to Wana Wana. A rifle shot rang out from ashore—the predesignated signal of recognition. Liebenow replied with a pistol shot into the air. Minutes later an exhausted Jack Kennedy was pulled aboard, and he directed the boat to the remaining survivors.

On crowded 157 there was great revelry, much handshaking, blackslapping, and joking (from a survivor: "What the hell took you so long?"). The wounded were taken below and treated by a pharmacist's mate, who decreed that both survivors and PT 157 men were in critical need of "medicinal treatment." So he passed out "torpedo juice" to all hands. Soon, as the Devil Boat got ready for the return trip, everyone joined in a medley of raucous songs, including:

We sent for the army to come to Tulagi,
But General MacArthur said "no."
He gave as his reason, it isn't the season,
And besides there was no U.S.O.

The natives Eroni and Biuku knew "Jesus Loves Me," so each song ended with "Jesus Loves Me."

When they reached the PT base on Rendova Island at 5:30 A.M., Lieutenant Liebenow was among those puzzled over how a fast and maneuverable PT boat could be rammed by a much more bulky destroyer. Liebenow put the question to Kennedy: "How did it happen?" The 109's skipper pondered the matter, then replied evenly: "Lieb, to tell you the truth, I don't know."*

---

* In 1960, during Sen. John F. Kennedy's successful campaign for the presidency of the United States, he equipped to Bill Liebenow: "If no one votes for me except those who claim to have been on your boat when it rescued me, I'll win easily!"

CHAPTER 11   Stuck on an Enemy-Held Reef

All during August, the shorelines of New Guinea and the Solomons were ablaze with gunfire as the Green Dragons and the *daihatsu* (barges) clashed violently almost nightly. The barges had been getting far the worst of it, and in the one month alone forty-eight of them had been sunk, badly damaged, or beached.

But the Japanese were flexible adversaries. Their barges were getting bigger—and tougher. They were plated with armor, and heavier guns—up to 40-mm—were mounted on them. PT skippers soon found that when they charged in to rake the barges with machine-gun fire, the bullets were ricocheting harmlessly off their sides. The *daihatsu* had indeed become formidable foes. No longer were they defenseless clay pigeons. In addition, the wily Japanese were rapidly installing coastal gun batteries and machine-gun positions along routes followed by the barges.

Despite the enemy's beefed-up defenses, on August 22 three boats were sent on a daylight raid into Webster Cove, near the Nipponese stronghold of Vila on the south coast of the Solomons island of Kolombangara. Each boat carried Army demolition teams, which were to slip ashore and blow up enemy installations.

At 7:30 A.M., the three-boat flotilla, led by Lt. David M. Payne in Lt. Sidney D. Hix's PT 108 (Plywood Bastard), was approaching

Webster Cove. PT 124 (Who-Me), skippered by Lt. Leighton C. Wood, dropped off to cover the entrance, while Hix's boat and Lt. Murray's PT125 edged on into the deathly stillness of the cove. Staring intently toward the brush-covered shoreline, tense crews manned battle stations but saw no indication of the enemy's presence. Suddenly, a raucous din erupted as machine guns, concealed all around the cove, opened with murderous crossfire. The Nipponese even had automatic weapons on platforms in trees.

Sid Hix's boat caught the brunt of the flying lead. Streams of bullets converged on it. Lieutenant Payne was struck almost immediately, and tumbled dead into the chart house. Another slug ripped into the head of Lieutenant Hix who was at the helm. But he put the wheel hard over to pull out his boat before collapsing. He died moments later. QM2 James G. Cannon, who had been hit in the face, shoulder, and arm, was bleeding profusely, and was only half-conscious; yet he crawled to the vacated wheel, pulled himself to his feet and, standing astride the dead body of Sid Hix, steered 108 toward Webster Cove's entrance.

All the while PT 108 was being peppered by a torrent of machine-gun fire, its own gunners had been blasting away at the unseen tormentors ashore. SC3 Jack O. Bell was killed while at his weapon, and all the other gunners save one were wounded. Sgt. J. E. Rogers of the Army's demolitions crew saw the forward 37-mm gunner cut down and, crouching over, edged toward the wounded men to give aid. A slug tore into Rogers, and he fell dead on the deck. Only one officer and two bluejackets on Plywood Bastard escaped being hit.

With the dazed Jim Cannon still at the wheel, PT 108 finally emerged from the deadly crossfire. But the boat was smoking, and several blazes were raging below. Crew members who could move went below and put out the fires that threatened to consume the bullet-riddled boat.

Lieutenant Murray, in 125, which had been trailing the ill-fated 108, at first was going to charge forward to Hix's aid, but when Plywood Bastard turned sharply, Murray turned also. So Murray's 125 escaped the worst of the Japanese fusillades, but was punctured with holes and one crewman was wounded by a slug.

One week after the bloody disaster at Webster Cove, Lt. Comdr. John Bulkeley, who had snatched General MacArthur "from the jaws of death" at Corregidor more than a year earlier, was prowling the

New Guinea coast on the black night of August 28/29. He was in PT 142 (Flying Shamrock), skippered by Lt. John L. Carey, and following was Ens. Herbert P. Knight's PT 152 (Lack-a-Nookie).

Thirty-two-year-old Bulkeley, the swashbuckler MacArthur called "the buckaroo with the cold green eyes," for months had been badgering Navy bigwigs in Washington to return him to combat duty in the Pacific. He had never been comfortable with the media or the public adulation heaped upon him after he had returned to the States as a living legend. Now, slipping along Vitiaz Strait in the blackness with other PT boatmen, Bulkeley was in his element. But on this night he was disappointed. His pair of boats had stalked the forbidding coast for many miles but had seen no sign of Japanese barges and were returning to base at Morobe before daybreak.

As the two Devil Boats were slipping past the Japanese-held town of Finschhafen, lookouts spotted three barges. The PTs charged the enemy vessels, and with a noisy burst of gunfire, sent one barge to the bottom. Bullets seemed to richochet off the other two barges, which were probably heavily plated with steel. So after making a wide circle, Ensign Knight's boat raced in and dropped a depth charge next to each barge. There were two mighty roars and geysers of water, but the explosives apparently had not fazed the tough targets. On Knight's heels, John Carey's 142 raced in, let two depth charges drop, and sank a second barge. The third barge remained defiant and refused to go down for the count.

"Pull up along side the bastard!" Commander Bulkeley ordered Carey. Once next to the barge, Bulkeley, Lt. Joseph L. Broderick, and Lt. Oliver B. Crager, whipped out their .45 Colts, and, like giant, armed cats, leapt softly onto the dark Japanese vessel. The PT officers were peering intently through the blackness when they spotted the dim outline of a helmeted figure slipping around the wheelhouse. In an instant, John Bulkeley, an expert marksman, lifted his pistol and squeezed the trigger. The dark figure collapsed in a heap, a neat bullet hole in the forehead.

Carefully and cautiously, the three Americans inspected the barge. They found twelve armed and fully equipped Japanese soldiers—all sprawled grotesquely in death. Bulkeley and the other officers scrambled back onto Flying Shamrock, and the two PTs pulled away. There was no time to be lost, for the series of explosions and Bulkeley's pistol shot no doubt alerted Japanese in and around Finschhafen. But before they raced away for home, there was one more item on the night's agenda: the 37-mm guns on Ensign Knight's PT poured eight or ten rounds into the thick hide of the stubborn barge and, finally, the vessel sank beneath the surface.

While the Devil Boats were continuing to tangle nightly with the heavily armed barges, a significant change in tactics had been made at Gen. Douglas MacArthur's headquarters: action along the lengthy road to Tokyo would be accelerated. So far, out of necessity, MacArthur's strategy in New Guinea and Adm. Bill Halsey's in the Solomons had been to hang on by their teeth for months and then to start snail-like advances. At this rate, slogging ahead through the snake-infested swamps and jungles a few hundred yards or even a mile at a time, it would take ten years to reach Tokyo. The brass knew that; so did the humblest PT crewman, airman, swabbie, foot slogger, and leatherneck caught up in the nightmare of the Pacific conflict.

General MacArthur would now employ leapfrog tactics. Once a star baseball player at West Point, the supreme commander used diamond terminology to describe his new strategy: "I will hit 'em where they ain't." Japanese strongholds would be bypassed, their supply lines strangled by PT boats, destroyers, and warplanes, and left to "wither on the vine"—that is, starve to death.*

MacArthur's new strategy of leapfrogging his forces along the rugged, 1,500-mile spine of New Guinea gave PT boats an even more crucial role in strangling Japanese supply lines and starving out by-passed Japanese strongholds. But more PT beef was on the way. Specht Tech, the PT boat training center at Melville, Rhode Island, had been steadily turning out skilled, eager skippers and crewmen; and boats for them were rolling off production lines in Bayonne, New Jersey, and in New Orleans.

At the same time, grizzled old PT skippers (aged early twenties to early thirties), who had been blooded in the Pearl Harbor and Philippines disasters, were trickling back to the South Pacific. They had been called home, mainly to teach Melville recruits, and even though

---

* Australian troops were still trying to root out bypassed Japanese bands in New Guinea when the war in the Pacific ended nearly two years later. This caused one "digger" (as the Aussies called themselves) to remark: "Blimey, mates, these Japs require a bloody lot of withering!" (As reported in *Time*, February 28, 1945.)

their function was crucial to the war effort, to a man the veteran skippers had been seeking to get back into the Pacific fight.

Among those at Melville were Lt. Comdr. John Harllee, whose PT squadron had shot down the first Japanese warplane in the Pearl Harbor attack. Harllee finally was given command of the new Squadron 12, early in 1943. He asked another Pearl Harbor veteran, Lt. Edward Farley, to come along with him as squadron executive officer.

Lieutenant Commander Harllee, who had graduated from the Naval Academy at age twenty and was the son of a Marine Corps brigadier general, and his squadron arrived in the combat area late in August. With them came the latest technological advances, ones that would have made John Bulkeley's mouth water when he was fighting the Japanese Imperial Navy in the Philippines with only a handful of leaking, obsolete PT boats.

Sophisticated radar would permit Squadron 12's skippers to "see" in the dark, not only to beat Japanese vessels to the draw (which could be the difference between life and death), but also to keep boats in position with each other at night and in bad weather. An electronic device, the fluxgate gyro-stabilized compass, would give the helmsman a true course, even when a Devil Boat was pitching violently in rough seas. (In contrast to the dead reckoning—that is, a seat-of-the-pants instinct—that John Bulkeley had to employ in March 1942 when he sneaked General MacArthur and his party through six hundred miles of Japanese-controlled and largely uncharted waters.)

Blasting the enemy had also been made more effective. The newly arrived PTs were equipped with side-launching torpedo racks instead of the heavier and more cumbersome torpedo tubes. This resulted in the boats being several tons lighter and therefore more maneuverable. And a PT's survival depended upon its speed and maneuverability.

Squadron 12 was scheduled to reach New Guinea in sections, and the first boats tied up at a base a mile up the Morobe River in early September. The Morobe was narrow, and the thick foliage overhanging its banks concealed the moored PTs from air observation. The base was a primeval leftover from the Stone Age. Stretching back a few hundred feet from the river, on the side of a brush-covered hill, the hideaway was dotted with shacks constructed by covering wooden frames with palm fronds and, in some cases, canvas. Dangling vines and foliage were so thick that only occasional rays of sunlight could penetrate to the ground, giving the locale an eerie atmosphere.

Here the PT squadron lived and worked. During the day it was so humid, so devoid of air, that the men were often gasping for breath and burdened by the disconcerting sensation of being strangled. Insects, especially mosquitoes, were abundant—and mean. The wretched sailors compared them to Japanese dive bombers. When it rained, footpaths turned into quagmires, at which times the men had to plod along in mud up over their ankles. Wits swore that they were going to wear bones in their noses, because then they would be just like the native headhunters living in almost identical conditions a short distance from the Morobe.

On the afternoon of September 21, Ens. Rumsey "Rum" Ewing, a tall, husky skipper who had been reared on a Wyoming ranch but now called St. Louis, Missouri, home, was summoned to Squadron 12's operations shack. Ewing and his PT 191 (nicknamed Bambi) had been at Morobe only a few days. Commander Harllee gave the twenty-two-year-old skipper the news: he was to go on his first combat patrol into Japanese-infested waters that night. The long, arduous weeks of training were over; the test of battle was at hand.

Ensign Ewing, who had been captain of his Dartmouth rowing team, was reassured to know that his experienced boss, John Harllee, also would make the patrol in Bambi. Lt. Robert R. "Red" Read would be going along in PT 133 (New Guinea Ferry).

As Ewing prepared his crew and boat for the night's mission, nagging doubts tugged at him. He tried to force the qualms to vanish; they refused. How would his eager, keenly trained but green crew measure up in the crucible of combat? More importantly, how would he, himself, react when the shooting started? Would he panic under fire at some crucial point, thereby costing the lives of his men? Then he remembered the words of the combat-tested instructor at Melville: "Going into battle, there are two kinds of men who are *not* afraid—liars and bigger liars."

To keep in perspective his own role as captain of PT 191, Rum Ewing recalled, almost word for word, what another South Pacific veteran had told his group of officers at Melville a few weeks earlier:

Maybe you won't like this, but you'd better—because it's straight from the shoulder. There are no heroes in a PT boat squadron. The boats themselves are the heroes. *No one man* stands out above the others. Each officer and member of the crew is just a plain American guy, in there pitching his best for his team-mates.

In the PT squadrons, the backbone and guts of the entire operation are the enlisted men. Never forget that! There must be discipline and respect for officers, yes. But, when you're in there delivering your Sunday punch, each man is on his own. And how good a teammate he is determines whether you come through or whether its taps for your PT boat and every man on her.

At dusk Ewing's and Red Read's boats slipped out of the Morobe River and headed for the Vitiaz Strait, the narrow body of water between New Britain and New Guinea and a thoroughfare for the Japanese barge traffic. Just after midnight, lookouts spotted a 125-foot cargo ship ten miles off Vincke Point. Ewing, followed closely by Read, charged the enemy vessel with all guns blazing, setting her afire. Moments later Commander Harllee on Bambi received an urgent radio signal: Jake and Pete (Nipponese float planes) were roaming the vicinity. So Harllee wanted to sink the burning diesel-powered lugger as quickly as possible. He rapidly gave orders: depth-charge her.

Two depth charges, weighing nearly four hundred pounds each, were in racks at the stern of each boat. They were released simply by unfastening restraining straps and letting the explosives roll into the water. With Rum Ewing at the wheel and Ens. Fred Calhoun at the stern, Bambi roared in. Calhoun released a depth charge that exploded twenty feet from the target. A torrent of water shot into the sky and cascaded onto the burning vessel. Red Read followed, with similar results from his depth charge. The wounded ship still refused to sink.

"Closer!" Commander Harllee exclaimed. "Get in closer!" Men on the PTs swallowed hard. Closer? How does one get closer than twenty feet from a target?

Ensign Ewing called out to Calhoun, "Let's change places." So the imperturbable Calhoun shrugged his shoulders, threw the throttles forward, and bolted ahead. On the stern, Ewing had fleeting second thoughts over the switch in assignments: it appeared that Calhoun was going to crash into the enemy ship. At the final split-second, Calhoun swerved to one side, barely missing the vessel.

Bambi's skipper instantly released the depth charge and virtually hurled it onto the enemy vessel's port deck, or so it seemed. An explosion ripped the night. Silhouetted figures were seen fighting the blaze furiously as the doomed ship sunk beneath the surface.

After regaining the open sea, Ensign Ewing turned to Fred Calhoun and exclaimed, "Cal, you're going to get into big trouble with Tojo. You scraped a lot of paint off that ship when you went past it!"

Heading back for the Morobe base, Commander Harllee mused, "That bowling-ball technique was a novel use of depth charges, wasn't it?"

Meanwhile, in the Solomons, the work of intercepting and sinking Japanese barges was being turned over to destroyers, as the focus of PT boat actions switched steadily to New Guinea. But shortly after dawn on September 30, four Devil Boats of Lt. Craig C. Smith's Squadron 6 were returning to their base at Lever Harbor. Tired, sleepy, even bored from the routine mission, crewmen glanced skyward and saw three Marine Corps Corsairs approaching. Real neighborly of the Marines to send out warplanes just to furnish them air cover, they quipped.

The Marine flight leader radioed the other two planes: "Don't fire. They're our PTs." One pilot understood the message, the third apparently did not. Even while the PTs made a sharp right turn (the standard recognition signal) the third Corsair swooped in with machine guns blazing and poured bullets into PT 126, as the startled Navy men scrambled for cover. Slugs ripped into an officer and two bluejackets, killing them instantly. Mild panic broke out among some on PT 126; it was always especially nerve-racking to be attacked by "friendly" aircraft. Without orders, a gunner opened fire, striking the Corsair. The plane flew onward for moments, then exploded in mid-air.

As night dropped over the southwest Pacific that same day, September 30, Ens. Rum Ewing, in PT 191, and Lt. Bob Lynch, in 68, departed Morobe to prowl the northeast coast of New Guinea. This was Ewing's first patrol as lead boat commander. Even though Lynch and his crew were from one of the old squadrons and had seen much action, Bambi was in the lead because its equipment was far more advanced.

Once the Devil Boats reached the open sea and were hidden by the night's blackness, half the crew stood watch, while the other half, in naval jargon, "crapped out" topside near their battle stations. Night patrols were tedious and uncomfortable; often the boats would travel 300 miles on a single mission. Bluejackets got what sleep they could, using their lifejackets for a combination pillow and mattress.

The watch had changed a couple of times as Bambi, followed by Read's 68, nosed its way up the coast. The boats had traveled about fifty miles when Ewing edged closer in to the shoreline and began cruising along on one engine, making about five knots, with mufflers closed. The idea was to make as little noise and wake as possible. Bob Lynch's boat was following in line.

Other than for the purring of one Packard on each boat, it was dead still. Binoculars in hand, skipper Ewing was standing in the cockpit searching for telltale signs of Nipponese barges: a bow wake, a dim silhouette, a tiny gleam of light. Gliding along less than fifty yards from the shore, Ewing was trying to decipher the significance of each shadow, each vague sign of the enemy's presence. Lookouts were doing the same. It was trying work. Two or three times each night the pair of PTs headed a mile or two out to sea for cigarettes and coffee. Then it was back to the perilous coastline where the boats resumed stalking the enemy.

The PTs were cutting across a small cove when Rum Ewing suddenly stiffened. He peered closely through the binoculars, then called out in a stage whisper to Joseph E. Davis, of Danville, Illinois, in the front turret: "Joe, what's that out there bearing about zero forty-five degrees?" Davis whipped up his glasses and moments later exclaimed, "Oh boy!" At the same time he began putting on his helmet and lifejacket. Ewing buzzed general quarters; there followed the usual organized chaos as men roused from deep slumber scrambled to battle stations. It was 1:05 A.M.

Two Japanese barges, moving very slowly, were seaward about one-half mile. To the PT crews, they were like big, fat ducks sitting out there in the water. They were low in the water, indicating heavy loads of supplies. Either the Japanese had failed to spot the lurking PTs, or had seen them and thought them to be friendly vessels. With a mighty roar, PT 191 charged toward the barges, followed by Bob Lynch's 68. Both boats poured fire into the leading barge, and it quickly sank.

Ewing's boat, with Lynch's following in its wake, made a large circle, then bore down on the second barge, which was now heading desperately for the black shore of the cove. When the Japanese vessel was less than a hundred yards from the beach, Ewing's boat caught up with it and raked it with automatic-weapons fire, then turned sharply away. Lynch's boat did likewise, but when it tried to turn there was a loud crunching sound as 68 ran aground on a reef, only some forty yards from shore.

Lying to out in the cove, Ensign Ewing received an urgent radio call from Bob Lynch: "We've run aground on a reef just offshore. Stuck fast. Can't get her to budge. Japs all over the beach."

"Don't run away," Ewing replied with levity that belied the gravity of the situation. "We're coming."

For the first time, Ewing and his crew noticed the fires that were burning about a hundred yards apart and on both sides of Lynch's stuck boat. When the two PTs had poured streams of tracer bullets into the two barges, some had overshot the target and raked the hillside beyond. Apparently this was a Japanese storage area, and the tracers had set fire to supply stocks. Advancing slowly and cautiously on one engine Bambi edged forward to the aid of the distressed boat and gently poked her bow up to Lynch's PT. The anchor line was passed over to 68, the plan being to secure the line to 68's bow so that Bambi could pull the boat off the reef. All the while, the blazes were growing larger and lighting up the beach.

Suddenly, large numbers of Japanese appeared and began dashing helter-skelter about the beach, only a stone's throw away. Their figures outlined eerily by the light of the flames, they were screaming and yelling wildly, apparently in a state of utter confusion. Probably this was the garrison manning the supply and ammunition base. The barges might have been caught just as they were coming in to unload.

It was a tense situation. The Americans had to fight a powerful urge to turn tail and run. But the anchor line was secured to the kingpost of each boat. Several times Bambi's groaning and protesting engines tried to dislodge 68. 68 would not budge. Many of the Japanese had lined up at the water's edge and were jabbering loudly. Perhaps they believed that the PTs were their own vessels and were shouting instructions on how best to handle the situation.

A few more attempts, all futile, were made to pull the boat free. Now Rum Ewing, Bob Lynch, and their executive officers held a hasty powwow on what to do next. Then *boom! boom! boom!* Three shore batteries had opened up. Were they shooting at Ewing's and

Lynch's boats? Or had they spotted other American vessels offshore? There were several moments of silence, and then Ewing called out, "Abandon ship!" The men on Lynch's boat needed no prodding. They were coming up out of the hatches like a pack of gophers and leaping onto Bambi. Up forward on 191, bluejackets were frantically pulling in the anchor line; they wished they could dig in to disappear between the coats of paint on the deck. Every few seconds the *boom! boom! boom!* burst forth anew.

Joe Davis in the forward gun turret, T. H. Dean, of Birmingham, Alabama, on the stern gun, and E. John Barton, of Dover, New York, in the aft turret, were gnawing at the bit. Their trigger fingers were itchy. The Japanese were still milling about on the beach, shouting and screaming, perfect targets in the light of the fires. Ensign Calhoun was on the bow of Bambi, helping the men from 68 aboard. In between those efforts, he stood there and shouted to the yammering Nipponese forty yards away, "Shut up, you goddamned sons of bitches!"

Some of the enemy soldiers, holding rifles overhead, were wading out toward the boats. They were shouting what sounded like, "Srendur! Srendur!" Apparently order had been partially restored on the beach after the chaos of the initial surprise, and an effort was being made to capture both the Americans and their Devil Boats.

At last, all hands were aboard Bambi, and Ensign Ewing backed away from ill-fated 68. To the Americans, it seemed like a century since Bambi had first reached Lynch's boat, but actually only a few minutes had passed. After pulling away an additional fifty yards from the beach, Ewing turned Bambi's starboard side to shore, in position to launch the PT's Sunday punch, as the Devil Boaters called it.

Each crewman on the 191 was eagerly fingering the trigger of some weapon from the arsenal of .30- and .50-caliber machine guns, and 20- and 40-mm cannon. In addition, Lieutenant Lynch and the men from 68 were sprawled topside on and under the torpedoes, each with a rifle or hand-held automatic weapon. The abandoned boat was directly between Bambi and the Japanese on the beach. Suddenly Ensign Ewing yelled, "Fire!" and there was an earsplitting din as every gun opened up. The enormous racket echoed for miles across the black sea and penetrated the thick jungle. Bullets poured into the Japanese, and, in a frenzy, they sought cover from the torrential rain of lead. Lynch's boat, the target of some gunners, burst into flame. More fires sprang up just behind the beach, as Japanese supply stockpiles were hit.

Relishing their work, the men continued to rake the beach until gun barrels were red hot and nearly all ammunition had been expended. Then Ensign Ewing called to John Calhoun at the helm, "Okay, Cal, let's head for the barn!" Calhoun threw the throttles forward and Bambi, like the thoroughbred she was, leaped forward and was soon swallowed up by the night. All hands looked back with grim satisfaction. What had been a series of fires at the Japanese supply base had now merged into one huge conflagration casting an orange glow into the night sky.

CHAPTER 12 Raid on a Secret Japanese Base

T he American war effort in the Pacific, by fall of 1943, was still an orphan, a stepchild at best, as far as the Joint Chiefs of Staff were concerned. Only 15 percent of production and fighting men was being allocated to the war against the Japanese empire. Adolf Hitler and Nazi Germany remained the number one target.

Eleven thousand miles from our nation's capital, supreme warlord Hideki Tojo and his Imperial High Command in Tokyo were taking a grim new look at their situation. Slowly, almost imperceptibly, the Japanese tide in the Pacific had begun to ebb. Defeats at Guadalcanal, in the Bismarck Sea, and on New Guinea's Papuan peninsula convinced Tojo that Japan had become overextended. Reluctantly, the Imperial High Command decided to draw in its horns. Under what was termed the "New Operational Policy," Nipponese forces would continue to contest savagely every foot of captured territory and hold present positions until the spring of 1944. By that time, significant fleet losses would be replaced and warplane strength would be tripled. Then—banzai! On to Australia!

But Douglas MacArthur had no intention of cooperating with Tojo's New Operational Policy. Like a skilled and cagey boxer fighting a much heavier foe, MacArthur continued to bob and weave, to keep the Japanese off balance, to "hit 'em where they ain't." In his series of leapfrog landings along New Guinea's northern coast, MacArthur's fighting men had seized Salamaua on September 12, Lae four days later. In the first combat employment of American airborne troops in the Pacific, the 503d Parachute Infantry Regiment bailed out over and quickly seized a key Japanese airfield at Nadzab. On October 2, Finschhafen fell to amphibious forces.

But these were only stepping-stones along the lengthy and tortuous road to Tokyo. They were but fortified American enclaves carved into the New Guinea coast, and the Japanese continued to hold long sections of real estate between these points. So Nipponese barges from New Britain, across the strait from eastern New Guinea, still departed nightly to run the PT boat gauntlet and bring in troops and supplies.

A key base for launching these barge runs to New Guinea was a few miles up the Pulie River, in southern New Britain. Due to the fact that it was far inland, shrouded by thick foliage, and on a barely navigable stream, the Japanese considered the terminal quite secure. To a degree, it was. American aircraft had been unable to locate it. PT boats had not yet tried to stick their noses into this hideout. They knew from countless patrols that barges had been coming out of the Pulie's mouth, but the precise location of the base remained unknown.

This juicy target continued to tempt the PT boaters. Finally, Lt. Oliver J. "Ollie" Schneiders, of Los Angeles, prevailed upon superiors to let him have a crack at it. Taking with him a nisei (Japanese-American) interpreter, Schneiders guided his boat to the mouth of the Pulie and started upstream. The starless night was dark and hot, quiet as a tomb. The only sounds were the faint purr of one muffled engine, the gentle lap of water against the bow, the muted whine of superchargers. A miniscule trace of light from the PT radarscope was the only challenge to the blackness. River banks, thick with trees and foliage, were only a few yards to each side of the boat—ideal locations for machine guns. Tension, thick enough to cut with a knife, gripped all aboard. Each knew that he could be nosing into a disastrous ambush. Nervously manning guns and trying desperately to penetrate the ink-black night, the men perspired profusely. Making five knots, the Devil Boat crept deeply and more deeply into the Japanese hideaway.

No American vessel had ever been up the Pulie. It was uncharted. One bluejacket, expecting to be raked by machine-gun fire at any moment, stood on the bow and repeatedly lowered a weighted line to measure the depth of the water. If the boat were to run aground, right in the enemy's backyard, it could be curtains for all on board.

Perhaps forty-five minutes after entering the Pulie—it seemed to those on board more like a lifetime—Lieutenant Ollie Schneiders detected the dim outlines of a group of huts and a small wharf jutting out into the river. Here it was—the Japanese barge terminal! Schneiders had a hasty, whispered discussion with the nisei, who, facing the huts and cupping hands to mouth, called out in Japanese: "Where can we tie our barge?"

Silence. A smothering pall of apprehension blanketed the Devil Boat. The occupants hardly dared to breathe. The PT was a sitting duck if ever there was one. Then from out of the darkness boomed a Japanese voice. Moments later lights flashed on. In plain view of the Americans were the structures at the base: huts, warehouses, sheds, all nestled between majestic palm trees.

A split second later: "Fire!" Schneiders shouted. Every gun on the floating arsenal began pouring streams of tracer bullets into the structures. Incendiaries ignited several small fires which quickly spread. The racket from the automatic weapons was deafening. Scores of Japanese, suddenly rousted from sleep, burst from the huts instinctively, ran directly into the American machine-gun fire and were cut down. Others headed frenziedly for the protection of the jungle. Now the entire base was a raging inferno. A mightly roar rocked the locale and an ammunition dump exploded with a mixture of fiery orange and black smoke.

The guns ceased firing. The eerie silence returned, punctuated by the angry crackle of flames. The PT men could see the crumpled forms of dead Nipponese on the shore. "Okay, let's haul ass!" a voice on the boat boomed out. There was no time for elation over wiping our an entire enemy barge terminal. No doubt the cacophony of spitting automatic weapons had alerted every Japanese "from hell to breakfast," as one anxious crewman observed. And there was only one avenue of escape: the same confining river route the PT had just traversed.

Hastily, Schneiders's boat started back. Moments later it ground to a halt. The PT had become stuck on the muddy bottom of the Pulie—right in the glare of the fire. The engines huffed and puffed, and in less than a minute the boat tore free. Boaters resumed breathing. To the astonishment of all aboard, the PT slipped back up the river without a shot being fired at it. Before daybreak, Ollie Schneiders and his bluejackets tied up at the rickety wharf at Morobe.

As the war in the Pacific inexorably widened in scope, so too did the operations of the Mosquito Fleet. New bases were being established in the western Solomons and on New Guinea. In early November, newly commissioned Squadron 21 arrived at the bleak Morobe hideaway. Led by thirty-six-year-old Lt. Comdr. Selman S. "Biff" Bowling, a Naval Academy graduate from New Albany, Indiana, Squadron 21's green but eager men were straining at the leash for action.

Earlier in the war, Biff Bowling had held a relatively cushy safe job as a staff communications officer with the South Pacific Amphibious Force, a function not to the liking of his combative spirit. So Bowling had volunteered regularly for patrols on Tulagi-based PTs, fallen in love with the Devil Boats, and badgered Navy brass until they assigned him to Melville, Long Island, where he formed and commanded Squadron 21.

Now, on arrival at the jetty at Morobe, the men of Bowling's squadron were greeted by the Old Salts (five weeks in combat) of Lt. Comdr. John Harllee's Squadron 12. Harllee's men noted promptly that Bowling's skippers were especially robust types. This husky collection had not been a coincidence. When Biff Bowling had returned to the States to fit out his own squadron, he was determined to get the biggest, roughest, toughest skippers he could locate.

As a result, Squadron 12 was rife with enough great professional and college football players to have formed a magnificent gridiron team. Among them were Ens. Ernest W. Pannell, a tackle with the famed Green Bay Packers; Ens. Alex Schibanoff, of the Detroit Lions; and Ens. Steven J. Levanitis, of the Philadelphia Eagles. Widely known college gridders were Ens. Bernard A. Crimmins, an all-American of Notre Dame; Lt. Paul B. Lillis, Notre Dame captain; Ens. Louis E. Smith, University of California halfback; Ens. Kermit W. Montz, Franklin and Marshall; Ens. William P. Hall, Wabash; Ens. Cedric J. Janien, Harvard; Ens. Stuart A. Lewis, University of California; and Ens. John M. Eastham, Jr., Texas A & M.

Bowling had also rounded up other prominent sports figures: Ens. Joseph W. Burk, holder of the world's record for single sculls (rowing); Ens. Kenneth D. Molloy, all-America lacrosse player from Syracuse University; Ens. James F. Foran, Princeton swimming champion; and Lt. John B. Williams, an Olympic swimmer from Oregon State.*

On the night of November 13/14, Lt. Hamlin D. Smith, in PT 154 (Tulagi Rot), and Lt. Michael R. Pessolano, in PT 155 (Ole Spooky), were prowling through the blackness a mile off Shortland Island, on a route barges were known to travel. Both Smith and Pessolano had binoculars to their eyes, looking for some indication of an enemy vessel. They had no way of knowing that at that precise moment Tulagi Rot and Ole Spooky were in the sights of a Japanese shore-based 3-inch gun-battery crew.

Suddenly the dark tranquility was shattered. *Boom! Boom! Boom!* Lightning-like flashes lit up the sky. Moments later three shells screamed toward the PT boats. Those on board ducked instinctively. A shell ripped into Ensign Smith's Tulagi Rot, causing a blinding explosion, tearing a gaping hole in the deck, and knocking out the steering mechanism. Men were blown topsy-turvy. Loud screams pierced the night as shrapnel ripped into flesh and bone. The pungent smell of cordite permeated the air. There were pitiful cries for help.

Bloody figures were sprawled about the deck. Lt. Joseph E. McLaughlin and QM2 Arthur J. Schwerdt had been killed, Lieutenant Smith and six bluejackets were wounded. Smith, half-conscious, gasped to MM1 John M. Nicholson, senior man remaining, to take over command of the boat. Somehow Nicholson managed to get the stalled engines going, and mangled Tulagi Rot limped toward the open sea.

As soon as Lieutenant Pessolano, in Ole Spooky, had seen shells landing around Tulagi Rot he quickly headed away from shore. But when he saw Smith's boat hit, he rapidly reversed course and raced toward the stricken PT. Nearing Tulagi Rot, whose rudder control

---

* No doubt the athletes' keen physical and mental skills, their demonstrated courage in rough-and-tumble competition, served them well in PT operations. Most of these Squadron 21 skippers would perform admirably in combat. But whether athletes, as a class, operated PT boats in a superior manner to nonathletes is open to conjecture.

had been knocked out, Pessolano tried to edge up close and collided with Smith's boat, ripping off Tulagi Rot's aft torpedo and tube. The boats untangled, and both managed to move farther out to sea.

Out of range of the shore battery, Pessolano came alongside Hamlin Smith's battered 154 and transferred the wounded to Ole Spooky. While 155 headed for its Treasury Island base, Pessolano stayed aboard Tulagi Rot and, using emergency steering control (a hand tiller), took the boat slowly to the base. It arrived more than two and a half hours after his own Ole Spooky.

At about this same time, Ens. Theodore Berlin, in PT 167, along with LCI gunboat 70 left Cape Torokina at midafternoon to escort LCT (landing craft, tank) 68 to Treasury Island. Torokina was on the northern coast of Bougainville, the largest of the Solomon Islands. At dusk the tiny flotilla was twenty-eight miles south of Cape Torokina after an uneventful journey.

Berlin and his executive officer, Ens. Paul B. "Red" Fay, Jr., were discussing the welcome quiet when suddenly those aboard heard the roar of airplane engines.* Men scrambled to battle stations just as twelve Japanese torpedo planes headed for their PT. Automatic weapons on the Devil Boat chattered. The first plane, the meatballs on each wing visible in the twilight, zoomed in so low crewmen topside ducked as it sheered off the PT's radio antenna. The torpedo plane flew on for nearly a mile, then began wobbling and crashed into the sea, the antenna's victim.

Moments after the torpedo plane had roared over the 167 boat, Berlin and his crew felt a jolt, but there was no explosion. The Americans continued to blast away at the buzzing swarm of Japanese warplanes circling menacingly. Then three torpedo planes headed for Berlin's boat, and the 20-mm gunners on the fantail poured tracers into the oncoming aircraft. The first plane started smoking, but continued to rush toward the Devil Boat. It plunged into the water so close to Berlin's PT that the fantail gunners were drenched by the enormous spout of water.

In the meantime, other planes had pounced on gunboat 70, whose gunners had been firing back furiously. Torpedoes and ammunition

* Years later, President John F. Kennedy appointed Paul Burgess Fay, Jr., Under Secretary of the Navy.

expended and darkness falling, the Nipponese planes flew off for home.

Ensigns Berlin and Fay promptly began inspecting their boat for damage. Going below, they reached the bow, and now they found what had caused the mysterious jolt when the first plane had sliced off the PT's antenna. The aircraft's torpedo had passed through the bow without exploding, leaving a gaping hole on each side of the boat. Pieces of the torpedo's fins and one of its rudders remained aboard, macabre souvenirs to remind the boat's personnel what might have been. The holes were considerably above the waterline, so there was no danger of 167 sinking.

Ensign Berlin took what his men called "our hole-ly boat" alongside gunboat 70, and found that it, too, had been the beneficiary of a minor miracle: 70 had an unexploded torpedo lodged in its engine room.

The following day, Radio Tokyo gave its version of the encounter: "Our courageous airmen sank one large carrier and one small carrier of Bougainville."

Over at Morobe, on New Guinea, during the first week in December, Lt. Comdr. Barry Atkins climbed on board Lt. Edward Farley's moored PT 190 early one afternoon. Atkins said he had a special mission for Farley and that 190 (nicknamed Jack O' Diamonds) should be ready to shove off at 4:00 P.M., only a few hours away. The task, which promised "excitement," was to transport an American and an Australian scout, together with nine natives who had undergone training, to a beach near Cape Gloucester on the western tip of Japanese-held New Britain. It was an especially sensitive island for the Nipponese, for their mighty bastion of Rabaul was located on its north-eastern tip.

The landing party, which would go ashore under cover of night, was to reconnoiter enemy positions and determine his strength around Cape Gloucester. That was all Commander Atkins knew about the urgent mission—or was willing to tell. If captured, Ed Farley and his men could not reveal to the enemy what they didn't know. Only later would Farley learn the purpose of his mission: General MacArthur's forces would conduct an amphibious landing at Cape Gloucester on December 26.

Not only would Farley's boat be heading directly into heavy Japanese concentrations, but the course through the Siassi Straits was a treacherous one. It was also the shortest route and offered the best possibility for getting through undetected. The success of the mission would depend a great deal upon Lt. Eric N. Howitt, Royal Australian Navy, who would pilot the PT through the Straits. In peacetime, the fifty-two-year-old Howitt had operated a copra plantation and had sailed the coastal waters of New Guinea and New Britain for more than fifteen years.

Jack O' Diamonds pulled out of Morobe at twilight. As expected, the trek through Siassi Straits was slow and tortuous. Lieutenant Farley was at the wheel and carefully heeded a continuing flow of instructions from the calm, imperturbable Howitt. It required more than an hour to negotiate the six-mile-long Straits.

It was just before 11:00 P.M. when the PT's radioman reported objects off the port bow showing on the radar. A short time later, lookouts on Jack spotted the dark outlines of four Japanese barges less than fifty yards away, moving in line in the opposite direction. Farley's gunners anxiously fingered triggers: this juicy target could be wiped out with one full-blown Sunday punch. Lieutenant Commander Atkins, aboard 190 as tactical commander, was confronted with a crucial decision: blast the barges or continue on the night's mission? Atkins chose to proceed.

Apparently the four barges were unaware of the PT boat. One by one they slipped past, as Jack, with engines muffled, crawled ahead in the opposite direction.

When the designated beach near Cape Gloucester was reached, Jack lay to a hundred yards offshore. The quiet was unearthly. Crewmen whispered that they could smell the Japanese cooking aromas. The night was black as ink, ideal for sneaking ashore—and for stumbling into enemy ambushes there. The American and Australian scouts, faces blackened, gear securely taped to prevent any telltale sound, gingerly climbed into a pair of rubber rafts and were followed by the natives.

These were tense moments. The slightest sound might betray their presence. Then someone on the boat inadvertently knocked an oar overboard. It made only a small splash, but to those of Jack O' Diamonds it sounded like a cannon going off. They were convinced that Tojo in Tokyo had been awakened by the noise.

The rafts, however, were paddled ashore soundlessly, and the landing party slipped onto the beach, hid the rafts in underbrush, and vanished into the jungle.

Lieutenant Farley had arranged earlier for brief radio contact so the boat would know if the party had landed safely and was on its way. Now, only a stone's throw from the beach, Lt. George Walbridge on Jack was closely monitoring a walkie-talkie. Some twenty minutes later, a loud voice with an Australian accent thundered over Walbridge's earphones: "Okay, Yanks, we're all set!"

Standing next to Walbridge, Ed Farley winced. The Aussie's booming remarks surely must have alerted every Japanese on Cape Gloucester. "Good luck!" Lieutenant Walbridge whispered.

Lieutenant Farley quickly gave the report to Lieutenant Commander Atkins on topside. He nodded his head, then called out in a stage whisper, "Now let's go get those goddamn barges we passed!"

As Jack O' Diamonds slipped out into the open sea, Ed Farley reflected on the lot of the landing party. Operating a plywood PT boat in combat situations is certainly no fun, he was fully aware. But scouting behind enemy lines, especially for long periods of time and perhaps a hundred miles or more from the nearest American, had to be one of the most perilous and gruelling tasks of war. Farley doubted if the two scouts and their eager natives would be heard from again.

Jack O' Diamonds scoured the waters until dawn in search of the four barges that had almost literally slipped through the Americans' fingers a few hours earlier. The hunt proved futile; the barges apparently long since had reached their destination, their crews not knowing how close they had come to sudden destruction.

That morning back at Morobe, Lieutenant Commander Atkins was still determined to nail the four Japanese barges. He ordered Lt. Alfred G. Vanderbilt, of New York City, a figure prominent in horse racing circles and scion of a wealthy, socially prominent east-coast family, and Lt. Ray Turnbull, of Monrovia, California, to track down and destroy those enemy vessels. That night, utilizing directions and other information obtained from Ed Farley, Vanderbilt, in 196 (Shamrock), and Turnbull, in 195 (Black Agnes), threaded their way through treacherous Siassi Straits and began prowling in search of their quarry.

It was just past midnight. High in the heavens the stars were twinkling. There was no moon, and visibility was limited. As Shamrock and Black Agnes cut softly through the night, their crews were startled suddenly. The sounds of singing—Japanese singing—wafted across the water. Moments later the dark hulks of two barges hove into view, only some forty yards away. As the Nipponese continued harmonizing, it seemed clear to Vanderbilt and Turnbull that the enemy was totally unaware of the PT boats only a hop, skip, and jump away from them.

In short order, the songfest was interrupted. A deadly salvo of automatic weapons and 40-mm fire from the Devil Boats raked the barges, at popgun range. Black Agnes and Shamrock then raced back and forth, firing into the enemy vessels. By the outlines of many helmeted heads, Turnbull and Vanderbilt knew the barges were filled with soldiers.

Racing in for a second strafing foray, Ray Turnbull spotted the silhouettes of two more barges, also crowded with helmeted heads. Turnbull's gunners raked them with fire, and the barges disappeared beneath the surface, leaving scores of soldiers floundering in the dark water. Vanderbilt, meanwhile, detected a fifth barge, and Shamrock crewmen peppered it with a torrent of bullets. The barge caught fire, then began to sink. Men on the Shamrock could see figures frantically fighting the blaze. Then a 40-mm shell tore into the disabled barge at the waterline, and it sank immediately.

With three down and two to go, Turnbull and Vanderbilt again turned their attention to the first pair of barges. The enemy vessels were lashed together, presumably to permit soldiers from one to transfer to the other less damaged craft. Aware that the Devil Boats were back after them, the barges separated and one tried to ram Black Agnes, whose gunners were firing furiously at the oncoming vessel. When barely fifty feet from Agnes, the barge seemed suddenly to lift out of the water. Its guns were blown in the air, its hulk riddled with holes. Illumination from Agnes' tracers revealed perhaps twenty Japanese soldiers sprawled dead on the barge's deck. Several Nipponese tried to escape by leaping overboard but were cut down in midair or after hitting the water. Then this barge and its companion vessel went under.

Reverberations from the midnight shootout off New Britain echoed all the way to the higher councils of war in the Japanese capital. The hated Green Dragons were moving steadily up the ladder of Nipponese Public Enemies. Tokyo Rose took angrily to the airwaves to denounce the latest "atrocity" committed by the Devil Boats; earlier she had labeled them the "Butchers of the Bismarck Sea." In the future, PT crews, if captured, would not be treated as honorable prisoners of war, Tokyo Rose exclaimed, but as "war criminals."

Two weeks after depositing the scouting party at Cape Gloucester, Lt. Ed Farley, in Jack O' Diamonds, returned to the same beach to retrieve them. Few on Jack expected the scouts to appear. But, exhausted yet chipper, the landing party did keep the prearranged rendezvous. Forty-eight hours later the American and the Australian scouts were at General MacArthur's main headquarters in Brisbane, pouring out a Niagara of details on Japanese troop strength, positions, and fortifications along Cape Gloucester.*

* Unfortunately, in the fog of war and with the passage of time, the names of the scouts, one American, one Australian, have vanished. But when MacArthur's troops stormed Cape Gloucester beaches a few days later, many survivors would unknowingly owe their lives to this pair of gallant and unheralded men and their native helpers.

CHAPTER 13   Two PT Boats vs Thirty-Five Dive Bombers

Ome of the most closely guarded secrets of the Pacific war was the existence of a cloak-and-dagger agency called the Allied Intelligence Bureau (AIB). Only a handful of officers even knew of its existence. The agency had been created hastily in Australia in early 1942 when General MacArthur realized he was fighting "blind." When the United States had been bombed into a global war at Pearl Harbor, neither its armed forces nor government had an intelligence service worthy of the name.

Under German-born, ponderous Maj. Gen. Charles Willoughby, MacArthur's intelligence chief, AIB was divided into several branches, including one involved with spreading propaganda, another that specialized in every form of sabotage, killing, and "dirty fighting," and a third (code name Operation Ferdinand) that had hundreds of Allied and native volunteers who, at great personal peril, served as coast watchers on scores of islands to report firsthand on Japanese ship and air activities.

Another top-secret Allied intelligence operation was a chain of U.S. Army and Navy radio listening posts that ringed the Japanese empire from Alaska to Australia. Hundreds of enemy ciphered messages were picked out of the air by the radio monitors, decoded, and rushed to high-level intelligence officers. Hush-hush agencies had been in operation at Pearl Harbor (code name HYPO) and at Washington D.C. (NEGAT), to uncover Japanese military secrets. These efforts were being matched at General MacArthur's headquarters by a unit whose code name was BELCONNEN. At a BELCONNEN listening post in northern Australia, the first week in December 1943, a Navy rating, his ear cocked to a receiving set, was furiously scribbling down a top-secret message being sent from Tokyo to field commanders in the southwest Pacific. Decoded, the message declared:

> At all costs, American PT boats must be smashed before we can reinforce garrisons now defending New Britain and New Guinea.

Early in December, to no PT man's regret, the hellhole of Morobe was unceremoniously abandoned. After nearly nineteen months of fighting, American and Allied foot sloggers had cleared the Japanese from the entire Huon Gulf region on the eastern tail of New Guinea. The PT base was now moved westward along the spine of New Guinea to Dreger Harbor, near Finschhafen. Men of Squadrons 12 and 21 greeted the move with mixed reactions. The new base would eliminate countless hours of "dead time" (that is, time consumed in reaching an area to be patrolled), save thousands of gallons of precious gasoline, and provide the PT men with a more comfortable and "half-civilized" mode of living. There were even drinks served at the officers's shack, a welcome switch from "torpedo juice." On the other hand, Dreger Harbor was virtually in the front lines: only six miles to the north, Australian "diggers" were slugging it out with Japanese soldiers. In the hush of the night, PT men lying in straw shacks or topside on moored boats could hear the artillery shells exploding.

Christmas was fast approaching. But the war raged on. On December 24, after a night on an uneventful patrol, Ens. Rum Ewing, in PT 191 (Bambi), and Ens. Herbert P. Knight, in PT 152 (Lack-a-Nookie), were returning to Dreger Harbor after dawn. It was difficult for the skippers and crewmen alike to realize that this was going to be Christmas Eve. It was hot, even stifling. The boats were nearing a small, bottleneck harbor near New Guinea's Gneisenau Point, a harbor PT men had long suspected hid some kind of Japanese operation, although air reconnaissance had not uncovered its nature.

Ewing and Knight hastily discussed the approaching mystery harbor and decided that they would poke their noses inside "just for the hell of it."

As the boats edged carefully through the entrance, all on board were electrified by what they saw: a Japanese submarine, one about 100 to 125 feet long. The men had long yearned to sink a submarine. Apparently unmanned, the underwater craft lay up near the beach. A heavily loaded barge, broadside to the sandy shore, lay next to it. On the other side of the submarine was a picket boat, seemingly awaiting repair.

Rum Ewing and Herb Knight threw throttles forward and roared toward the beach. Their itchy-fingered gunners fondled triggers. Ashore a group of Japanese ran about, shouting and gesturing toward the onrushing Devil Boats, then raced frantically for the nearby jungle. Shouts of "Fire!" rang out on Bambi and Lack-a-Nookie, and a torrent of bullets and shells tore into the three enemy craft. During a brief lull in the firing, a loud hissing noise like escaping compressed air was heard coming from the submarine. Its stern was on the beach, and it began to settle by the bow, finally coming to rest on the bottom in six feet of water.

The skippers could see that the sub's hull had been badly shot up, so they circled and made another run, riddling the barge and picket boat with both shells and bullets. Both vessels were destroyed. Not a shot had been fired at the PTs.

The youthful bluejackets were jubilant. They wanted to board the cigar-shaped submarine, hitch a line to it, and tow it more than a hundred miles back to base. But Ewing and Knight, wise old heads of twenty-two and twenty-three, counseled against such an enterprising effort to corral a prize of war in such a unique manner. "We've tempted fate long enough for one day," they exclaimed. But before roaring out of the narrow-necked harbor, the PTs poured incendiary bullets into the living and supply straw shacks, leaving the Japanese base a blazing inferno.

Arriving back at Dreger Harbor several hours later, Lieutenant Commander Harllee sent for Ensigns Knight and Ewing. He had just heard about their spontaneous bolt into the small confined harbor.

Harllee read the riot act to the two skippers for their "impulsive behavior" that "could have endangered boats and crews." Then, with a twinkle in his eye, Harllee added, "Off the record, that was goddamned good work!"

Ewing left the headquarters shack and reported to his sweating crew: "I'll bet we're the only bunch of bastards that ever sank a Jap submarine and caught hell for it!"*

Although disappointed over being unable to tow home the Japanese underwater craft they had helped bag, Ensign Ewing's crew had cause for elation. Before the boat left the States the previous May, Ewing's father, Nathaniel, a St. Louis insurance executive, had promised Bambi's men a $1,000 prize should the PT boat sink a submarine or destroyer or a ship of comparable size, the money to be split up equally. Forbidden to give specifics on actions, Rum Ewing wrote his father: "Christmas Eve was payday for us from you."

On receipt of his son's letter, Nathaniel Ewing paid off promptly. Accompanying his check for $1,000 (a tidy sum in 1943) was a note: "I have never been so pleased to be a thousand dollars lighter."

Christmas Day was typically hot, breathless, cloudless. The Navy made a valiant effort to bring a little "home" into the lives of the PT boat crews at Dreger Harbor (and elsewhere in the Pacific). Turkeys were distributed to each PT boat—birds that were half-cooked in many cases. PT cooks, enterprising men accustomed to being confronted with the unexpected, recooked the turkeys.

On Ed Farley's moored boat, Squadron 12 leader John Harllee was guest of honor for Christmas dinner. In a display of naval democracy, Lieutenant Commander Harllee, other officers, and bluejackets were shoehorned into the tiny mess compartment below and, elbow-to-elbow, knee-to-knee, devoured juicy pieces of turkey plus all the trimmings. Then Farley passed out the cigars he had long hoarded for the occasion.

By the close of 1943, the lethal Green Dragons had become an ever-increasing torment to the Japanese in the southwest Pacific. What

---

* Three weeks later, after Allied ground troops had overrun Gneisenau Point, Lt. George Vanderbilt, Intelligence officer of Squadron 12, examined the underwater vessel sunk by Bambi and Lack-a-Nookie. It had heeled over on its side in eight feet of water.

especially frustrated the Nipponese was that they seldom had the opportunity to retaliate due to the will-o-the-wisp modus operandi of these swift, spunky hornets that struck unexpectedly and with great fury, then raced away to be gobbled up by the night. But a chance to realize long pent-up dreams of retaliation would not be long in coming.

Shortly after sunrise on December 27, a pair of PT boats, Bambi, under Rumsey Ewing, and Jack O'Diamonds, skippered by Ed Farley, were ready to head for home after a fruitless night of prowling up and down the southern coast of New Britain off Cape Peiho. In Farley's boat were Lt. Henry M. S. "Swifty" Swift, who was in tactical command, and Lt. Eric Howitt, the Australian who had acted as a scout at Cape Gloucester.

Reluctant to return empty-handed, the PTs poked their noses into Marije Bay, and finding no sign of the enemy set a course for Dreger. They had already tarried too long, the officers agreed. It was 7:35 A.M.

Ed Farley turned the wheel over to his executive officer, Lt. William N. Bannard, and went below for coffee. (Bannard was the son-in-law of PT boat builder Preston Sutphen of Electric Boat Company, Elco, in New Jersey.) On Bambi, Rum Ewing had the wheel, and his number two man, Fred Calhoun, a Colorado rancher from Delta, was stretched out on a bunk below, encumbered only by a pair of socks.

Almost at the stroke of eight bells (8:00 A.M.), a Japanese plane dove from a cloud bank toward the Devil Boats. There was the eerie swishing sound of a falling bomb, and then a loud explosion. Jack O'Diamonds seemed to lift out of the water. Ed Farley peeked from the chart house just in time to see a thirty-foot geyser of water leap into the air, then splash down on his boat's deck.

"That was close!" Lieutenant Bannard at the helm called out, belaboring the obvious. Then: "Here come more of the bastards!"

On Bambi, Ensign Calhoun, nimble of mind and body, hit the deck, and in one motion reached for his shorts and had them on before the bomb geyser had returned to the sea. Men on both boats leaped to their guns and aimed streams of lead at the enemy plane. Amid the cacaphony of noise from the spitting PT machine guns, Calhoun dashed to the cockpit, scanned the sky, and nudged Ewing with his elbow. "Do you see what I see?" he exclaimed.

Ewing squinted upward to the north, then to the west. "My God!" he replied.

They saw more warplanes approaching, swarms of them, perhaps thirty, maybe thirty-five, even forty of them. No one had time to count. Val and Zeke dive bombers. They were soon circling high above, like starving vultures over a wounded animal.

Men on both boats were grim faced. One bluejacket on Bambi exclaimed, "Keee-ryst, the whole Nip air force has showed up!"

Ensign Ewing broke formation to divide the targets. Far off in the distance, directly over the course to Dreger Harbor, low storm clouds—good for cover—were spotted. But could the PTs reach them in time?

Now the first dive bombers were peeling off and zooming down toward the Devil Boats, which began to take frenzied evasive action. The Vals were greeted by heavy bursts of machine-gun fire, too, but loosed their bombs anyway. Hard on their heels, four Zekes, with the sound of screaming banshees, swung downward. The bombs rained down all around the beseiged little boats. Gunners on Bambi and Jack were blazing away, and one Val, trailing a long plume of black smoke, glided for about a mile and then crashed.

Concussions from bomb explosions caused Bambi and Jack O'Diamonds to pitch and heave like children's toys in a bathtub. But their machine guns continued to spit lead at their tormentors. A Zeke climbed steeply, then went into a sharp dive and plunged into the sea. But in waves of three and four, the planes pressed on with the attack.

None of the veteran PT men had any illusions as to their chances. With a little luck, we have perhaps fifteen minutes to live, Fred Calhoun reflected. While gunners kept their barrels hot, radiomen on both boats were calling Finschafen frantically for air support. That was the PTs' only slim chance for survival.

"Have you reached them yet?" Ed Farley shouted above the din to his radio operator. A bomb exploding directly in Jack's path sent up a geyser that drenched the boat.

"No, sir," the operator replied.

"Why not?"

"Circuits are all busy!"

Now the Vals and Zekes, hovering menacingly above, began strafing runs. GM Edmund "Buzz" Barton, a twenty-two-year-old from Dover, New Hampshire, was blasting away at a Zeke that was roaring downward with nose cannon blazing. One shell tore into Barton's twin-mounted fifties and knocked one gun from its base. The blast bolted Barton over, but he was unhurt. A jagged, white-hot sliver of shrapnel from the same shell ripped into Ensign Ewing's abdomen and emerged from his back. Ewing, seriously wounded and paralyzed, slumped to the cockpit floor, a stunned look on his face. He lay there racked with pain and unable to move a muscle, yet fully aware of each howling bomber roaring toward Bambi from the clouds.

At the same time Ewing was cut down, a chunk of shrapnel tore into Ensign Calhoun's hip. With a stream of blood flowing down his leg, Calhoun struggled to the cockpit and grabbed the wheel. While zigzagging the boat desperately and also directing gunfire, he had to stand astride Ewing, for in their fight for survival no one could take time to remove the skipper.

Bombs seemed to be exploding closer and closer to Bambi. As each Val or Zeke dove and released its lethal cargo, Calhoun could see it coming and took violent evasive action. Yet, as a bomb plummeted downward, Calhoun told himself, "This one will blow us to hell!" He was struck by a curious thought: if the plywood Bambi were to receive a direct hit, how many millions of matchsticks would result?

Despite the rain of Japanese bombs and machine-gun bullets being hurled at the two dodging, darting Devil boats, the enemy was paying a price. Two more Vals were shot down by the American gunners. A few others limped home trailing traces of smoke. But no one on Bambi or Jack felt exhilaration; there was too much grim, unfinished business at hand.

At Bambi's stern, Chief Motor Machinist's Mate Thomas H. Dean, of Miami, Florida, and Motor Machinist's Mate August Sciutto, of Brooklyn, New York, were firing their 20-mm gun. A Japanese shell struck the barrel of the weapon and richocheted into its magazine, exploding six or eight shells. The two men's faces were instantly transformed into bloody masks. Slivers tore into Sciutto below each eye, and another lodged in his brain. He collapsed.*

Dean was struck in the forehead, stomach, foot, and had the fingers of his left hand mangled. Yet he crawled slowly forward from the fantail and insisted that he be allowed to continue the fight. But

---

* August Sciutto remembered nothing until he awakened in a hospital in Brisbane, three weeks later. He would carry the metal sliver embedded in his brain because doctors were unable to operate on it.

he was taken below by Motor Machinist's Mate First Class Victor A. Bloom, of Lynn, Massachusetts, for fear that, in his intense pain, Dean would stumble overboard.

Still the Nipponese planes came. Bambi was already riddled with bullet and shell-fragment holes, and an eighteen-inch hole had been blown in her port side. Now another specter reared its ugly head: bomb fragments had hit water jackets on two engines, and jets of hot water were spurting through the engine room. The starboard intake manifold also was hit, and the supercharger forced gasoline flames into the engine room. Bambi stood in mortal danger of going dead in the water.

Bloom, senior engineer on Bambi, knew that the gas tanks were hit and leaking and might burst into flame or explode at any moment. Although painfully scalded by the spurting streams of hot water, Bloom, working against time, taped and stuffed the leaks, then, with great presence of mind, closed off the tank compartment and smothered the space with carbon dioxide. All the while Bloom was laboring, he could hear bullets periodically ripping through Bambi's thin skin.

At his post in the cockpit where he had been spinning the wheel to dodge falling bombs, Fred Calhoun heard RM John Fraser, of Rockville Centre, New York, shout from below: "The fighters have heard us. The say to hang on for ten more minutes and they'll be here!"

A tingle of faint hope flowed through those on Bambi. Tired and near collapse, Calhoun looked down between his feet where Ewing lay ashen faced. Calhoun was convinced his friend was a goner. In his desperation, he called down to Radioman Fraser the only thing that had come to mind: "Tell them if they can't get here in five minutes they might as well not come."

But they did come. And within the crucial five minutes. Off in the distance men on Jack O'Diamonds and Bambi could discern the flight of American Eagles, like the U.S. cavalry of the Old West, riding to the rescue at the last minute. Perhaps forty planes in all— P-40s and P-47s—streaked in and tore into the Japanese aircraft, which promptly turned and headed for their base at Rabaul. Every man aboard the pair of PTs who was not too wounded to care gave a rousing cheer of jubilation. Perhaps they would live to see another sunset after all.

Not many of the Vals and Zekes made it home. In addition to the four planes shot down by the PT gunners, sixteen more were downed by the Eagles in dogfights in the chase back to Rabaul. When the Army Air Corps took over the fight, Bambi's exhausted men flopped to the deck. The death struggle had lasted for perhaps forty-five minutes; to the Americans, it had seemed a lifetime. Now the fright that had gripped Bambi's young crew (a few were not long out of high school) manifested itself. Two or three—brave boys all, who had come through unflinchingly when the chips were down—broke out in soft sobs. Others tried to sit upright, but could not due to jerking muscles. Etched into each face was that haunted look of fighting men who have just come face-to-face with the Black Angel of Death and have somehow been spared.

Bambi, battered and bruised, limped onward and, hours later, made Dreger Harbor under her own power. Although Jack O'Diamonds had been buffeted and pitched about by at least a score of bombs that had barely missed, the boat had emerged relatively unscathed.

That night from the Japanese capital, Radio Tokyo related to *tanaka* (Nipponese equivalent of John Q. Public) a stirring account of that morning's battle. Said the excited announcer: "Off the southern coast of New Britain, our courageous airmen sank an entire flotilla of American PT boats without the loss of a single airplane."

Ens. Rum Ewing confounded the prediction of his pal Fred Calhoun that the skipper was "a goner." A few days later, Ewing and Tom Dean were lying side by side on cots in a makeshift hospital at Dreger Harbor. Although badly shot up and in pain, both men were in good spirits and joked about their wounds. Referring to the hunk of jagged metal that had ripped into his abdomen and come out his back, Ewing quipped to a visitor: "The only thing they could find wrong was that there's a shaft of light running clear through me—and that's against Navy regulations."

CHAPTER 14   Agony on a Raft

At General Douglas MacArthur's headquarters in Brisbane the first week in January 1944, an intense reappraisal of the strategic situation in the southwest Pacific was in progress. It had taken the Allies a year to claw forward 240 miles northwest of Buna. There were still 2,240 miles to go to reach the supreme commander's primary objective—Manila, in the Philippines. Manila was still as far from MacArthur's grasp as Chicago is from Los Angeles. At the current pace, it might take ten years to reach the Philippines, another five years to push on to Tokyo.

MacArthur saw only one solution for accelerating the tempo of the Allied advance: lengthen the leapfrog jumps rather than increase their number. His eye was on the Vogelkop Peninsula at the far western tip of New Guinea. Beyond that lay the Moluccas, an ideal springboard for the Philippines. But to reach the Moluccas, MacArthur would need one more base in the Bismarck Sea. The Admiralty Islands, three hundred miles northwest of Dreger Harbor, would fill this need. He would get there in one mighty leap.

General MacArthur's staff was flabbergasted over the proposal. It would mean the greatest gamble yet in the southwest Pacific, they argued. A recon party that had slipped ashore on Manus Island, the largest in the Admiralties, and on Los Negros, the second largest, reported them to be "lousy with Japs." Staff officers pointed out that the closest Allied base was at Finschhafen, three hundred miles away, too far to reinforce the beachhead. MacArthur, calmly puffing on his corncob pipe, replied evenly he would reinforce by air. What if the Admiralties' airstrips aren't in American hands? They will be, MacArthur assured them. Target date for invading the Admiralties was set for the final week in February.

While major strategic decisions were being thrashed out in the rarified atmosphere of high command, Ens. Ernie Pannell, the brawny Green Bay Packers' tackle, in PT 324, and Ens. Frederick C. Feeser, in PT 363 (Ace's Avenger), were stalking the coast of New Guinea on the night of January 7. They caught four barges, loaded with perhaps 150 Japanese soldiers, heading for the enemy stronghold of Madang.

Pannell and Feeser charged forward and were met by a torrent of fire from the barges. All PT guns were blazing. Almost at once GM1 Frank C. Walker, firing a 37-mm gun on Feeser's craft, was knocked down by a slug that ripped into his abdomen. Bleeding profusely, Walker struggled to his feet and continued to shoot until the PTs had finished their run. Then he collapsed.

Some of his mates carried the unconscious Walker below. His face was nearly white, his blood was saturating the bunk. Briefly Walker regained consciousness and whispered to comrades, "Did we get them?" Assured (correctly) that the four barges and 150 of the emperor's soldiers had been sent to the bottom, Walker gave a weak smile. Then to the man who would replace him, the wounded sailor said, "Get those guns cleaned up, son." Moments later Frank Walker was dead.

All along the rugged northern coast of New Guinea, the Japanese were finding it increasingly difficult to bring in supplies to their isolated garrisons. During the three months of November 1943 through January 1944, PT boats had sunk 147 barges. In their desperation, the Nipponese were employing submarines for resupply missions in much larger numbers. Snooping PT boats periodically discovered rafts carrying rubber bags of rice, tins of dried fish, and waterproof boxes of medical supplies. The submarines had surfaced offshore, loaded supplies on rafts, then submerged. It was hoped that the tide would carry the floating supplies to the beach where they would be retrieved.

Gen. Charles Willoughby, MacArthur's intelligence chief, was accumulating much evidence that the Devil Boats were achieving their mission of strangling the Japanese barge traffic. Australian troops, hacking their way along the New Guinea coast, reported finding the carcasses of ten pack animals that the starving Nipponese had slaughtered and eaten. At another locale, the Aussies discovered the grisly remains of five Japanese cadavers that had been cut up, cooked, and seemed to have been devoured. One captured Japanese, who was a living skeleton, told interrogators that, in desperation, foraging parties had been sent deep into the jungle in search of food. On occasion, the POW stated, these search parties failed to return. Apparently they had been captured and eaten by native headhunters.

Late in February, newly promoted Lt. Fred Calhoun, who had been wounded in the hip when Bambi was badly shot up by Japanese warplanes, returned to active duty with Squadron 12, just in time to be sent on a special mission. Native coast watchers had reported that the Japanese had occupied a mansion at Higgins Point on Rooke Island and were using it as a headquarters. Calhoun was ordered to blast the mansion off the map.

An Australian civilian was brought aboard Calhoun's PT to navigate through treacherous reefs just offshore from the target, which sat on a hill overlooking the sea.

Reaching the objective, Calhoun lay to just offshore and his gunners began firing into the sturdy mansion. The bullets and shells seemed to be having little effect. The Aussie suggested to the skipper, "Raise your gunfire a little, because the lower floor is concrete." The gunners complied, and in minutes the structure collapsed into a pile of masonry and wood splinters.

Now the volunteer navigator pointed to a clump of trees. "You might want to send a few bursts in there," he stated. "There's a building hidden in among those trees, and the Nips are probably using that, too." The PT gunners opened a torrent of fire, and as bullets and shells defrocked the trees of their leaves, the building became visible. It also was blasted apart.

As the PT set a course for home, the curious Lieutenant Calhoun asked the Aussie, "How in the hell did you know the layout so well back there?"

With no display of emotion, the Australian replied, "Because I built the place with my own hands and lived there with my family 'til the bloody Japs showed up."

Late in the afternoon of February 27, General Douglas MacArthur strode briskly up the gangplank of the cruiser *Phoenix* in Milne Bay. It was the first Navy vessel he had been on since leaving Lt. John Bulkeley's PT 41 in the Philippines nearly two years earlier. That night *Phoenix* sailed for the Admiralties and the biggest risk MacArthur had taken to date. At dawn, the invasion armada dropped anchor in Hayne Harbor off Los Negros, and Maj. Gen. Innis P. "Bull" Swift's 1st Cavalry Division stormed the beaches. Four hours later, Douglas MacArthur went ashore in a driving rainstorm.

The supreme commander walked right into a buzzsaw. Cavalrymen (they had long since been divested of horses) in steel helmets and battle fatigues were lying prone in the mud, engaged in a fierce firefight with entrenched Japanese. Conspicuous in his salmon trenchcoat and gold-embroidered hat, MacArthur strolled casually about as anxious aides tried to get him to take cover. As bullets whizzed past like angry bees, a young cavalry lieutenant tugged at the supreme commander's sleeve, pointed toward a path, and exclaimed, "Pardon me, sir, but we killed a Jap sniper there just a few minutes ago!" The general, without missing a draw on his corncob, replied evenly, "Fine, lieutenant, that's just the thing to do with them."

Splattered with mud, soaked to the skin, MacArthur reboarded the *Phoenix* late that afternoon, satisfied that the operation was in good shape. Six days later, American troops were in firm control of both Manus and Los Negros.

Hard on the heels of Douglas MacArthur's three-hundred mile leap, new PT bases were established rapidly at Seeadler Harbor in the Admiralties and at Talasea on the northern coast of New Britain. From Talasea, the doughty Devil Boats were prowling as far eastward as Cape Lambert, only forty miles from the Japanese bastion at Rabaul. Now there were four distinct areas of PT operations: the Admiralties, the northern New Guinea coast, and northern and southern New Britain.

On the night of March 6/7, a pair of PTs, their crews at battle stations, were stealing into New Guinea's Hansa Bay, a Japanese stronghold 135 miles northwest of the boat's base at Saidor. Typically, the Devil Boats were looking for trouble. Lt. Comdr. N. Burt Davis, Jr., Squadron 24 skipper, was aboard Lt. Carl T. Gleason's leading PT 338 (Grey Ghost), and following was Ens. Henry W. Cutter's PT 337 (Heaven Can Wait).

Commander Davis glanced at his watch. It was 2:05 A.M. The

bay was ghostly quiet. Minutes later Davis picked up a radar target, about a mile ahead and close to shore, and the Devil Boats began creeping up on their quarry. Crew members soon spotted two Japanese luggers moored together, about four hundred yards to the front. Suddenly the eerie silence was shattered as machine guns on shore opened up with withering blasts of fire.

Davis quickly issued orders, and as the pair of PTs started to make a run to strafe the machine guns on the beach, other automatic weapons around the rim of the bay began aiming bullets at the boats. Now loud booms erupted as a large-caliber battery, perched on dominating Awar Point at Hansa Bay's entrance, sent shells screaming into the water around the Devil Boats. Commander Davis knew that he and his men had walked into an ambush.

Gunners on the PTs returned the fire, as streams of tracer bullets zipped through their plywood craft. Then an explosion rocked Ensign Cutter's Heaven Can Wait as a shell tore into the engine room, knocking out the three Packards and causing fuel tanks to burst into flame. Motor Machinist's Mate Third Class Francis C. Watson was hurled to the deck. He struggled to his feet and saw Motor Machinist's Mate First Class William Daley, Jr., stagger out of the blazing engine room, his clothing saturated by blood. Daley had been struck by shrapnel in the neck and jaw.

Moments later Ensign Cutter called out: "Abandon ship!"

Crewmen pitched the oval-shaped balsa life raft into the water and began jumping overboard and scrambling onto it. Daley, dazed, badly burned, still bleeding profusely, got into the water unaided; Ensign Cutter and Ens. Robert W. Hyde, seeing Daley about to go under, swam to him and towed him to the raft. Already undergoing the tortures of the damned, Bill Daley's pain was made even greater by salt water seeping into his wounds.

The raft, only seven feet by three feet, could not hold the entire crew, so some men had to hang onto it while still in the water. Then the crew began paddling desperately, with a few swimming alongside, to put distance between themselves and the blazing PT before it exploded.

In the meantime, the ill-fated craft's patrol companion, PT 338, had bolted outside the bay to escape the rain of lead into which the boats had stumbled. When Cutter's boat failed to join Grey Ghost,

Commander Davis ordered 338's skipper, Lieutenant Gleason, to rush back into Hansa Bay. Just inside the entrance 338 was grasped by relentless searchlight fingers, and the big guns on Awar Point began shelling the boat, driving it back out to sea. Several times during the remaining hours of darkness, Davis tried to slip back into the bay, but each time Grey Ghost was met by a torrent of fire. At dawn, the Squadron 24 skipper reluctantly gave the order to return to base. In the daylight, 338 would be a sitting duck for Japanese warplanes and shore batteries.

All the while, Ensign Cutter and his men had been paddling the balsa raft. They had been fighting a heavy current, and after two hours were only seven hundred yards from the smoking, smouldering Heaven Can Wait. About 4:15 A.M. a terrific blast rocked the raft as the doomed boat blew sky high.

An hour later, Bill Daley died. Never once had he cried out in agony or complained. Gentle, quivering hands lifted Daley off to his final resting place in Japanese-held Hansa Bay. Now three officers and eight bluejackets remained on and beside the tiny raft.

As streaks of gray broke through the black sky, the marooned men were convinced that their remaining minutes of life were few. The raft was still inside Hansa Bay, a mile from the entrance, and in daylight gunners on Awar Point could pick them off, like shooting fish in a barrel. But for some reason, not a shell was fired at the little knot of Americans. And now Providence took a hand: a powerful current swept the raft out through the bay's entrance toward Manam Island, six miles offshore.

Ensign Cutter decided to head the raft toward Manam where the men might find food, water to drink, or be able to steal canoes or even a sailboat. Throughout the hot, humid afternoon the PT men paddled arduously, but each time they neared the island, the current shoved them back out to sea. Spirits plummeted. The men were famished, thirsty, exhausted.

That night two logs floated up to the raft. Cutter and Ens. Bruce C. Bales climbed aboard the logs and set out to paddle to Manam. If they could reach it they would try to locate a boat and return to pick up the others. After paddling vigorously for three hours, the two were exhausted and had to abandon the effort. The capricious current swept Bales and Cutter and the raft back together again.

About an hour after the two officers had cast off on the logs, QM2 Allen B. Gregory and Ensign Hyde started swimming for Manam Island. Neither would be heard from again.

During the night, Cutter, TM2 Morgan J. Canterbury, and TM3 Edgar L. Schmidt became delirious, mumbling incoherent phrases, visualizing sumptuous feasts. Suddenly Canterbury leapt into the water and tried to swim away. Harry E. Barnett, a strong swimmer, tried to rescue Canterbury, but could not locate him.

By dawn, their second day on the raft, the men had been carried by the tricky current around to the northern side of Manam, a mile from the beach. Ensign Bales, Motor Machinist's Mate Third Class Evo A. Fucilli, and Edgar Smith set out to swim for the beach. None was heard from again. Ship's Cook Third Class James P. Mitchell also started for the shore, but when only fifty yards from the beach he spotted several Japanese soldiers, so he swam back to the raft, arriving there exhausted. Clearly, that island was out as a place of refuge.

With nightfall, the weary men on the raft thought they saw a small boat putting out from the shore and heading toward them. Hallucinations? Or were the Japanese coming out to machine-gun them? The more lucid of the survivors watched intently. This was no fantasy, they agreed. Several men could see machine guns on the craft. The mystery boat veered to one side and began circling the raft slowly at a distance of about two hundred yards. There appeared to be two men in the boat, which continued its surveillance until 4:00 A.M., when a sudden squall whipped up eight-foot waves. When calm returned, the boat had disappeared. Another unexplained enigma in the fog of war.

At dawn on March 9, only five men remained on the raft. They were near the end of their endurance: starving, mouths like cotton from no water, exhausted, lips cracked and parched from the blast-furnace rays of the tropical sun, faces covered by beards. A few yards away, they spotted an overturned Japanese collapsible boat floating past. It was crude and only fifteen feet long, but in comparison with the fragile little raft, the canoe looked like a luxury ocean liner. They righted it, bailed out the water, and climbed aboard.

And, under the circumstances, there was a feast to suit a king. Jim Mitchell spotted a crab clinging to the canoe and with a display of dexterity born of desperation caught it. The hapless creature was torn apart and devoured. A couple of hours later the crab breakfast was supplemented by a drifting coconut plucked from the water.

That night and the following morning, March 10, were spent in sheer agony. By now the bodies of the remaining five survivors were covered with saltwater sores. Even the strongest hearts had begun to lose hope. Suddenly, at about noon, the men in the canoe were electrified: they heard the roar of airplane motors and saw three American B-25s winging toward them. Cutter furiously waved his arms, trying to identify his group by semaphore. The twin-engine planes circled the canoe, then zoomed in low and dropped a box. It promptly sank to the bottom. Now came two more boxes and a small package attached to a life preserver, all of which landed a few feet from the canoe. In the containers were food, water, medicines, and cigarettes. Also included was a chart showing the canoe's position, and the most welcome of all, a note that read: "Catalina will pick you up."

The next morning the big flying boat, covered by a pair of P-47 fighter planes, landed near the canoe and took aboard the five men. Two hours later they were back at Dreger Harbor.*

In the meantime, PT Squadrons 18 and 21 set up shop at Seeadler Harbor, at the elbow of Los Negros Island in the Admiralties. Gen. Bull Swift's cavalrymen were still cleaning out nearby die-hard bands of Japanese, and snipers hidden around the harbor occasionally sent potshots into the Devil Boats at anchor. But the Japanese high command had decided to write off the Admiralties, so the role of the PTs there had changed. Instead of sinking barges bringing in troops and supplies, the boats would prevent Japanese soldiers from fleeing. On the night of March 11/12, a pair of Squadron 18 PTs under Lt. Henry "Swifty" Swift spotted nine Japanese soldiers in a native canoe near Pak Island. As the boats drew nearer, one of the Nipponese stood up, pulled the pin from a grenade, and blew up himself and three companions. One who survived the blast refused to surrender and was shot; the other four men were taken prisoner.

On board the PT, one of the Japanese asked for pencil and paper and wrote (later to be translated):

---

* A tiny life raft adrift in a vast, trackless ocean is a difficult object to spot. For five days, since PT 337 was lost, aircraft by day and PTs by night had been searching vigorously for the survivors.

My name is Kaminaga. I worked in a Yokohama war factory
as an American spy. I set fire to Yokohama's arsenal. Later, I
was conscripted into Japanese army. I was very unhappy. To
repay your kindness I will work as a spy for your American
army.

Private Kaminaga was turned over to U.S. army interrogators,
who declined to accept his offer to serve as a spy.

As the closest Japanese airstrip was 150 miles away, PTs in the
Admiralties could operate in the daytime. And due to a dearth of
barges, skippers sought out other profitable targets. On the morning
of March 20, Lt. Cedric Janien, the former Harvard football star, in
PT 321 (Death's Hand) and Lt. John F. Ganong, in PT 369 (Sad
Sack), roared up to Loniu Village, a Japanese supply center on Los
Negros. As the boats cruised along the shore, gunners poured fire
into the buildings, but they refused to burn.

"This calls for more direct action," Janien declared. Along with
several heavily armed crewmen, Janien and Ganong went ashore in
a rubber dinghy. They carried with them two buckets of gasoline.
Crouched in a clump of bushes, the two men looked around and spotted a juicy target: some twenty-five camouflaged buildings. Under the
wooden structures were hidden thirty-one canoes, large ones capable
of carrying thirty men each. But where were the Japanese manning
this base?

There was no time to ponder that question. The men rapidly poured
gasoline on the canoes and on a few buildings, one of which was
crammed with ammunition. They torched the fuel-soaked objects, then
hightailed it back to their boats for more gasoline. There Lieutenant
Janien found the first tangible evidence that there were Japanese around:
one of his officers had been wounded by a sniper's bullet.

All the while, the ammunition building had been exploding. As
Janien, Ganong, and the others paddled to shore once more they were
more cautious; the exploding ammo could have alerted every enemy
soldier for miles. Hastily, they sloshed gasoline over several buildings
filled with tons of food and supplies and set them ablaze. As they
scampered for their concealed dinghy, the sound of roaring flames
behind them was music to their ears.

Lt. Cmdr. Robert
Leeson (PT Boats,
Inc.)

Lt. James R. Thompson
(PT Boats, Inc.)

Devil Boaters haul in a survivor of a sunken Japanese ship. The prisoner
appears to be unconscious but helmeted man at right has weapon in the
event of treachery. (U.S. Navy)

Elco PT boats at Mios Woendi, near Biak, Southwest Pacific. (U.S. Navy)

Crew member stands guard at twin-mounted .50 caliber machine guns as PT boats return to base (National Archives)

*Studying captured Japanese weapons aboard PT tender **Hilo,** L to R: Lt. Donald F. Seaman, intelligence officer for PT squadrons (Seventh Fleet); Lt. Cmdr. Robert Leeson, leader of Squadron 7; Cmdr. Biff Bowling, PT commander, Seventh Fleet; and Lt. Cmdr. John Harllee, Bowling's Chief of Staff. (PT Boats, Inc.)*

General MacArthur heads for the Leyte landing beaches aboard PT 525 on 24 October 1944. L to R: Lt. Alexander W. Wells, skipper; General MacArthur; Cmdr. Selman S. "Biff" Bowling; Lt. Gen. Walter Krueger, leader of Sixth Army. (U.S. Navy)

Ensign Dudley J. Johnson (PT Boats, Inc.)

Lt. Richard W. "Bill" Brown (PT Boats, Inc.)

Lt. Cmdr. Francis D. Tappaan (U.S. Navy)

Lt. Byron F. Kent (PT Boats, Inc.)

There was nothing remaining to salvage after PT 320 received a direct bomb hit in Leyte Gulf 5 November 1944. (U.S. Navy)

*Crew members of PT boat tender **Willoughby** depart to rescue survivors from burning LST, hit by Kamikaze in Leyte Gulf. (PT Boats, Inc.)*

Electrician's Mate Joseph J. Burke (left) found himself in a dilemma after Davis's Raiders (below) wiped out a Japanese camp on a tiny island off Leyte. (PT Boats, Inc.)

PT boats being bombed in Leyte Gulf. Gunners are firing back. (U.S. Navy)

Burning of the Devil Boats at Samar. (PT Boats, Inc.)

Lt. A. Murray Preston receives the Medal of Honor from President Truman. (U.S. Navy)

President John F. Kennedy and John D. Bulkeley, wartime comrades in the Pacific, greet each other at the White House in 1962. (Author's Collection)

CHAPTER 15   Ordeal on a Wandering Fuel Barge

Early in April, General MacArthur was about to make his boldest leap to date along the jungle road to Manila and Tokyo. Despite vigorous protests from his staff that the operation could meet with disaster, MacArthur was going to spring 400 miles westward along the coast all the way to Hollandia in Dutch New Guinea, a point two hundred miles behind Japanese strongholds at Madang, Hansa Bay, and Wewak.

MacArthur's staff and commanders wanted to seize Wewak first before leaping to Hollandia. But the supreme commander brushed aside this proposal. Wewak was precisely where the Japanese thought he would hit next, MacArthur declared, so all combat troops had been rushed from Hollandia to Wewak to counter the next American blow. Hollandia was ripe for plucking—and MacArthur intended to pluck it. "This operation will advance our timetable by six months," he pointed out.

In strategic deliberations with his staff, MacArthur held a trump card he could not show them: his code busters had already advised him that the Nipponese had virtually denuded Hollandia.

On the afternoon of April 15, a naval task force (code name Reckless) with 60,000 American troops aboard set out on the thousand-mile, circuitous trek to the MacArthur-chosen objective. On the bridge of the destroyer *Swanson*, Lt. Gen. Robert L. Eichelberger, who would command the assault, gazed in awe at the mightiest sea armada thus far assembled in the Pacific. There were hundreds of ships, escorted by battleships: cruisers, destroyers, sub chasers, and carriers with their swarms of fighter planes and dive bombers.

What a stark contrast to the early lean days, Eichelberger reflected. Ten months earlier, when he led an amphibious assault at Nassau Bay in northeast New Guinea, there had been but thirty landing craft (compared to 280 in the Reckless force). The "naval escort" had consisted of two PT boats, which, though their skippers were stout of heart, had the effect of beebee pellets in a shotgun war.

Shortly after dawn on April 22, troops of the 24th and 41st Infantry divisions stormed ashore simultaneously at Tanahmerah and Humboldt bays, thirty miles apart, on either side of Hollandia. A third landing was made at Aitape, midway between Hollandia and bypassed Wewak. Dazed and confused by the unexpected lightning bolt two hundred miles behind their forward bases, the Japanese troops melted into the jungles. MacArthur secured the entire Hollandia region at a cost of only 150 American lives.*

Feverish work began at once to develop Hollandia rapidly as a major naval and air base for future leapfrog operations. The landings had isolated the Japanese 18th Imperial Army, some 50,000 men, around Wewak and Hansa Bay. To keep this strong force from being resupplied by barge, two PT squadrons were rushed to Aitape four days after the assault, and a few days later another PT squadron moved farther westward to Humboldt Bay, in Hollandia.

Almost at once the Devil Boats tangled with barges in which the Japanese were trying to bring supplies to the marooned 18th Imperial Army. On the night of April 28/29, two PTs, skippered by Ens. Francis L. Cappaert and by Ens. Louis A. Fanget, shot up and sank three barges in Nightingale Bay, east of Wewak. One of the enemy vessels had been carrying two artillery pieces and some forty-five men.

---

* Even the chief of naval operations, Adm. Ernest King, MacArthur's longtime arch foe, admitted begrudgingly that MacArthur's Hollandia operation was a "masterful stroke." But American media gave it scant attention: there had not been enough bloodshed to warrant front-page headlines.

As the soldiers floundered about in the dark waters, the PT crews tried to take prisoners—a difficult task at best. Some Nipponese chose to die for their emperor and deliberately drowned themselves rather than be pulled aboard the boats.

Over the months, the PT men had become quite adept at hauling in prisoners in similar situations. Their technique was to bop an enemy soldier or sailor over the head with a boat hook and, in effect, reel his unconscious form onto the deck. Another modus operandi was to lower a cargo net over the bow of the PT boat. As crewmen held them by lines around their waists, two men climbed down the net. They would club a floating Japanese over the head with a blackjack and put a line around him so that he could be hauled aboard. If heavy bops on the head failed to render the enemy soldier or sailor unconscious, the Japanese would resist bitterly efforts to reel him in and, in many cases, would try to kill himself and the PT crew by detonating a grenade.

Despite strenuous efforts, only two Japanese were pulled alive from the dark waters of Nightingale Bay by Cappaert's and Fanget's crews. One of the prisoners, who lay gasping on the deck of Cappaert's PT, kept pointing to himself and declaring, "Me officer. Me officer." In cracked English, Me Officer (as the PT men started calling him) said that more barges were heading for Nightingale Bay.

Ensigns Fanget and Cappaert deployed their boats and awaited developments. Less than thirty minutes later, the men heard the soft murmur of engines on the calm waters of the bay as three more barges approached. Suddenly a mighty roar echoed across the bay as the PTs opened fire and sank all three of the vessels. One PT edged up to a floating Japanese, and the crew administered him the boat-hook treatment. The semiconscious officer clutched tightly to a box and, after being hauled to the deck, resisted efforts to take it from him. Later it would be learned that the container held secret documents, and the officer had been assigned the task of delivering them to the Japanese commander at Wewak.

As soon as the pair of PTs had returned to base at Aitape after a productive night in Nightingale Bay, Me Officer proved to be a bonanza of Intelligence information when questioned in Japanese by American officers. He reeled off a lengthy list of barge movements: numbers, times, destinations, cargoes. Armed with this detailed schedule, PT boats sallied forth to Wewak and Hansa Bay on five consecutive nights, lay in wait, and sank fifteen barges and a picket boat and shot up eight other barges.

While events of great magnitude were unfolding around Hollandia, several hundred miles to the east, on the night of April 28/29, two PT boats, 347, under Lt. Robert J. Williams, and 350, skippered by Lt. Stenley L. Manning, were stalking the black coast of New Britain west of the Japanese stronghold of Rabaul. PT 347 (Zombie) became stuck on a reef. PT 350 (Shifty Fifty) was still trying to pull Zombie loose, at 7:00 A.M., when two U.S. Marine Corps Corsairs zoomed in with machine guns blazing and poured bullets into the boats. Three men on Shifty Fifty were killed. Believing the planes to be Japanese, gunners on the PTs opened fire and shot down one Corsair.

Back at the PT base at Talasea, Lt. James R. "Red" Thompson, leader of Squadron 25, received a radio report of the attack. He urgently contacted Cape Gloucester with a request for air cover, then jumped into Lt. James R. Burk's PT 346 and raced for the scene of the shootout at Cape Pomas.

Meanwhile, the pilot of the remaining Corsair had radioed his base at Green Island in the Solomons that he and his partner had strafed "two 125-foot Japanese gunboats." As a result, Green Island operations officers ordered twenty-two fighters and dive bombers to race to the site and finish off the "enemy" vessels.

The groundwork for disaster had been laid. The Green Island air base was located in Admiral Nimitz's South Pacific area and the Cape Gloucester airfield, to which Lt. Red Thompson had appealed for air cover, was in MacArthur's southwest Pacific zone. So the two American air bases, although geographically close, were operating independently of each other.

When Lieutenant Thompson reached Cape Pomas where Zombie was still stuck on a reef, he began directing operations to free the boat. (Badly shot up and with three men dead, Shifty Fifty had returned to its base.) Suddenly Zombie's skipper, Lt. Bob Williams, called out, "Planes approaching from the north." Thompson put his binoculars on the flight and replied, "It's okay, they're the air cover I requested from Cape Gloucester." Salvage work resumed. But it was not the air cover arriving; it was the twenty-two American warplanes from Green Island with orders to "finish off" the pair of "Japanese gunboats."

Suddenly, with a mighty roar of engines, the American planes pounced on the pair of PTs. Bombs were exploding in the water on all sides of the boats before the PTs had a chance to start identifying themselves. But the aircraft continued to drop bombs and strafe, and finally the PT gunners opened fire, shooting down a Hellcat. Riddled with bullets and shell fragments, both Devil Boats plunged to the bottom.

A Catalina (Black Cat) flying boat was sent from Green Island to try to find the Hellcat pilot, but the search proved to be futile. The Catalina did pick up thirteen surviving PT men. Only when the flying boat returned to Green Island did air operations officers learn that one of the war's most devastating friendly-fire tragedies had occurred: fourteen PT men and two pilots were dead; twenty-one PT men were wounded.

Two nights later, on May 2, a pair of Squadron 7 boats sank two barges, shot up four more, and were returning to base when PT 114 (Buccaneer) went aground on a reef barely four hundred yards off Kairiru Island near the Japanese stronghold of Wewak. Dawn was approaching fast. Orders were given to abandon ship, but when Buccaneer's torpedoes and depth charges had been jettisoned, it was light enough for the companion boat, PT 144 (Southern Cross), to pull it off the reef. It was now 6:30 A.M.

When feverish preparations had been underway to abandon Buccaneer, secret codes and other confidential documents had been placed in a rubber raft. The raft was to have been tied to the stern of Southern Cross, but in the confusion the raft had been permitted to float away.

As the two PTs headed toward their base, an officer called out: "The codes on the raft! Where in hell is the raft?" There was a rush for the fantail. Raft and secret codes were not there. In Japanese hands, those documents could have been highly damaging.

Reaching Aitape, the skippers sheepishly reported the loss, and Lt. Comdr. Robert Leeson, leader of Squadron 7, promptly set out to search for the missing raft. He rode in PT 129 (Artful Dodger), skippered by his brother, Ens. A. Dix Leeson. With the Artful Dodger was Ens. Edmund F. Wakelin's PT 134 (Eight Ball). Late in the afternoon, the raft was spotted—on a beach near Yarin on Kairiru Island.

A hurried powwow of officers was held. The raft was in full view of a native village, and nearby, the skippers knew, was a Japanese shore battery of big guns. In addition, there was a Nipponese building of some sort within six hundred yards of the raft. Without further ado, Bob Leeson stripped to his undershorts and plunged into the water. In broad daylight, expecting to hear the angry chatter of enemy machine guns at any moment, Leeson swam the four hundred yards to the raft.

Hurriedly, he looked in the rubber vessel and was greatly relieved to see the pile of confidential documents, presumably intact. Towing the raft behind him, Commander Leeson made the gruelling swim back to the waiting boats. Moments later there were loud barks down the shoreline; a gun battery barely a half-mile away began sending shells toward the pair of Devil Boats. With a noisy revving of engines, the PTs raced out to sea.

But Commander Leeson was not yet ready to call it a day. After dark, Artful Dodger and Eight Ball once more slipped in to the Kairiru shoreline and soon were involved in a fierce shootout with three heavily laden barges. The Devil Boats sank two of the barges and shot up the third. Then a shell from a shore-based gun tore into the Leeson brothers' PT, ripping a fourteen-inch hole in an exhaust stack and starting a fire under one engine. MoMM2 Clarence L. Nelson grabbed an extinguisher and put out the fire, but not before he was overcome by carbon dioxide and exhaust fumes. Helping Nelson fight the blaze that threatened to consume the boat, MoMM3 A. F. Hall also keeled over, unconscious. Ens. Richard Holt dashed into the engine compartment and began administering artificial respiration, and eventually revived the two bluejackets, who had been on the verge of death.

Operating on two engines, Leeson's boat led the way closer to the shore, where the pair of Devil Boats unleashed a barrage of twenty-four rockets in the direction of the flashes from the land-based battery. The Japanese guns fell silent, and now the boats headed for home.

On the morning of May 17, Lt. George Sprugel, of Williams, Iowa, was standing on the deck of the PT boat tender, Oyster Bay, which was anchored in the bay at Hollandia. Sprugel was furious. He had just left the Oyster Bay quarters of Lt. Comdr. Robert J. Bulkley, Jr., the newly appointed commander of Squadron 12, veteran of the Solomons and New Guinea. Bulkley had just given an assignment to

Sprugel that was most distasteful to the young skipper. Sprugel was to take two bluejackets and ride a nonpowered barge with 250,000 gallons of high octane gasoline to a new, advanced PT base at Wakde Island.*

Only the previous day, Douglas MacArthur had leapfrogged 125 miles to Wakde, 2 miles off the New Guinea coast and directly opposite the wild jungle region called Toem-Sarmi. Wakde, on which were located several Nipponese airstrips, was only two miles long and a mile wide. But the Japanese had holed up in caves, and when elements of the 41st Infantry Division hit the beach, the eight hundred defenders put up such a fierce and organized resistance that it required two days of continuous action before the Americans wiped out the garrison.

Now on the deck of the *Oyster Bay*, Lieutenant Sprugel was describing the mission to the two men who would go with him, SF1 M. L. Harvey and MoMM1 Anderson. Harvey, at forty-seven, was twice the age of Sprugel. A native of Maine, the shipfitter had survived a year and a half of combat with the Army in France during World War I, and was one of the most popular men in PT boat Squadron 12.

Neither man tried to conceal his disgust over "playing nursemaid to a goddamned fuel barge." These men were accustomed to darting, slashing attacks in speedy PT boats and now they had been consigned to riding a wallowing barge that was being inched along by a seagoing tug. How boring an assignment could one get?

The following morning the tug and barge crawled out of Hollandia, and after thirty interminable hours of being broiled by the tropical sun in the day and chilled by showers and cold spray at night, Sprugel, Harvey, and Anderson arrived at Wakde. They were behind schedule. PT boats needed fuel for an urgent mission still farther to the west, so the tug and fuel barge anchored at the entrance of the harbor. One by one, the Devil Boats came alongside, fueled up and raced seaward on their night's mission.

Just as the last thirsty PT had ingested its fuel, unexpected orders

---

* Lt. Comdr. Robert J. Bulkley, Jr., is not to be confused with Lt. Comdr. John D. Bulkeley of MacArthur/Corregidor fame.

were received by the tug. The plan had been for the tug to tow the barge to a permanent mooring spot inside the harbor. But now the tug was ordered to join a convoy leaving Wakde before dark bound for Hollandia.

The tug chugged off, leaving the unpowered fuel barge floating helplessly. By semaphore, Lieutenant Sprugel signaled the harbormaster to send a craft to tow the barge into the harbor. Just before dark, an LCM (landing craft, medium) appeared, but was not strong enough to do the job. The three PT men were growing increasingly apprehensive. Dusk was approaching, and soon Japanese planes from nearby fields would be coming. Sprugel and his men ranted and raved. They made grim jokes as to how close to the moon they would be blown if a bomb were to hit their barge with its tons of high-octane gasoline.

A larger landing craft arrived. It failed also, and departed. The curtain of night fell over the Wakde harbor. A brisk wind stirred the water. Sprugel and his men had no means of steering their clumsy craft, and the chain was too short for the anchor to bite into the bottom. There was no night signalling equipment aboard. The three men were adrift and helpless.

The barge floated aimlessly out to sea. On the mainland two miles across the channel, American forces held a beachhead, but if the barge were to meander west of there it would be either an easy target for Nipponese shore batteries or might even drift onto the shore in enemy-held territory.

During the night there was a heavy downpour, and with it the wind howled and whipped up large waves. The barge's deck was awash with angry breakers. No one on board could tell where they were or in which direction the raft was going. Artillery explosions on the mainland indicated that the coast was on the port side.

Now a new fear struck George Sprugel and the others. They knew the U.S. Navy had thrown up an antisubmarine screen of destroyers north and west of Wakde. Would their own ships blast them out of the water—and up to the moon? Only later would the PT men learn that, indeed, their barge had drifted unmolested and unchallenged through the destroyer screen presumably on full alert for unidentified craft.

Daybreak found the wandering barge about four miles offshore and twelve miles west of Wakde, deep in Japanese-controlled territory. An enemy airfield at Maffin was only four miles away. Now a new menace arose: two American P-38 fighter planes began circling the barge. Lieutenant Sprugel started signalling furiously to identify his craft as friendly and in need of assistance. An alarming question occurred to Sprugel: From the air did the unmarked American barge look any different than an unmarked Japanese barge?

Then the pair of twin-boomed Lightnings, their fuselages glistening in the rays of the early morning sun, peeled off and zoomed downward toward the barge. At the last minute, the P-38s leveled off, wigwagged their wings in recognition, and flew away. Sprugel, Anderson, and Harvey let out a collective sigh of relief.

All morning the barge drifted onward, inexorably moving deeper into Japanese-controlled waters and closer to shore. Just before 2:00 P.M., there was a crunching sound as the fuel carrier grounded on a reef only seventy-five yards from shore. The stranded PT men were within a stone's throw of the enemy's Sawar airfield, and no doubt Japanese soldiers were nearby along the shore, although none could be seen.

Now there was an even more haunting prospect than sudden death at the hands of the Nipponese. The heavy surf was crashing over the reef, causing the barge to quiver and groan as though it were being thrashed about by some huge supernatural force. Highly inflammable 100-octane gasoline was spilling out, and even one spark from the grinding metal of the hull could turn the vessel into an instant fireball.

The barge and its cargo obviously were doomed. So the PT men debated over swimming ashore and taking their chances there or paddling out to sea in a rubber dinghy and hoping for the best. Moments later their minds were made up for them: Japanese along the beach began to pepper the Americans with rifle fire. Crouching low and clutching carbines, the three Devil Boaters dropped the dinghy overboard and scrambled into it; then they began paddling madly seaward. There were only two paddles, and the angry swells and wind caused the rubber raft to heave and pitch and threaten to capsize at any moment.

The Japanese on shore began hurling streams of machine-gun tracers toward the huddled, waterlogged Americans, but the violent up-and-down pitch of the dinghy made it an elusive target. Progress was tortured. As two men rowed, the third one fired a carbine at their tormentors. When they were only a hundred yards from the gasoline barge (which had started to break up), the enemy opened up with a 3-inch gun. A shell burst directly over the bobbing dinghy, sending a sliver of hot metal into M. L. Harvey's head, killing him instantly.

Anguished by the loss of their comrade, Sprugel and Anderson summoned up their tiny reserve of energy and continued to paddle. Three hours after leaving the reef, they were only a mile out to sea— and the gun was still firing at them periodically. A half-hour later, when the two men had reached the end of their tether, an APD (high speed transport) happened by. Anderson took off his shirt and, standing up, waved it furiously while Sprugel struggled to keep the raft from capsizing, cheating Neptune of two more victims. The APD sent a landing boat to pick up the two PT men and Harvey's body.

SF1 M. L. Harvey, age forty-seven, fearless fighter, revered by all in Squadron 12, was buried at Hollandia the next day. Tears rolled down the bronzed cheeks of comrades young enough to have been his sons.

CHAPTER 16   Hide-and-Seek on an Enemy Island

B ack in the States on June 3, readers of the *New York Times* noted a headline buried deep within the newspaper:

GI'S MOPPING UP ON BIAK

The source of the story was an upbeat communique from the headquarters of Southwest Pacific Command in Brisbane—fifteen hundred miles from the island of Biak. Actually, the battle situation was precisely the opposite: American foot soldiers and tankers were slugging it out with the Japanese on Biak in some of the most brutal fighting of the war.

Biak, perched in the mouth of Geelvink Bay, New Guinea's largest inlet, had been assaulted on May 27 by a task force built around the 41st Infantry Division in what was to have been yet another hit-'em-where-they-ain't leapfrog operation 185 miles west of Wakde. Intelligence had reported little indication of Nipponese presence on the sun-baked island. But the enemy was there in strength—nearly 10,000 of them—supported by tanks and big guns. They were dug in along cliffs overlooking the American landing beaches, concealed in countless caves, and huddled in underground bunkers.

Foot by foot in bloody clashes, the Japanese were rooted out by

GIs wielding rifles, machine guns, BARs, flame-throwers, bayonets, trench knives, and mortars. Huge amounts of gasoline were poured down into caves and set afire, incinerating the Japanese holed up there. At dawn on June 22, hundreds of Nipponese shouting banzai! charged American lines and, to a man, were cut down. Resistance on Biak had ended.

The stench on the island was sickening. The burned and butchered bodies of thousands of Japanese littered almost every square foot of ground, corpses so numerous they could not be counted. Thus concluded the mopping up of godforsaken Biak.

Six days after the initial assault had been made on Biak, the major PT boat base in New Guinea was moved hundreds of miles forward, from Dreger Harbor to Mios Woendi, a small atoll ten miles south of Biak. Mios Woendi was a tropical paradise to Devil Boaters who had known only interminable months on islands infested by pestilence, swamps, mosquitoes, snakes, crocodiles, headhunters, and tangled jungles. Mios Woendi had beautiful white sandy beaches and was festooned with palm trees.

Within forty-eight hours of the first PTs moving into Mios Woendi, Warhead Torpedoman Seaver of the Bitchin' Witch and a few comrades were tuned to their favorite radio personality, Tokyo Rose. She played their favorite American tunes to gain their attention and related sexual encounters in the most graphic terms, which gained even greater attention. Then she would slip in her propaganda pitch for the night.

"Hello, you sexy fellows in PT Boat Squadron Twelve," she cooed. The ears of Warhead Seaver and the others perked up. "We know where you are," she continued. "We'll be over to see you in the morning. Nighty night."

Shortly after dawn, a Zero zoomed in just above the waves, dropped a bomb that exploded close to the fantail of PT 190 (Jack O'Diamonds), and scurried for home. For two weeks after Tokyo Rose's surrogate paid his call on Mios Woendi, the PT men manned battle stations just before daybreak. But no Japanese warplane returned.

But out to sea and around Biak it was a different matter. On the morning of June 12, Carolina Chile (PT 326), skippered by Lt. Ken Molloy, the all-America lacrosse player from Syracuse University, set out from Mios Woendi to patrol off Biak. It was the job of the Devil Boats to blockade Biak to keep the Japanese from bringing in supplies and reinforcements. Suddenly, from out of the sun, four Zekes pounced on Carolina Chile. Four bombs exploded less than seventy feet from the boat. PT gunners began throwing up lead, and a 40-mm shell ripped into a Zeke. It caught fire and splashed into the sea. Now the three remaining Zekes spotted a juicier target nearby, the destroyer *Kalk*. Gunners on the *Kalk* downed a second Zeke, but the destroyer took a direct bomb hit that heavily damaged her superstructure. Raging fires broke out below decks. Four officers and twenty-six men were killed; four officers and thirty-six men were wounded.

On Mios Woendi, Devil Boaters had been watching the entire action, which had taken place in a matter of a few minutes. As soon as the *Kalk* was hit, every PT in the lagoon charged out at full throttle, headed for the stricken ship. One after the other, the PTs edged alongside the destroyer which continued underway to avoid bombs, and removed the wounded. PT officers began immediately to administer first aid while their boats raced to LST 469, which had a surgical team aboard.

That same night, Lt. Bill Bannard, son-in-law of a PT boat manufacturer, in Jack O'Diamonds, and Lieutenant James C. Higgins, in Green Hornet (PT 146), were patrolling the northern side of Biak where the Japanese were trying to slip in troops. Lookouts spotted the outlines of three barges and the helmeted heads of perhaps two hundred men. Suddenly, with a loud roar the two Devil Boats unleashed their Sunday punches. The unsuspecting Japanese never knew what hit them. Within three minutes two hundred members of the 202d Pioneer (Engineer) Unit and the three vessels were sent to the bottom. Among those who drowned was the unit's leader, Lieutenant Commander Nagata.*

Meanwhile, in Japan, the home front was being regaled nightly over Radio Tokyo about "glorious victories" by the emperor's armed forces. But at his headquarters outside the capital, supreme warlord Hideki Tojo had to take a more starkly realistic view of the situation in the Pacific. The mighty Imperial war machine, which thirty months earlier had broken loose with the brilliance of Halley's Comet, had begun to fade. MacArthur's force had been leapfrogging up the spine of New Guinea, and now had nearly reached its western tip. Admiral Nimitz's men had been pushing steadily westward in a series of bloody,

---

* As reported later by a Japanese survivor.

brutal battles on tiny islands and coral atolls. Now the two powerful Allied forces were threatening to converge on the crucial Philippines from the south and from the west. For the first time, General Tojo had inner doubts as to the outcome of his goal to drive the white devils from the Pacific.

In Dutch New Guinea, at the western end of the world's second largest island, PT boaters found a new and ambitious ally. Natives, extremely loyal to the governing Dutch and who hated the Japanese, often paddled out from shore in canoes to idling Devil Boats and told interpreters where there were Japanese camps concealed along the coast. Armed with this intelligence the boats would shoot up the enemy camps, then return a few days later to obtain firsthand reports from their native informants on the results of their strafings.

As a result of the PT and air blockade, the Japanese in Dutch New Guinea were starving. Desperate for food, they were easy prey for natives who lured small groups of them away from their camps with promises of something to eat. When a safe distance away, the New Guineans jumped the weakened Japanese and locked them in stockades. When a PT boat would show up a few days later, the still-starving enemy soldiers would be handed over to the Americans. On occasion, as many as thirty Japanese POWs were taken in tow by the PT men.

General MacArthur was now ready to leap forward once more. He would strike at the island of Noemfoor, west of Biak and perched in the wide mouth of Geelvink Bay. In preparation for this imminent landing (set for July 2), a pair of Devil Boats landed a reconnaissance party at Bani Point, on Noemfoor, then picked up the scouts after midnight.

The skippers were Lt. Kermit Montz, a former football star from Franklin and Marshall University, in PT 331, and Lieutenant Cyrus R. Taylor, once a star back on the Yale University football team, in the Bitchin' Witch (PT 193). Known to crew and fellow officers alike as The Cypress, the brawny, six-foot-two Taylor was one of the most highly respected skippers in the Motor Torpedo Boat service. Adored by his young crew, a man among men, Cy Taylor had gained almost legendary status for his feats of derring-do in countless attacks against enemy barges, destroyers, and shore batteries.

The Bitchin' Witch may well have seen more combat patrols (each an adventure in its own right) and been involved in more shoot-outs than any American PT boat. "She's a temperamental old bastard," a teenage crewman exclaimed. She had a wicked and stubborn personality, with a tendency to balk in tight situations. But Bitchin' Witch was loved by her crew. The crew regarded their gung-ho skipper with a curious mixture of awe and apprehension. A few months earlier, The Cypress's boat was making the first daylight mission along the New Guinea coastline northwest of Saidor. "Hot damn," The Cypress exclaimed in glee as the boat set out. "This daylight will be a good chance to catch those Jap bastards with their pants down!"

Whispered a not-so-enthusiastic Warhead Seaver to a comrade, "Yeah, and this daylight will sure handicap the vision of those Jap Zeros when they catch us with our own pants down a long way from home."

Later in the day, a young crewman named Sparks was scanning the coastline carefully with binoculars. Seaver, in a stage whisper, called out in mock menace, "Sparks, you goddamned fool, put those binoculars down. Do you want The Cypress to pull in there and twist them damned Japs' whiskers? You know damn well that's what he'll do if you spot a lousy barge. I don't wanna be no dead hero!"

"Don't worry about it," another chimed in. "We all know The Cypress is immortal. As long as we're with him, nothin's going to happen to us."

That night the Bitchin' Witch roamed far behind Japanese positions, and the enemy got careless. Lieutenant Taylor spotted a light, then another and another, and finally a whole string of them. No doubt about it: this was a large Nipponese encampment. Men sprang to their guns, and as the PT cruised slowly along the beach, she unloaded her Sunday punch into the camp. Not a shot was fired from the shore as the boat raced away.

"Hot dog," roared The Cypress. "It wasn't daylight, but we sure as hell caught the bastards with their pants down!"

Now, four months later, The Cypress was not yet ready to return to base, even though he had completed his mission of picking up the scouts. He began prowling the north coast of Noemfoor. Two barges were detected near the shore, and the Bitchin' Witch charged them with all guns blazing. One vessel sank promptly, but the other, burning fiercely, continued to float. Taylor made a wide circle, then came in again to finish off the burning barge. Hard on Bitchin' Witch's heels was Lieutenant Montz's PT. Suddenly there was an enormous crunching sound, and crews on the PTs were knocked off their feet. Both of the boats had piled onto a reef a short distance from the blazing ammunition barge. With only one screw remaining undamaged, Kermit Montz managed to back PT 331 off the reef. But Taylor's craft refused to budge.

Ammunition on the Japanese barge began exploding and kept it up periodically for three hours as The Cypress and his men labored to refloat the Bitchin' Witch. Light from the explosions kept the stranded boat illuminated. Suddenly, just before 4:30 A.M., an alarming panorama unfolded: Japanese trucks raced up and came to a halt on the beach barely a half-mile away. It seemed clear to the harried PT men that the enemy was moving in guns to fire virtually point-blank at the stranded boat.

Lieutenant Taylor had no recourse. He gave the orders to abandon ship and for the crew to scramble onto Montz's PT which was lying to nearby. Most of the crew shoved off in rubber boats for 331. Lieutenant Taylor and three others remained behind to destroy secret materials. Then Taylor, below deck, dumped gasoline into the bilges to make certain that the redoubtable Bitchin' Witch would be totally destroyed.

Suddenly there was a terrific explosion. The gasoline had apparently ignited prematurely. Flames shot high in the air, lighting up vast reaches of the bay and coastline. Looking on in horror from the 331 and the rubber raft, the crews saw a few heads bobbing about in the water near the burning boat. Moments later they spotted the dark silhouette of a man (who proved to be The Cypress) staggering through the roaring flames. The figure jumped overboard.

Lieutenant Montz promptly called for volunteers to go after the four floundering crew members. It would be a perilous mission. To a man, the crew quickly volunteered. Several shoved off in a rubber boat. One by one three Bitchin' Witch men, dazed and burned, were hauled from the water. Cy Taylor was the last man to be reached. He had been horribly burned and was in excruciating pain, pain rendered even more intense by the salt water. Yet he did not utter a moan or a cry.

Back on PT 331, Lieutenant Montz and the others were growing more apprehensive by the moment: the Japanese at the truck were rolling up what appeared to a 3-inch gun. The rescuers paddled back furiously to 331 where they had great difficulty lifting the 225-pound, agonizingly burned Cy Taylor six feet up to the deck from a bobbing and pitching rubber raft.

It was finally accomplished, and The Cypress was taken below and given morphine. At full throttle, PT 331 raced off. White flashes were seen along the shoreline, as the Japanese gun opened fire. Shells followed the speeding boat until it was far out to sea.

Halfway back to Mios Woendi the 331 was met by a boat carrying Lt. Comdr. Bob Bulkley (who had been notified by radio of the disaster), a doctor, and two medical aides. They treated Taylor, who was rushed on to Biak where he was taken aboard a hospital ship.

That night Lt. Cy Taylor, the immortal, the indestructible, died.*

The passing of The Cypress cast a thick pall of gloom over every PT boat in the southwest Pacific. But the war against Tojo had to go on. In the blackness of July 7/8, PT 329, skippered by Lt. Bill Hall, a former football great at Wabash University who came from Dayton, Ohio, and PT 161, commanded by Lt. Rogers V. Waugh, were stalking the New Guinea coast off Cape Oransbari. Hall's radar picked up a 150-foot lugger, a wooden hulled vessel powered with diesel engines, creeping along in the shadow of tall shoreline cliffs. With Lt. Stuart Lewis, the former University of California football player from Whittier, California, steering 329 as Bill Hall directed the gun crew, the two boats slipped closer, and at barely seventy-five yards unleashed their Sunday punches into the lugger.

Almost at once the Japanese vessel gurgled and sank out of sight. Around it the sea was dotted with bobbing heads. A few of these floating enemy soldiers were administered the boat-hook massage and their unconscious forms pulled onto the PT decks. One swimmer was more nimble than the others and avoided several swipes. "Haul the bastard aboard, anyhow!" someone called out.

"To hell with him!" another exclaimed. "Let him become shark's food."

The belligerent Japanese, kicking, squirming, and cursing loudly, was hauled aboard PT 329. He was a lieutenant colonel, one of the highest ranking prisoners of the New Guinea campaign. As soon as he regained his feet, the Nipponese officer whipped out a pistol and

---

* The PT base at Mios Woendi was renamed Camp Taylor in honor of this gallant and much loved officer.

aimed it at the closest bluejacket. Lt. Bill Hall lunged at the colonel and smashed his hamlike fist into the captive's mouth. The POW was knocked sprawling before he could pull the trigger.

Hall saved his crewman's life, but his fist was severely bruised and cut. A few days later it became badly infected and required that the skipper be hospitalized. In a liberal interpretation of regulations, Hall was awarded the Purple Heart. A week later he returned to his boat, only to meet the jibes of his officers and crew as "the only United States Navy officer to receive the Purple Heart for being *'wounded in the face of the enemy.'*"

On the following night, Lt. Charles A. Black and a party of scouts scrambled silently over the side of a PT boat and began paddling a rubber dinghy toward the shore of Roemberpon Island, in southwestern Geelvink Bay. Faces blackened, clad in dark clothing, armed to the teeth with tommy guns and nasty looking trench knives, Black and his men stole onto the beach, trotted to a clump of vegetation, crouched, and listened. The only sound was the eerie rustling of tree leaves in the soft ocean breeze.

Charlie Black's mission was to reconnoiter the beaches and make contact with friendly natives, for MacArthur was to strike yet another blow on Roemberpon within a few days. Black was well suited for the task, as he spoke Javanese and a few native dialects, and was the free spirited type ideal for these perilous reconnaissance missions on Japanese-held islands.

Soon it was daybreak. The PT boat had pulled out to sea. Just as they were starting to slip along the edge of the beach, a chilling sound of raucous Japanese voices reached the scout's ears—probably officers shouting commands. The invaders had been detected. All that day, while the Nipponese were beating the bushes looking for the Americans, Black and his scouts were pushing inland to a native camp where Operation Ferdinand coast watchers were known to be.

Black and his party reached the camp where the PT skipper was given extensive information on Japanese troop strength and gun positions. Then about ten of the natives insisted on accompanying the Americans back to the beach as a kind of bodyguard-in-force. One native advanced well ahead of the others, and he returned excitedly to give Charlie Black a piece of startling information: the Japanese had found the hidden rubber dinghy and were strung out along the beach waiting to ambush the Americans when they came back. Again the islanders came to the rescue. They told Black where they had concealed a canoe along the beach in a locale not guarded by the enemy.

Twilight in the southwest Pacific is but a brief interlude between sunset and night, but Charlie Black used what there was of it to allow his party to steal as close as possible to the canoe. When it was nearly time to scramble into the canoe and shove off for a prearranged rendezvous with an offshore PT boat, Black spotted a chilling sight: four Japanese with bayonet-fixed rifles walked up and took a stand precisely at the point from which the canoe would have to be launched.

There seemed no way out of the predicament. Time was running out. The Japanese dragnet was growing tighter. If the Americans did not get off Roemberpon Island that night, they were doomed, no doubt to hideous deaths. Only one course of action remained for Charlie Black: boldness. It was now dark, and his features could not be discerned by the enemy. So the lieutenant left the brush and began walking nonchalantly toward the four Nipponese sentries. The enemy soldiers looked up at the silhouetted figure but—a mistake on which Black was literally staking his life—thought the American was a comrade. Certainly a hunted quarry would not be strolling calmly along the beach toward them.

When he was only ten feet from the enemy soldiers, Black whipped up the pistol he had been holding behind his back and shot all four unsuspecting Japanese. But the sharp pistol reports alerted every enemy soldier in the region, and the Americans could hear shouts and the rustling of underbrush as more Japanese raced for the site.

Offshore, Lt. Paul T. Rennell, of Southport, Connecticut, in tactical command of a pair of Devil Boats, saw the muzzle blasts from Black's pistol. He promptly realized that the scouting party was in trouble, and despite the peril to his PTs ordered them to close in to the beach. As the harsh shouts of the closing-in Japanese rang in their ears, the Americans scrambled out of the brush and waded out to the PT boats.

Pulled out of the water and onto the deck, Charlie Black collapsed from exhaustion and, gasping for breath, looked up at Lieutenant Rennell and exclaimed, "God bless these damned PT boats!"

CHAPTER 17 Defiant Rescue of a Downed Pilot

The struggle for the godforsaken jungle and mountain mass known as New Guinea finally was drawing to a close. On July 30, General MacArthur's troops splashed ashore at Sansapor, clear out on the western tip of the Vogelkop Peninsula and the final whistle stop on New Guinea. Sansapor, 250 miles west of Camp Taylor, the PT base at Mios Woendi, was seized as a site for airfields to cover future leaps toward the Philippines.

Left behind along the rugged fifteen-hundred-mile coastline of New Guinea were an estimated 200,000 of the Japanese emperor's troops, scattered mainly in small bands. They were doomed to starvation.

For more than two years, Douglas MacArthur had been obsessed with returning to the Philippines, liberating its 18,000,000 hard working, loyal citizens, and "lifting America's flag from the dust," as he phrased it. Two years earlier he had impressed Filipinos with the stirring pledge: "I shall return!" Through the interminable months of Japanese brutality, Filipinos had been sustained by that promise from a man they trusted and idolized: *I shall return!*

Standing on the porch of his hideaway bungalow near Port Moresby on the balmy night of August 3, General MacArthur faced northward, puffed on his corncob pipe, and remarked to visiting Generals Krueger and Eichelberger, "Gentlemen, I can almost see Manila now!"

Indeed he could. By Pacific distances, the Philippines were just over the horizon from Sansapor.

By mid-August, the motor torpedo boat squadrons, which had played a crucial role for twenty-one months in blunting General Tojo's headlong lunge for Australia, had just about run out of customers. For the entire month, only eight barges had been sunk. An advance PT base had been set up on Amsterdam Island near Sansapor and the coastlines in the region were prowled nightly, but few Japanese vessels were detected. Tojo had been pulling out his remaining forces from western New Guinea for several weeks, and the evacuation was nearly completed.

As a result of the Americans gaining control of nearly all of New Guinea, Japanese airpower had virtually vanished, and Devil Boats were stalking the coast in daylight at more frequent intervals. On the morning of August 10, Lt. Ken Molloy, the lacrosse star, in PT 326, and Lieutenant James N. Elliott, Jr., in PT 325, were returning to base after a fruitless night of barge hunting. They came upon a group of natives in three canoes off the southern tip of Roemberpon Island. The New Guineans managed to convey the fact that the Japanese had camouflaged and concealed a barge nearby and agreed to lead the PTs there.

Weaving through treacherous reefs as far as they could, the boats had to halt short of the barge hideout. The natives would go no closer during daylight for fear of snipers; they said that Japanese were in the vicinity. Fire could not be poured into the barge because it was partially concealed behind rock outcroppings. So Lieutenant Molloy dismounted a .50-caliber machine gun from the deck, scrambled with it into a rubber dinghy, and rowed to shore. With him in the landing party were GM2 William Boldt, TM2 Peter Kolar, and TM3 Wilbur Burkett.

Expecting at any moment to be fired on by concealed gunners, the PT men charged up the beach to a point fifty yards from the barge and rapidly set up the machine gun. In staccato fashion they poured five hundred bullets into the vessel and set it afire. Not wishing to press Lady Luck any further, the men quickly dismantled their weapon, hurried back to the waiting PTs, and raced away. Behind them a towering column of black smoke from the blazing barge reached into the clear morning sky.

Morotai is an egg-shaped island some forty-five miles long and lies about halfway between Sansapor in New Guinea and Davao Gulf in Mindanao, the southernmost major island in the Philippines. MacArthur planned to seize Morotai as an air and naval base before leaping on to Mindanao.

On September 15, MacArthur struck at Morotai with a task force under the command of Rear Adm. Daniel "Uncle Dan, the Amphibious Man" Barbey. As usual, the four-star General MacArthur accompanied the task force. Leaving his flagship, the cruiser *Nashville,* the supreme commander headed for shore on the heels of the first wave. Near the beach, his Higgins boat grounded on a rock—much to the chagrin of the youthful coxswain. Impatient to get ashore, MacArthur ordered the ramp lowered and promptly stepped off—into chest-deep water.

While younger men struggled to keep up, MacArthur waded ashore. He was in high spirits. There was no opposition. Douglas MacArthur was within 300 miles of the Philippines. Again he gazed northward toward General Tojo's stolen empire, toward Manila and Bataan and Corregidor. It wouldn't be long now. "They're waiting for me up there," he remarked to an aide.

The following day Comdr. Selman "Biff" Bowling, who had come to the southwest Pacific several months earlier as a squadron skipper and was now commander of all motor torpedo boat squadrons of Rear Adm. Thomas C. Kincaid's Seventh Fleet, arrived at Morotai with the tenders *Oyster Bay* and *Mobjack* and forty-one PTs. The Devil Boats had their work cut out for them. Twelve miles across the water from Morotai is the much larger island of Halmahera (170 miles long), and on it were some 37,000 Imperial soldiers and marines. It was the job of the PTs to constantly patrol the twelve-mile strait and prevent the hordes of Nipponese on Halmahera from crossing over to Morotai.*

Early on the morning of D-day-plus-1 at Morotai, a flight of carrier-based fighters had just completed a strafing sweep over Halmahera and were returning to their ship when Ens. Harold A. Thompson's plane was struck by antiaircraft fire over Wasile Bay, sixty miles south of Morotai. Although painfully wounded by shrapnel, Thompson managed to throw open his canopy and bail out. He parachuted into

---

* Working in relays, the PT boats kept the 37,000 hostile Japanese bottled up on Halmahera for eleven months, until the end of the war.

the water a few hundred yards from the beach. As the ensign floundered about in the water, a Catalina flying boat zoomed in and dropped a rubber raft.

Thompson inflated the raft and climbed into it. The raft began drifting toward the enemy-held shore, and when it nestled up to an unmanned Japanese cargo ship some 150 yards from the beach, the pilot tied the raft to the vessel's anchor chain. A short time later a Catalina tried to land nearby to rescue Thompson, but was driven off by a torrent of fire from shore.

Ensign Thompson could not have picked a worse place to get shot down. Wasile Bay on Halmahera has a narrow entrance, and the approach was protected by several shore batteries and heavy mine concentrations. The downed pilot took hope from the fact that his squadron mates, working in relays when fuel ran low, continued to circle menacingly overhead and drop down on occasion to strafe the shore when it appeared that the Japanese were trying to reach Thompson. But night would arrive in a few hours, and with it the Navy pilot would be doomed.

In the meantime, Ens. Hal Thompson's plight was radioed to Adm. "Uncle Dan" Barbey, commander of Morotai amphibious forces, who ordered Cmdr. Biff Bowling to report to him immediately. Bowling took along his intelligence officer, Lt. Donald Seaman, Lt. Arthur Murray Preston, skipper of Squadron 33, and Lt. Swifty Swift, leader of Squadron 18.

Hopping into a PT, the four officers raced to Barbey's flagship and were escorted at once to the admiral's cabin. Barbey tersely outlined the situation at Wasile Bay and asked, "Can the PTs get the Navy pilot out of there?" Bowling and his three experienced officers had no illusions about the task. If ever there was a suicide mission, this was it. Plunging in broad daylight into the narrow entrance of a bay guarded by numerous batteries and minefields held little promise for survival. The Japanese would know that a rescue effort was imminent; they would be alert and primed, licking their chops as they waited for the quarry to enter the trap.

Commander Bowling, known as a man of great personal courage, told Barbey frankly, "It looks like a mighty dangerous mission to me. I'd hate to have to *order* my PTs to go in after the pilot."

"I agree," the admiral replied evenly. "I have no intention of ordering the PTs to go in."

Biff Bowling glanced at his young skippers. Their faces were grim.

But he could tell by the look in their eyes that each was thinking: we can't stand by idly while that pilot dies; let's go in and get him— come what may. The PT skippers knew pilot Hal Thompson, known personally to none of the Devil Boat men, would not have hesitated a moment in coming to their rescue had they been stranded under Japanese guns and in danger of imminent death.

"Well, admiral," Bowling declared solemnly, "I feel confident that with air cover I can find two volunteer boat crews to try it." Knowing that the PTs would run into a buzzsaw at Wasile Bay, Bowling added, "Provided the officer in charge will have complete discretion in the matter and could turn back, breaking off the attempt without fear of censure or criticism if at any time it appears necessary to avoid losing his men and boats."

"I can't ask for more than that," Uncle Dan Barbey exclaimed.

With that, Lieutenants Preston and Swift blurted out in unison, "I'd like to take two boats from my squadron and try."

Biff Bowling pondered the situation. Since Swifty Swift's squadron was scheduled to go on patrol that night, Bowling selected Murray Preston. Now Don Seaman spoke up. He pointed out that he had studied the strait leading into Wasile Bay and could be of great assistance to the rescue operation. He pleaded to go along. Commander Bowling, not wishing to lose his intelligence officer, who probably knew more about the region than any PT man, approved the request— reluctantly.

Thirty-one-year-old Murray Preston, of Washington, D.C., rushed back to his base and quickly assembled the officers and crews of PT 489 (Eight Ball), skippered by Lt. Wilfred B. Tatro, and PT 363 (Ace's Avenger), under Lt. Hershel F. Boyd. Preston explained the rescue mission, omitting none of the perils, and asked for volunteers. Every officer and bluejacket stepped forward.

Lt. Murray Preston's background hardly seemed one that would produce a gung-ho Devil Boat skipper. He had graduated from Yale University and Virginia University Law School. When called into service with the Navy in 1940 he had been practicing law in Washington D.C. Friendly, courteous, well liked by his men, Preston was now faced with perhaps the most difficult mission he had yet encountered.

The squadron leader climbed onto Eight Ball with Lieutenant Tatro and, with Ace's Avenger following astern, raced off southward at full throttle. Every second counted. As the boats cut through the water, Lt. Robert Stanley hurried to the chart room on Eight Ball and began poring over a map of the Wasile Bay region. He swallowed hard. The approximate location of the downed American pilot was barely a few hundred yards from an operating Japanese airfield.

Nearing the relatively narrow entrance to Wasile Bay, the PT men caught their first glimpses of the mountainous masses on both sides of the entrance. No doubt Japanese guns were positioned on the over-looking heights. Now another specter emerged. "Where in hell is our goddamed air cover!" rang out from both Eight Ball and Ace's Avenger. Navy planes from the carrier *Santee* had not arrived as planned.

Predictably, the Nipponese were alert and waiting. When the PTs were four miles from the Wasile Bay entrance, a big gun opened fire and dropped shells all around the pair of zigzagging boats. Now two more heavy guns joined in; Lieutenant Preston gave the order to pull back seaward at full throttle. In their hasty retirement to regroup, the boats had to bolt through a suspected minefield. Each man, expecting to be blown to smithereens at any moment, held his breath.

Just as the Devil Boats had moved outside the range of the big shore batteries, the planes from the *Santee* roared in. Murray Preston gave the order: "Head for the entrance!" At the wheel of Eight Ball, Lieutenant Tatro threw the throttles forward and the boat leaped ahead, followed closely by Ace's Avenger. This was it!

The Navy planes were swooping down on both sides of the en-trance like gigantic hawks pouncing on prairie chickens. Men on the approaching PTs felt like cheering as bombs exploded and machine guns rattled. The euphoria was short-lived. Enemy guns continued to boom. Both PTs were taking violent evasive action as they charged through another suspected minefield. It took the PTs twenty minutes to reach the entrance of Wasile Bay, which was no more than seven miles wide at any point.

As the boats charged inside the Japanese noose, a mighty ca-cophony echoed across the water. The scores of enemy guns ringing the bay joined in the all-out effort to annihilate the pair of impudent Green Dragons. Gunners on Eight Ball and Ace's Avenger were blast-ing away at the unseen targets on shore; they were achieving little, but fighting men always receive a morale boost when they are able to shoot back.

Despite the fury of fire directed at them, the PT boats sped on-ward, heading toward an anchorage filled with small vessels. "There he is!" someone on Eight Ball shouted above the roar of the engines. Those on board saw Ensign Thompson, huddled in his raft tied to the anchor chain of a cargo ship, about the length of a football field from shore. A fighter plane from *Santee* swooped along the nearby beach, laying smoke to blind Japanese gunners there. As Ace's Avenger lay to, ready to provide extra gun cover, Eight Ball edged up to the enemy ship, and went still in the water only a few feet from the downed pilot's raft.

The Eight Ball was standing so close to shore that crewmen felt they could reach out and shake hands with the Japanese—or pitch a grenade at them. Eight Ball's only protection was the thin layer of smoke that was rapidly dissipating. The Devil Boaters saw immediately that Thompson was wounded and having great difficulty in casting loose from the anchor chain. Watching the pilot struggle, the PT men were growing increasingly nervous. Through the thinning smoke screen they could spot the roof of an airplane hangar above the trees on a nearby hill.

Sizing up the situation, Lieutenant Seaman and MoMM1 Charles D. "Happy" Day plunged into the water, swam to the raft, and towed Thompson back to Eight Ball. As the exhausted pilot was hauled aboard, Lieutenant Preston called out, "Let's get the hell out of here!" Apparently aware that the hated Devil Boats had snatched a victim from under their noses, Nipponese gunners around the bay sent scores of shells screaming toward the PTs as they raced for the entrance. Getting out was more perilous than getting in.

At last Eight Ball and Ace's Avenger were out of range. All aboard let loose with sighs of relief. In broad daylight, the plywood boats had been under constant fire for two and a half hours. "You know," a teenager muttered philosophically to a comrade, "I ought to have my head examined for volunteering for something like this!"

While a stirring footnote in history was being written indelibly at Wasile Bay, far to the north in Tokyo the Imperial High Command was growing increasingly desperate. With the American invasion of Morotai, the Philippines were threatened. And if MacArthur seized the Philippines, the Land of the Rising Sun would be cut off from the oil of the Dutch East Indies, the lifeblood of the emperor's generals and admirals. But the Japanese high command was convinced Imperial forces could smash MacArthur's looming invasion of the Philippines and had drawn up a do-or-die plan, code name Operation

Shōgō (Victory). Every available soldier, airplane, and ship would be hurled against the Americans.

Hirohito had always allowed his generals and admirals to run the war as they saw fit, but when General Tojo had called at the royal palace to offer his resignation, Hirohito readily accepted. His dreams of unprecedented conquest and of driving the white devils out of the Pacific gone up in smoke, Tojo vanished from the public eye into a sort of limbo.

In the meantime, General MacArthur began preparations for his next leapfrog operations: to the southern Philippine island of Mindanao on November 15 (two months in the future) and the central island of Leyte on December 20. But the audacious Adm. Bull Halsey, one of the handful of Navy brass with whom MacArthur had rapport, proposed that timetable be scrapped in favor of a bolder leap.

Warplanes of Halsey's powerful Third Fleet had pounding Japanese bases in the Philippines for several days, and the admiral had reached the conclusion that the central islands were "a hollow shell, with weak defenses and skimpy facilities." The Bull described Leyte as the "vulnerable belly of the Imperial dragon."

MacArthur was electrified by Halsey's suggestion, which the Joint Chiefs of Staff approved promptly. Mindanao (held tightly by Japanese forces) would be bypassed; MacArthur would hit Leyte. The timetable was rolled back by two months: A day at Leyte would be October 20.*

On learning of the approaching invasion of the Philippines at Leyte, Comdr. Biff Bowling had his exhilaration tempered by a difficult problem: how would he get his PT boats from Mios Woendi to Leyte, a distance of some twelve hundred miles? It was too far for the relatively tiny boats to make in one hop. Even if the weather was good and the thirsty PTs were refueled by tenders at sea, so much gasoline would be consumed that little would remain in the tenders to conduct combat operations at Leyte.

Bowling decided the best transport method would be by LSD, a

---

* Douglas MacArthur refused to use the term "D day" in his Pacific operations. He growled to his staff that Gen. Dwight Eisenhower had "monopolized" the term in Normandy. The two four-star theater commanders were not mutual admirers.

combination of ship and floating drydock that could swallow a half-dozen Devil Boats in its maw. This idea was quickly squashed: the LSDs were needed for other more urgent purposes. It was finally decided to send PT boats and tenders on a course through Paulau, in the Marianas, which Admiral Nimitz's forces had seized at the same time MacArthur was invading Morotai.

A week before A day at Leyte, Commander Bowling sailed from Mios Woendi in *Oyster Bay,* with two other tenders, two Army vessels, a seaplane tender named *Half Moon,* and forty-five Devil Boats under the tactical command of Lt. Comdr. Bob Leeson. It would be the largest and longest movement of PTs under their own power during the war; Bowling had his fingers crossed. His normal concerns were hardly relieved by his departure date: Friday the 13th.

On Monday, October 16, Douglas MacArthur, drawing serenely on his corncob pipe, led his staff aboard the cruiser *Nashville* at Hollandia for the two-day voyage to Leyte. (Three small islands in the mouth of Leyte Gulf would be seized before the A day assault.) The supreme commander was in good humor. For more than two and a half years he had been focusing on this moment. Only a year earlier, MacArthur reminded his staff officers, they had been bogged down in the sweltering heat and swamps of New Guinea, fifteen hundred miles away from the nearest Filipino. Now the Great Return had been launched with 200,000 troops and the more than seven hundred vessels of Adm. Tom Kincaid's Seventh Fleet.

The *Nashville* dropped anchor off the landing beaches in Leyte Gulf at midnight of A day-minus-1. The moonless sky was black. On this eve of what the Japanese high command had been calling the "decisive battle of the war" in the Pacific, Douglas MacArthur paced the cruiser's bridge. His thoughts harked back emotionally to March 1942 when he, his family, and key personnel had escaped from Corregidor in John Bulkeley's PT 41. On all sides of him now, he knew, were hundreds of vessels of the powerful Seventh Fleet. What a stark contrast to those bleak early days in the Philippines, MacArthur reflected, when his "fleet" was commanded by Bulkeley, a two-striper (lieutenant junior grade), and consisted of four decrepit, leaking PT boats.

CHAPTER 18   Ambush in Surigao Strait

At dawn of October 20, a mighty roar echoed across placid Leyte Gulf as hundreds of warship guns began shelling the beaches relentlessly. The abrasive rays of the early morning sun cut through the haze and clouds of smoke that veiled the barely visible shore. On the bridge of the *Nashville,* Gen. Douglas MacArthur, his face impassive, casually smoked his pipe and peered through his sunglasses at the orange bursts of shellfire exploding in the thick underbrush on the hills and the glistening sands of the landing beaches.

Soon the smoke parted briefly, and off in the hazy distance the supreme commander spotted the roofs of the small city of Tacloban. The view caused his heart to skip a beat: Tacloban had been MacArthur's first assignment after leaving West Point forty-one years before.*

The general watched the scores of Higgins boats, looking like waterbugs scurrying about a small pond, heading for the beaches with hundreds of grim-faced assault troops. He scanned the skies for hostile aircraft. Soon warplanes bearing Rising Sun emblems roared over

---

* In what may have been the most flagrant understatement of World War II, General MacArthur later wrote: "This was an emotional moment for me."

and began pounding the vast array of ships and bombing and strafing the beaches. Admiral Halsey had been wrong. The Japanese were not nearly as weak in the central Philippines as the Third Fleet commander had been led to believe. Rather the Nipponese had, in the words of a MacArthur staff officer, been "playing 'possum,'" hoarding their might until MacArthur had committed himself.

Later on that A day, Gen. George Kenney made another alarming discovery. Due to Leyte's unstable soil, airfields there could not be used during the rainy season. And the rainy season was nearly at hand. For the first time since he had launched his hit-'em-where-they-ain't campaign in Papua, New Guinea, more than two years earlier, Douglas MacArthur would be fighting without land-based air cover. His air support would be limited to the carrier-based warplanes of Bull Halsey's Third Fleet.

As was his wont, MacArthur went ashore on the heels of his initial assault waves. Fifty yards from shore the landing boat ran aground, and the supreme commander and his party had to wade to shore. There large numbers of Japanese snipers, hidden in trees or crouched in *tako-tsubo* (the Nipponese term for foxholes), were steadily picking off GIs. A conspicuous figure in his gold-braided cap and khaki uniform, Douglas MacArthur stood on a little knoll and calmly lit his pipe. Waving out the match, he began strolling inland. Around him, and along a twelve-mile stretch of beach, thousands of Gen. Walter Krueger's Sixth Army troops were pouring ashore.

That afternoon on the beach, with the crack of Japanese rifles furnishing background accompaniment, General MacArthur stood before a portable radio microphone to deliver a two-minute address that would be carried throughout the islands. Only longtime confidants noticed that his hands were shaking with emotion. Uncharacteristically, he had to clear his throat several times. A torrential downpour of rain erupted, and offshore the warship guns boomed. The supreme commander, outwardly the picture of serenity, began speaking: "People of the Philippines, I have returned . . ."

That night, back on the *Nashville,* Douglas MacArthur slept like the proverbial log. Just before retiring, he had heard Radio Tokyo declare: "We know the war criminal MacArthur is aboard the *Nashville.*" The announcer added that "our valorous airmen will never allow" the cruiser to leave Leyte Gulf. It was probably only an educated guess—but the broadcast resulted in a lot of nervous men aboard the supreme commander's flagship.

Early on the morning of A-day-plus-one, the first Devil Boats roared into Leyte Gulf after their twelve-hundred-mile trek from Mios Woendi. Along the way the boats had refueled from tenders, which in turn had refueled from tankers. As Comdr. Biff Bowling had predicted, the PT men arrived off Leyte nearly exhausted, their bodies and minds badly battered from endless hours of pounding on a trip as far as the distance between Kansas City, Missouri, and New York City. That same night, however, the Devil Boats were out stalking the Japanese along the coasts of the central Philippines.

During the first three nights at Leyte, PT skippers claimed to have sunk seven barges and a small freighter and to have shot up several other smaller craft. On October 23—A day-plus-three—ten boats of Squadron 12, under Lt. Weston C. Pullen, Jr., along with five PTs of Squadron 7, skippered by Lieutenant Commander Leeson, were ordered to move to Liloan, on Panaon Island off southern Leyte. It looked like a routine assignment, a precautionary move, of the type bomber crews called a milk run (where no violence was anticipated). None of the PT boaters heading toward insignificant Panaon Island had any way of knowing that within twenty-four hours they would be embroiled at the center of one of the Pacific war's most crucial actions, an all-out Japanese naval effort to destroy General Mac-Arthur's bridgehead on the western shores of Leyte Gulf.*

Panaon Island had been secured by the Army as a base for the Devil Boats, whose mission was to guard Surigao Strait, a narrow passage between Leyte and Mindanao. Even as Lieutenant Commander Leeson's and Lieutenant Pullen's boats were tying up at Panaon, a mighty Japanese armada was steaming to the northeast at full speed, bound for the strait, which empties into Leyte Gulf.

With the Philippines threatened, the Imperial High Command in

---

* Surigao Strait, and the waters of the Mindanao Sea to the south, was the scene of one of three great naval engagements, fought simultaneously, which collectively became known as the Battle for Leyte Gulf. It would be history's mightiest sea battle.

Tokyo had launched Operation Shōgō, a final roll of the dice for victory in the Pacific. Three great naval forces were converging on MacArthur's Leyte Gulf beaches: the Center Force (most powerful of the three) was approaching from the west; the Northern Force, heavy with aircraft carriers, was steaming southward from Japan; and Vice Adm. Shoji Nishimura's Southern Force was coming up from the south.

On October 24, reconnaissance planes spotted the Center Force heading for Leyte Gulf through San Bernardino Strait, and Nishimura's Southern Force, steaming for Surigao Strait. Hurried conferences were held at the highest levels, and it was decided that Admiral Kincaid's Seventh Fleet (often called MacArthur's navy) would confront Nishimura's armada, while Bull Halsey's more powerful Third Fleet would intercept the Japanese Center Force. At this time, American naval brass was unaware of the carrier-heavy force bearing down on Leyte Gulf from the north.

Admiral Kincaid promptly rushed Rear Adm. Jesse B. Oldendorf, with the Seventh Fleet's six ancient battleships, eight cruisers, and twenty-five destroyers, and twenty-four more PT boats to block Surigao Strait. Taking full advantage of the geography in the area, Oldendorf, a cagey Old Salt, set up an ambush for the oncoming Admiral Nishimura. His battlewagons, cruisers and destroyers were strung out across the northern entrance to Surigao Strait. South of these heavy ships, the thirty-nine Devil Boats were deployed along the shorelines at a point where the Japanese armada would have to reform into column to negotiate the narrow passage.

Like cavalry scouts in the days of the frontier, who would slip ahead of the main body, conceal themselves, and send back word of approaching bands of hostile Indians, the PT boats' primary function was to alert Oldendorf's heavies.

It was approaching midnight of October 24. Onward through the night came the Japanese Southern Force. On the bridge of the mighty battleship *Yamashiro,* Admiral Nishimura stared intently ahead. Nishimura, as well as Vice Adm. Takeo Kurita, commander of Center Force, had sailed on the mission with great forebodings. Weaving in and out of islands, neither Nipponese force would have air cover, and the admirals feared stumbling into American naval ambushes.

On the cruiser *Louisville,* Jesse Oldendorf was rubbing his hands in glee. Here was every Old Salt's dream: an enemy fleet rushing headlong and blindly into his ambush.

Ens. Peter R. Gadd, in PT 131 (nicknamed Tarfu), looked at the luminous face of his watch.* It was 10:15 P.M. Tarfu was stationed outside the southern entrance to narrow Surigao Strait, off Camiguin Island. Suddenly Gadd tensed. His radar had picked up two targets, and as Tarfu headed for them, the two blips divided into five. A light fog lifted, and Ensign Gadd and his crew could discern what appeared to be a destroyer, two cruisers, and two battleships. The "cavalry scouts" tried to flash word back to the main body: "hostile Indians" approaching. But they could get no response on their radios.

With Tarfu were Lt. Joseph A. Eddins's PT 152 (Lack-a-Nookie) and Lt. Ian D. Malcolm's 130 (New Guinea Krud). Although boring in on the enemy force, the Devil Boats were still three miles away, too far to launch torpedoes effectively. Suddenly loud booms erupted and dazzling flashes illuminated the seascape. The enemy ships had spotted the oncoming PTs and opened fire; the first salvos straddled the boats. Not wanting to engage in a slugging match with steel monsters perhaps a hundred times their size, the Devil Boats quickly laid smoke, spun around, and sped away.

Boom! Boom! Boom! The battleships sat back and continued to fire at the wildly zigzagging PTs and illuminated them with starshells. In the meantime, the Japanese destroyers gave chase. Members of the New Guinea Krud's crew were knocked to the deck; an 8-inch shell had struck the forward torpedo a glancing blow, shattering the warhead, ripping up deck planking, and passing through the bow above the waterline. Neither the shell nor the torpedo exploded; no one was hurt.

Shells continued to land all around the racing Devil Boats. Lt. Joe Eddins was at the wheel of Lack-a-Nookie when a large shell ripped away the 37-mm gun at the bow, killing the gunner, stunning the loader, and knocking down the skipper and others on deck. A fire broke out on the boat. Eddins regained his feet and looked back over his shoulder. The enemy destroyers were still in hot pursuit.

As crewmen fought the blaze, the closest destroyer caught Lack-a-Nookie in its blinding searchlight beam. Eddins ordered that two

---

* Tarfu was a popular expression among American fighting men in all theaters. It was an acronym for Things Are Really Fouled Up.

depth charges, set at one hundred feet, be dropped and that the 40-mm gun crew should begin shooting at the searchlight. Moments later the light beam vanished.

The Nipponese destroyers chased the three hated Green Dragons for twenty-three minutes. Lieutenant Malcolm on the battered New Guinea Krud located Tarfu, but Lack-a-Nookie had become separated. Reaching Ens. Dudley J. Johnson's PT 127, near Camiguin Island, Malcolm told of the violent clash, and at ten minutes after midnight, Johnson made the first radio report to Admiral Oldendorf on the *Louisville*.

In the meantime, crewmen had put out the fire on Lack-a-Nookie, and Lt. Weston Pullen, in tactical command of the three PTs, and the boat's skipper, Joe Eddins, surveyed the damage. The shell had caved in the bow, but the boat could still make twenty-four knots. Pullen and Eddins had no intention of calling it a day—or night. Lack-a-Nookie roared off in pursuit of the now withdrawing Nipponese destroyers with the intention of launching a torpedo attack. The enemy warships were making at least twenty-two knots and had a big lead, so, after trying for an hour to catch up, Pullen and Eddins had to call off the chase.

At about 11:50 P.M., Lt. Comdr. Bob Leeson, in charge of three PT boats at the southern entrance to the strait, picked up radar targets ten miles away. The boats headed for the quarry, but became separated due to the blackness and heavy rain squalls. Leeson, in Lt. Edmund F. Wakelin's PT 134 (Eight Ball), spotted the outlines of what he thought were two battleships and three destroyers at three thousand yards range. Moments later a powerful searchlight beam grasped Eight Ball, and then shells splashed around the boat, exploding both in the water and overhead. Chunks of white-hot metal hissed around crew members on deck.

Undaunted, Eight Ball bored ahead for five hundred yards, all the time firing automatic weapons at the warship silhouettes. Two torpedoes were launched, but the Japanese vessels continued on course. Eight Ball then headed for the shoreline shadows at Panaon Island and lay in wait for another target. It was not long in coming. Four destroyers filed past barely a half-mile seaward. Leeson launched his last torpedo, but apparently it missed.

Another of Leeson's boats, 137, skippered by Lt. Isadore M. Kovar, was hunting in the blackness and the periodic rain squalls. Its generator had failed, leaving the boat without radar or radio transmission. But at 3:35 A.M., Kovar detected a Japanese destroyer and closed to within nine hundred yards. Now the moon was shining brightly, and a disappointed boat crew saw its torpedo pass harmlessly under the beam of the destroyer.

Then the enemy vessel bathed PT 137 in the brilliant beams of her searchlight, and turned the seascape into high noon with starshells. Shells began exploding around the PT boat, and Lieutenant Kovar was turning the wheel hard to race away when those on board heard an explosion. Crewmen turned just in time to see flames shoot into the sky on the far side of the destroyer. Mike Kovar's torpedo, while missing its target, had continued onward and plowed into the unseen light cruiser *Abukuma*. The blast killed some thirty men, wounded several score, and slowed the cruiser to ten knots. *Abukuma* limped into a port on Mindanao, where, the following day, she would be detected and sunk.

All over the southern portion of Surigao Strait countless battles took place between the darting, slashing Green Dragons and Admiral Nishimura's much more heavily armed warships. The seascape was a montage of sweeping searchlight beams, long chains of tracer bullets crisscrossing the water, fiery orange torpedo explosions, and the jagged white muzzle blasts of Japanese big guns. Ten miles north of where Lieutenant Commander Leeson's boats had tangled with the enemy warships, Lt. John M. McElfresh, in PT 490 (Little Butch), picked up four targets rounding the end of Panaon Island, eight miles to the south. Along with Lt. Harley A. Thronson's PT 491 (Devil's Daughter) and Lt. Richard W. "Bill" Brown's PT 493 (Carole Baby), McElfresh roared off toward the oncoming warships.

One moment the moon was shining brightly, and the next rain squalls made it so dark that the skippers could not see the bows of their boats. Suddenly, the three PTs emerged from a squall and came face to face with a Japanese cruiser and three destroyers. The nearest enemy warship was only seven hundred yards away—popgun range. Little Butch promptly launched a pair of torpedoes, and moments later the boat was caught in a searchlight beam. Searchlights flashed on other warships, and heavy salvos from big Nipponese guns exploded on all sides of the little boats, deluging their decks with torrents of water and shrapnel.

McElfresh's craft, though naked in the relentless glare of a powerful searchlight, continued on and launched two more fish at the leading destroyer, now barely four hundred yards away. On Carole

Baby, Lt. Bill Brown spotted a large flash at the destroyer's waterline and heard a loud explosion. At the same moment, the warship's searchlight went out. Brown was convinced that one of McElfresh's fish had found its mark.

Now McElfresh's Little Butch was the target of many guns, all seeking to blow it to perdition. One shell blast knocked out the PT's searchlight, a second ripped into its side above the waterline. On deck, TM3 Arthur G. Peterson was struck by shrapnel and knocked down. Struggling to regain his feet, he staggered to the smokescreen generator and turned it on before collapsing.

Then the Japanese fury focused on Brown's Carole Baby. One large shell tore through the boat from side to side, above the waterline. Moments later another missile plunged clean through the engine room, blasting to pieces the auxiliary generator, damaging the engines, and ripping a hole below the waterline. Even though Carole Baby appeared doomed and he probably soon would find himself floundering in the water many miles from shore, MoMM2 Albert W. Brunelle whipped off his own lifejacket, stuffed it into the hole in the side, and went to work to keep his battered engines running.

At the same time, yet another shell ripped away the chart house canopy, killing two bluejackets and severely wounding Lieutenant Brown, the second officer, and three other men. The blast blew everyone in the cockpit clear to the aft of the boat. Although seriously wounded, Ens. Robert E. Carter, the second officer, stumbled back to the cockpit over the blood-washed deck and regained control of Carole Baby. As Al Brunelle kept the damaged engines running, Bob Carter, weak from loss of blood and his vision hazy, steered for Panaon Island. By the time Carole Baby reached shore, the engines were nearly submerged. At daylight, the tide lifted the mortally wounded craft from the beach, and a short time later Carole Baby disappeared beneath the waves in deep water.

As cavalry scouts, the PT boats had done their job. Admiral Nishimura's armada was flushed by the Devil Boats as soon as it steamed between the islands of Camiguin and Bohol at the southern entrance to Surigao Strait. Not satisfied with merely reporting positions of the Japanese vessels to Admiral Oldendorf, the PTs got in many licks of their own with torpedoes and deck guns, and threw Nishimura's force into confusion. But in the process, ten of the thirty-nine Devil Boats involved in the action were riddled by gunfire.

Onward, toward Leyte Gulf and MacArthur's bridgehead, steamed the Southern Force. As it neared the northern entrance to Surigao Strait, an enormous crescendo of noise erupted, punctuated by jagged, lightninglike flashes that lit up the shoreline for miles. Every gun on the battleships *Maryland, California, Tennessee, West Virginia,* and *Mississippi,* along with those of the cruisers and destroyers, rained shells onto the hapless, staggering Japanese warships. Fire-direction officers on the heavies, through steady reports from the cavalry scouts, knew in advance almost to the minute when the enemy vessels would be in range.

American gunners concentrated on the mighty *Yamashiro,* and repeated salvos crashed into her, knocking out three gun turrets and setting her ablaze. Explosions deep within her bowels rocked the battleship. From *Yamashiro's* bridge, Admiral Nishimura shouted an order over the ship-to-ship communications system: "Proceed and attack all ships!" On all sides Nishimura could see his warships burning fiercely.

Moments later a shell struck the bridge, killing Admiral Nishimura. His second-in-command took over and, following his chief's final order, directed that the *Yamashiro,* now a blazing inferno, continue to move forward, toward the belching American guns. Twenty minutes later, with a gigantic shudder, the battleship plunged to the bottom of Surigao Strait.

In its headlong charge through Surigao Strait, Nishimura's Southern Force had been wiped out. With the light of day would be seen nothing remaining on the calm waters but bits and pieces of floating wreckage and streaks of oil.

While the fight was raging in Surigao Strait, a short distance to the north Admiral Kurita's Center Force had sailed through narrow San Bernardino Strait (which had been left unguarded in a high-level communications mix-up) and on into Leyte Gulf. General MacArthur's bridgehead, and the thin-skinned transports offshore, might have been in mortal danger. As it happened, however, Kurita was confronted by a small task force of escort carriers and destroyers under Rear Adm. C. A. F. "Ziggy" Sprague. Against great odds, Sprague's outgunned and outnumbered little force held off the powerful Nipponese fleet of battleships and cruisers, until Admiral Kurita, fearing that he had sailed into a trap, fled back through San Bernardino Strait.

Shortly afterward, Adm. Bull Halsey's scout planes spotted the Japanese Northern Force of carriers and supporting warships, and in a running fight as the enemy carriers turned tail and steamed for Japan, Halsey's pilots virtually destroyed the Nipponese flotilla.

The Imperial High Command's plan to wipe out MacArthur's bridgehead on Leyte and seize the initiative in the Pacific had met with stark disaster. In three days of naval battles around the Philippines, the Japanese had lost four carriers, one battleship, six cruisers, and four destroyers, and suffered heavy damage to fifteen other major warships. The Imperial Fleet had been reduced to mere-nuisance level.

But the warlords in Tokyo still had an ace up their sleeves. They would unleash upon the unsuspecting Americans invading the Philippines a frightening weapon the likes of which mankind had never known and against which there was no defense.

CHAPTER 19 A Rain of Human Bombs

At an airfield outside Manila shortly after dawn on October 25, Lt. Yuro Seki of the Japanese Imperial Navy was steeling his spirit for an ordeal he was facing. Twenty-three-year-old Seki knew that by noon he would be dead.

Yuro Seki was a pilot and a good one. He had graduated with honors from the Imperial naval academy, and only a week prior to being rushed to the Philippines to meet the American invasion threat, he had been married. Handsome, soft-spoken, pleasant, well liked by fellow pilots, Lieutenant Seki had volunteered a few days earlier to lead the first suicide attack against the hundreds of American vessels on Leyte Gulf.

On this beautiful morning, Seki's thoughts flashed back to five days earlier when an Imperial Navy admiral, his voice quivering with emotion, gathered Seki and twenty-four other pilots around him and declared:

> Japan faces a terrible crisis. The salvation of our country is beyond the power of ministers, the general staff, and lowly unit commanders like myself. It is now up to spirited young men such as you.

These "spirited young men" were being asked to become human missiles, to deliberately crash their warplanes into MacArthur's ships in Leyte Gulf. Lieutenant Seki was hardly aware that he would be the forerunner in a revolutionary type of warfare—suicide missions by piloted aircraft—that would eventually threaten American victory in the Pacific. He and the hundreds more who would volunteer to become human bombs were called Kamikazes. The name, meaning Heavenly Wind, was derived from a landmark in Japanese history. In 1570, a Mongol emperor organized a large amphibious force to invade Japan, a small nation that was virtually defenseless. But the gods sent the Heavenly Wind in the form of a typhoon that scattered the Chinese fleet and blew the vessels back onto the China coast.

Now, nearly four centuries later, Lt. Yuro Seki and four other pilots climbed into their Zeros. Bombs were strapped to the wings of each warplane. Seki was ready to die for his Emperor. (The preceding night he had sent his beautiful young wife back in Tokyo a few locks of his hair and clippings from his finger nails.) With a raucous revving of motors, the five Zeros zipped down the runway and lifted off.

Later that morning in Leyte Gulf, thousands of American eyes were warily looking skyward from warships and cargo vessels and PT boats, for Adm. Tom Kincaid's Seventh Fleet had been under periodic bombing and strafing attacks for four days and nights. Then a flight of five Zeros flew in at one thousand feet, and a terrific racket echoed across the gulf as hundreds of antiaircraft guns opened fire on the intruders. These were Yuro Seki and four other human bombs.

Quickly each Kamikaze pilot picked out a target, peeled off, and dived. Four Zeros missed their targets—barely—and plunged into the water. The fifth Kamikaze crashed onto the flight deck of the escort carrier *St. Lo,* setting her ablaze. Thirty minutes later, the blackened, twisted wreckage of the *St. Lo* sank beneath the waves.

Among the gunners blazing away at the Kamikazes were those on the PT boat tender *Willoughby.* As were men on scores of other vessels in Leyte Gulf, *Willoughby's* officers and bluejackets were in a state of open-mouthed astonishment, unable to comprehend how other human beings could commit suicide by crashing their planes into ships. Most dismissed the Kamikaze attack by Lieutenant Seki and his four pilots as an isolated incident by a handful of "gung-ho Japs."

This viewpoint would soon be smashed. Heavenly Wind aircraft, in increasing numbers, would continue to go after American vessels of all types, and the hated Devil Boats and their tenders would be singled out for special attention. On the following day, October 26, the tender *Wachapreague* was heading for Leyte Gulf with a group of the PT boats that had battled Admiral Nishimura's ill-fated Southern Force in Surigao Strait. Suddenly, from out of a cloud bank, five Kamikazes roared down toward the *Wachapreague,* whose gunners opened fire, as did those on the PTs. Within minutes, one aircraft was downed, and shortly afterward two other Kamikazes plunged into the water. The peripatetic Eight Ball (PT 134), which always seemed to have a knack for being in the center of the hottest actions, was hardest hit: one man killed and four wounded by bomb fragments.

When the action simmered down, Lt. Comdr. H. A. Stewart, skipper of the *Wachapreague,* remarked dryly to staff officers: "Apparently the enemy is somewhat hostile to anything connected with PT operations."

Commander Stewart's words would prove to be prophetic. That same night, Ens. Paul H. Jones's PTs 132 (Little Lulu) and 326 (Green Harlot) crept into a dark cove and opened fire on two barges loaded with fuel and ammunition. Towering plumes of fire shot into the sky, and shells began exploding, lighting up the cove and the shoreline for miles. PT men could see the dark figures of surviving Japanese crewmen leaping frantically overboard, and minutes later the barges sank. Green Harlot and Little Lulu had a long trek home, and dawn's first light caught them out on the open sea.

No one saw it coming. A lone Zero swooped down and dropped a bomb that exploded barely ten yards from Little Lulu, killing two bluejackets, and wounding Ensign Jones, his second officer, and eight other crewmen. Disaster had struck like a bolt from the blue.

On the following night, Lt. Comdr. Francis D. Tappaan was in charge of a pair of Devil Boats stalking the north coast of Leyte. It was raining hard, so hard that Tappaan could barely see the bow of his boat from the cockpit. Suddenly, as though activated by a switch, the downpour halted. Visibility improved markedly. At once, from the dark sky, four Zeros dropped on Tappaan's PTs 523 and 525, bombing and strafing the boats. PT 523 took the brunt of the short, savage assault: eight of its men were killed; Commander Tappaan and two other officers, six bluejackets, and an Australian war correspondent were wounded.

In the meantime, the ground fighting on Leyte had turned into a bloody, yard-by-yard slugging match. The Japanese soldiers, always clever and tenacious, had to be dug out of foxholes, caves, and bunkers with flamethrowers, bayonets, grenades, rifles, and automatic weapons. But the weary, waterlogged, fever-racked GI infantrymen clawed ahead steadily, and by the first week in November the Japanese had only their stronghold at Ormoc Bay, on the west side of Leyte, for bringing in reinforcements and supplies.

Nightly, Japanese convoys, guarded by destroyers, slipped into Ormoc Bay. For it was on Leyte, not Luzon as MacArthur had predicted, that the emperor's forces would fight it out to determine who would be landlord of the Philippines. As a result, Ormoc Bay would become the principal hunting ground for the Devil Boats.

It was black and moonless on the night of November 9/10. Lt. Murray Preston, who had rescued the downed pilot in Wasile Bay, was in command of PTs 492 and 497, which were stalking the southern entrance to Ormoc Bay. All hands were at battle stations. The Devil Boats had stuck their noses almost into the harbor of the Japanese bastion.

Lieutenant Preston glanced at his watch: it was 1:14 A.M. God, it's quiet! the skipper reflected. Suddenly, lookouts spotted the outlines of three destroyers slipping around the northern end of Ponson Island. Quickly, Preston called out orders, and the two Devil Boats maneuvered into position. Each PT launched all four of its torpedoes. Moments later a fiery ball leaped into the black sky from the last destroyer in line. Clouds of smoke engulfed the warship. Preston's boats turned hard rudder right and began racing away; moments later shells were screaming into the water around them.

Lieutenant Preston was convinced that at least one torpedo had scored a bull's-eye. One of the three destroyers had disappeared from his radar screen. As the peacetime lawyer glanced back through binoculars, he could see the silhouettes of only two destroyers.

Back at his base the following morning, Murray Preston was jubilant as he told of his fish crashing into the Japanese warship and the pyrotechnics that had resulted. "Looked just like an old-time Fourth of July back home!" he exclaimed.*

---

* Lt. A. Murray Preston, one of the two PT men in the Pacific to receive the Medal of Honor, switched from law to banking after the war. He died on January 7, 1968, at his home in suburban Washington, D.C.

Hardly a night went by in which a shoot-out failed to erupt in or outside Ormoc Bay. On the night of December 11/12, PT 492 (Impatient Virgin), skippered by Lt. Melvin W. Haines, and PT 490 (Little Butch), led by Lt. John McElfresh, were prowling outside the bay when Haines's radar indicated a target four miles away. Stealthily, like huge cats, the Devil Boats slipped into firing position between the target and the beach. As Haines and McElfresh had hoped, this maneuver threw the target into sharp outline—the 330-foot-long destroyer *Uzuki*.

All hands on Impatient Virgin and Little Butch were almost fearful of breathing, lest even that sound give away their presence to the destroyer; she was only a few hundred yards away. So far, there had been no indication that *Uzuki* was aware of her peril. On board the PTs came the muted order "Fire!" and several torpedoes raced toward the unsuspecting warship. Moments later, two enormous explosions at the destroyer's waterline split the night. Oil, water, flames, and debris were hurled hundreds of feet into the air. The 1,315-ton *Uzuki,* without as much as a groan, plunged to the bottom in less than a minute, taking hundreds of crewmen with her.

Two nights later, two PTs led by Lt. Roger H. Hallowell bolted right into Ormoc Bay, torpedoed and sank a two-hundred-foot submarine chaser and a patrol boat, then raced away as angry Japanese guns on shore opened fire on the violently zigzagging boats.

Elsewhere along the black coasts of the central Philippines, the Devil Boats, in the words of an official report, had been "raising merry hell with the Nips." They shot up or torpedoed and sank a long list of freighters, luggers, gunboats, barges, and minesweepers.

Not all the mayhem was being inflicted on the Japanese from the decks of Devil Boats. Among those looking for action of another type was a group of fifteen volunteers from Lt. Comdr. N. Burt Davis's PT Squadron 24. Heavily armed and clad in jungle-camouflaged clothing, Davis's Raiders, as they were known, specialized in landing behind Japanese lines and shooting up camps, gun positions, and supply bases.

Early one morning the second week in December, Commander Davis was visited by a group of agitated natives. They said twelve to fifteen Japanese soldiers had taken over their tiny island, booted out the native families, and then moved into their huts. Davis quickly rounded up his Raiders and, together with the natives, scrambled aboard

PT 338. The islanders guided the Americans to a beautiful little island, complete with white sandy beaches and a blue lagoon.

Davis's Raiders paddled ashore in rubber boats and crept inland. They spotted the huts from a clump of brush where they were hiding. A few Japanese were strolling about, others were lying on cots, none appeared to be aware that there was an American within fifty miles. Suddenly an earsplitting roar engulfed the tropical island, as the Raiders let loose with rifles and automatic weapons. It was over in less then a minute. An eerie silence fell. Then someone set fire to the huts.

EM2 Joseph J. Burke, a nineteen-year-old Raider from Philadelphia, was staring at the score or so of lifeless, bullet-riddled bodies sprawled there when something to one side caught his attention. He swung around to see an unarmed Japanese soldier standing scarcely ten feet away. Burke could tell by the man's face that he was frightened. Every bit as scared as I am, the American reflected.

The enemy soldier put his hands on his head in surrender, and Burke searched him. Commander Davis walked up, clutching a tommy gun. In rapid-fire fashion, the teenager explained to the squad dog that the enemy soldier was unarmed and wanted to surrender. Burke was concerned that Davis would order him to shoot the prisoner on the spot. The thought deeply disturbed the youth. Shooting a Japanese in armed combat at a distance is one thing, gunning down an unarmed soldier face to face is another, Burke warned himself.

Burt Davis stared expressionlessly at Burke for several moments. Finally the commander said, "Okay, Burkey, take him to the boat." The electrician's mate felt as though a battleship anchor had been removed from his back.

Now Burke saw that the Japanese was wounded. He pitched his rifle to a comrade and motioned to the enemy soldier to put his arm around the American's neck. They staggered off toward the beach. This is crazy, Burke reflected. Minutes ago I was trying to kill this man, now here I am helping him—and even feeling sorry for him.

Climbing aboard the Devil Boat, Burke saw that another prisoner was aboard. He asked the cook to bring soup for the Japanese, but they would not eat it. Then Burke knew why they refused: the Japanese were afraid it was poisoned. The youngster consumed a spoonful from each bowl, and then the POWs began gulping it down eagerly.

As Joe Burke watched the men eat, he noticed a Japanese flag wrapped around the waist of the soldier he had escorted to the boat. Burke removed it as a souvenir, only to find that the flag was covering a gaping hole in the soldier's side that was covered with maggots. Soon Burt Davis and his Raiders scrambled back on the 338 and, mission completed, roared off toward home.

As mid-December neared, General MacArthur was ready to make another gigantic leap forward, this time to the large primitive island of Mindoro, 290 miles northwest of Leyte Gulf. The southern Mindoro landing beaches would be less than 200 miles from MacArthur's primary objective—Manila Bay, where lay the Philippine capital and two locales he considered hallowed soil, Bataan and Corregidor. Mindoro would provide air bases and be the final stepping-stone to Luzon.

Leyte had seen some of the most bitter, exhausting, rugged fighting that the veteran American combat soldiers would ever know. Casualties had been heavy. But for the Japanese, Leyte had been a debacle. The Nipponese had lost (or would lose) some 65,000 first-rate troops, nearly all of their fleet, and virtually all of their air force except for the Kamikazes. But the Special Attack Corps (as the Japanese called the Kamikazes) was growing steadily. Each day scores of pilots were volunteering, eager to become human bombs. Minimal training was needed to crash an airplane into an American vessel; the primary ingredient was a fanatical desire to die for the emperor.

MacArthur's planned leap to Mindoro would be an audacious one. The Joint Chiefs of Staff had cabled him that the operation was "too daring in scope, too risky in execution." The Mindoro landing beaches were within easy reach of Japanese warplanes, including many Kamikazes, based at airfields around Manila, the supreme commander was warned. But intelligence sources and his own intuition told MacArthur that Mindoro was lightly defended and could be seized at minimal cost. He would ignore his bosses in Washington.

On the bright afternoon of December 12, two squadrons of PT boats, under the tactical command of Burt Davis, sailed out of Leyte Gulf as part of a large convoy carrying assault troops to Mindoro. All eyes scanned the cloudless skies on the lookout for suicide aircraft. So likely were air attacks, no PT tender was taken along; the ponderous mother craft would be extremely vulnerable.

The invasion convoy got a taste of what was in store for it on the afternoon of the second day at sea, December 13. A Kamikaze crashed into the cruiser *Nashville* within a few feet of the cabin MacArthur had been occupying during the Leyte landings. Several men were killed and a few score were wounded.

On the heels of a heavy bombardment by American warships, assault troops stormed ashore at 7:00 A.M. on December 15. As General MacArthur had predicted, there was virtually no opposition, and before noon four abandoned airstrips had been seized for Gen. George Kenney's fighters and bombers. But the Imperial Air Force—now mainly Kamikazes—reacted to the Mindoro landings, so close to Manila, like an angry colony of wasps whose nest had just been disturbed by an intruder.

Thirty minutes after H hour, Lieutenant Commander Davis led five Devil Boats into Mangarin Bay, which was to be the squadrons' base on Mindoro. Minutes later, the Special Attack Corps struck. Eleven warplanes flew over, and three of them dove on a destroyer in the bay and were shot down by the combined gunfire of the PT boats and other vessels. A fourth Kamikaze swooped down on Ens. J. P. Rafferty's PT 221 (*Omen of the Seas*). Perspiring gunners on *Omen* blasted away; just before the suicide plane reached the boat it caught fire, spun to one side, and crashed into the bay.

The other seven Kamikazes in the flight went after a group of slow-moving LSTs, being escorted by eighteen PT boats, that was approaching the bay. Lt. Comdr. Alvin W. Fargo, Jr., skipper of Squadron 13, had seen the Kamikaze flight as it drew closer and had quickly ordered his Devil Boats to race forward to get between the vulnerable LSTs and the suicide planes. Fargo's boats had barely executed the maneuver when seven planes peeled off and strafed the hated little Green Dragons. Automatic weapons on the PTs blazed away, and three of the aircraft were destroyed.

But four Kamikazes got through the hastily thrown-up PT boat screen and dove on the clumsy LSTs. Two planes were downed by the combined fire of PTs and LSTs, but the remaining pair of human bombs crashed into two LSTs. A mighty roar spread across the seascape, and fiery plumes of flame and black smoke reached skyward. Both LSTs, burning brightly, sank within minutes. More than two hundred survivors of the doomed ships were fished from the water by the PT boats.

By the following morning, nearly all of the Mindoro PT boats were in Mangarin Bay. PT 230 (Sea Cobra) was cruising out to sea when Lt. Byron F. Kent, the boat's captain, looked up and saw three Kamikazes diving on his craft. Kent threw the throttles forward and began zigzagging. The first plane had nearly reached his boat. Now began a lethal guessing game between Devil Boat skipper and suicide pilot. The stakes were enormous: the lives of fifteen Americans. The diving Kamikaze would try to anticipate, at the final moments, in which direction, left or right, the Green Dragon would swerve and would aim for that point. The boat skipper would wait until the last split second, after the human bomb had committed his direction, before veering sharply to one side or the other to avoid being pulverized.

This time Lieutenant Kent guessed correctly. At the last moment, he turned hard right rudder and the Zero plunged into the bay a mere thirty feet from the PT and at the precise point the boat would have been had the skipper chosen to swerve left.

Hard on the first plane's heels, the second Kamikaze roared downward. This time Kent gave a hard left rudder at the last minute, and the Kamikaze hit the water only forty-five feet from the racing PT. Undaunted by the fate of his two fellow pilots, or by the streams of tracer bullets converging on him from Sea Cobra's gunners, the third Zero zoomed downward, its engine screeching. Again the guessing game. Kent made a violent swerve; the plane struck the water and exploded just off Sea Cobra's stern, which lifted out of the water as though the boat were a child's toy in a bathtub. Those on deck were deluged with flame, smoke, debris, and water. All on board were knocked to the deck, groggy, but alive—thanks to a cool skipper who had guessed correctly. Three times.

All the while, eight more suicide planes had pounced on other PT boats that were darting about Mangarin Bay. They dodged, feinted, weaved, and switched speeds to avoid the plunging Kamikazes, like talented halfbacks evading tacklers on broken-field runs. A plane crashed ten yards in front of Lt. Frank A. Tredinnick's PT 77 (Galloping Ghost), which was nearly capsized by the concussion. Lt. Harry E. Griffin, Jr.'s PT 223 had an even closer call; a Kamikaze hit only ten feet away. And a suicide plane literally scraped the paint off the hull of Lt. J. R. Erickson's PT 298 (Big Time Charlie).

On the next afternoon, three Kamikazes struck at Mangarin Bay, and all were shot down. Twenty-four hours later three planes arrived, and one dove on PT 300 (ironically named Kamikaze Val). Lt. Comdr.

Almer P. Colvin, skipper of Squadron 16, waited until the last split second and turned hard right. He guessed wrong. This time, the human bomb won the guessing game. The Kamikaze smashed into the boat, slicing it in half. Bodies were flung about like rag dolls. Commander Colvin was seriously wounded, as were two officers and four bluejackets. Four men were killed and four were missing. Only one crewman escaped unscathed.

As serious a threat as were the Kamikazes, another major menace was bearing down on the Mindoro landing beaches from the sea.

CHAPTER 20 Inferno on the *Orestes*

L ate on the morning of December 26, an Army pilot, scouring the sea some eighty miles northwest of Mindoro, flashed back an alarming report: he had spotted a Japanese naval force of one battleship, one cruiser, and six destroyers steaming hell-bent for the Mindoro landing beaches. This was the second enemy flotilla detected that day in central Philippine waters. A force of cargo ships and troop transports had been sighted slipping out of Subic Bay, in southern Luzon.

The reports touched off a flurry of activity on- and offshore from the Mindoro beachhead. A hurried conference of commanders concluded that the Japanese had launched a coordinated amphibious operation to drive the Americans from Mindoro. The only naval force in the region to confront the onrushing Nipponese armada was Lt. Comdr. Burt Davis's PT boat squadron. On N-day-plus-eleven, the crucial hours of the Mindoro invasion were at hand.

Brig. Gen. William C. Dunckel, the stocky, black-haired commander of ground troops at the bridgehead who had been painfully wounded when the Kamikaze crashed the *Nashville,* hastily deployed elements of the 503d Parachute Infantry Regiment and the 24th Infantry Division to meet the invasion threat. General Kenney's fighter-bombers lifted off from the captured Mindoro airstrips to pound both of the Japanese naval forces. And Lieutenant Commander Davis sent about half of his Devil Boats roaring out of Mangarin Bay to disrupt any invasion force before it hit the beach.

Davis had concluded that his Mosquito Fleet could help throw back the Japanese threat best by attacking the thin-skinned transports with torpedoes as they closed on the beach, and then to rake landing barges filled with soldiers with automatic weapons fire as they were making runs for the shore.

The Devil Boat squadron skipper dispersed eleven other PTs, all in poor condition due to heavy duty during the preceding twelve days, around Mangarin Bay to conduct, if need be, a last-ditch defense of the American main inner anchorage on Mindoro.

North of Mangarin Bay that night, Lieutenant Commander Fargo, skipper of Squadron 13, was peering through the blackness from the cockpit of one of the four Devil Boats in his patrol. Shortly after 8:30 P.M., Fargo saw what happened to be heavy antiaircraft fire on the horizon and estimated the site to be forty miles northwest of Mangarin Bay. No doubt about it, Fargo decided, this was the Japanese warship force under attack by Kenney's fighter-bombers. The flashes on the horizon continued at intervals for nearly an hour.

Suddenly, at 9:15 P.M., Commander Fargo picked up several blips on his radar. Only minutes later, the squadron leader and his men detected the clear outlines of six ships, less than four miles in the distance. Moments later, the men became acutely aware that the enemy force had spotted them also. Jagged flashes of light pierced the night sky, and screaming shells from heavy guns on the Japanese warships landed in the water around Fargo's boats.

Fargo was itching to attack, even though the odds would have been heavily against four PT boats slugging it out with six destroyers and a cruiser. But his orders had been specific: scout and report *only,* do not attack until the Japanese approach the beach in the probable landing area. Reluctantly, Fargo flashed the order: spin about and head back toward the Mindoro bridgehead. Two or three destroyers took out after the Green Dragons, and for nearly an hour a wild chase resulted. The PTs were zigzagging furiously, and shells from the destroyers' guns were splashing into the sea all around them. Finally the enemy warships broke off the pursuit.

The sighs of relief on the four PT boats would be short-lived. Minutes later, crew members heard the angry roar of aircraft diving toward them and bombs began bursting near the boats. One exploded just off the stern of PT 77 (Galloping Ghost), wounding the captain and eleven men and badly damaging the craft. A bomb detonated close by PT 84 (Peacock Lounge), blowing a bluejacket overboard.

Suspecting that the planes were American, their pilots confused by the blackness and the battle raging off Mindoro, Commander Fargo called out to anxious gunners: "Hold your fire! Hold your fire! They're friendly!"

"Some goddamned friends!" an angry and frightened bluejacket called out to the loader of his 40-mm gun.

Not a return shot was fired by the disciplined Devil Boat crew, even as the fighter-bombers returned and strafed the PTs heavily.

Alvin Fargo was furious, too—at the "friendly" aircraft that had shot up his boats and wounded a large number of his men, and at the Japanese destroyers that had been aiming shells at his boats for nearly an hour. He radioed Lt. Comdr. Burt Davis and requested permission to "go after the goddamned Japs." "No," Davis replied, "have Eighty-four escort Seventy-seven back to base." Then, Davis ordered, Fargo should take his two remaining PTs southward through the strait between Ilin Island and Mindoro to be in position to intercept the enemy's transport force in case it tried to land troops on the southern Mindoro beach.

At about the same time that Fargo's boats were being attacked by "friendly" warplanes, far to the north a pair of PTs led by Lt. Philip A. Swart were off the northwestern tip of Mindoro. On board Lt. E. H. Lockwood's PT 221 (Omen of the Seas) and Lt. Harry Griffin's PT 223 were an Army radar team and six guerrillas. Swart's mission was to land the party at Abra de Ilog, on northern Mindoro, where they would observe and report on Japanese activity in the narrow strait between Mindoro and Luzon, the latter heavily garrisoned by the Japanese.

It was shortly before midnight when Lieutenant Swart received an urgent radio signal from Lieutenant Commander Davis: report back to Mangarin Bay at the highest possible speed. The two PTs would be needed in the last-ditch effort to break up the impending Nipponese landing.

Meanwhile, the enemy warship force, blasted by American planes for more than two hours, had had enough. The flotilla reversed course and headed north to its home base. It was spotted by Phil Swart's two Devil Boats that were racing south. PT 223 loosed two torpedoes, and moments later a flash was seen from the third ship in line, and a heavy explosion reached the ears of the Devil Boatmen.

Only later, from Japanese crewmen hit on the head with boat-hooks and fished from the water by PT crews, would Lieutenant Swart and his men learn that they had administered the coup de grace to the 2,000-ton destroyer *Kiyoshimo,* one of the newest and most powerful in the Japanese navy. *Kiyoshimo* had been crippled by bombs in the air attack and sank after the PT torpedo plowed into her.*

As the days passed, the fury of the Special Attack Corps became more intense. On the morning of December 28, Capt. George F. Mentz, on the PT tender *Orestes,* was leading a convoy bound from Leyte Gulf to Mangarin Bay. From there it would launch diversionary attacks against southern Luzon prior to the main landings scheduled for January 9, 1945. Halfway to Mindoro a swarm of Kamikazes pounced on Mentz's force of PT boats, cargo ships, and LSTs. The human bombs plunged into an LST and the cargo ships *John Burke* and *William Ahearn.* Loaded with ammunition, *John Burke* disintegrated in an enormous roar that could be heard for twenty miles. The blast sunk a nearby freighter. PT 332 (Black Hawk) was five hundred yards away, but the concussion ripped open its seams and stunned crew members.

All the way to Mangarin Bay, for four days and nights, Captain Mentz's lumbering convoy ran a gauntlet of suicide aircraft. Eighteen Japanese Kamikazes, torpedo-bombers, and fighter-bombers had been downed, and several ships had been hit by the time Mentz's flotilla pulled into its destination. Sick bays were filled with Americans wounded in the bitter actions.

On the afternoon of December 30, an unnatural silence hung over Mangarin Bay, where Captain Mentz's vessels squatted like brooding hens. It was a welcome relief to the battle-weary crews. Nerves unwound. Muscles relaxed. Perhaps the Kamikazes had had enough. Or

---

* Japanese records examined by U.S. Navy officers after the war are unclear as to whether the mission of the Japanese naval force was to invade Mindoro. Its mission may have been to bombard the four American airfields on the bridgehead.

maybe they were running out of suicide-bent pilots. Then, at 3:05
P.M., they struck. One Kamikaze plunged into the tanker *Porcupine*,
one crashed into the destroyer *Gansevoort,* and a third dove toward
the tender *Orestes.*

Gunners on the *Orestes* and her surrounding pack of Devil Boats
laced the onrushing suicide plane with heavy automatic-weapons fire
and set it ablaze; it struck the water only a few yards to one side of
the PT tender. The Zero skipped on the surface and plunged into the
guts of the *Orestes.*

An enormous explosion shook the tender. Scores of bodies were
hurled every which way. The blast pitched many into the water. Almost at once the *Orestes* was engulfed in a sheet of fire that quickly
spread to ammunition boxes on deck. Twenty- and 40-mm shells detonated, adding to the horror of the inferno.

On the bridge, Captain Mentz lay crumpled in a bloody heap, and
next to him, fatally wounded, was Comdr. John Kremer, Jr., his chief
staff officer. Sprawled on the decks were scores of mutilated men,
many burned to a crisp. Scattered about the burning *Orestes* were the
mutilated lifeless forms of crew members.

Nearby in the bay, Burt Davis looked on at the anguish of those
on the *Orestes.* Davis knew that an even greater holocaust loomed
for the stricken tender: if the blaze reached her 37,000 gallons of
high-octane gasoline and her large supply of stored torpedo warheads,
the *Orestes* and all aboard would be blown to eternity. Yet Davis
never hesitated: led by himself, PT boats around Mangarin Bay rushed
to the side of the burning vessel, and many officers and bluejackets
scrambled aboard to search for and remove the wounded.

The tense PT men knew the peril. Each step could be their last
one. But they probed every nook and cranny, carried out mangled
and hideously burned men. Comdr. A. Vernon Jannotta, who had
taken charge of the task force after Mentz and Kremer were cut down,
brought a pair of LSTs alongside the tender, and hoses were carried
aboard. Ninety minutes after the human bomb had struck, the flames
were under control.

The *Orestes* had suffered heavily: six officers and fourteen bluejackets were killed; thirty-seven men were missing; seven officers and
eighty-six crewmen were wounded. But an enigmatic Fate was not
finished with the tender's survivors. Twenty-four hours later, on New

Year's Day, a Japanese plane flew over Mangarin Bay and dropped a single fragmentation bomb. It killed eleven survivors of the *Orestes* inferno and wounded ten others.

As Kamikazes continued to pound American vessels around Mindoro, in Manila, two hundred miles north of MacArthur's bridgehead, Gen. Tomoyuki Yamashita was fully aware that the climax of the war in the Pacific was at hand—that the Americans were about to strike at the key island of Luzon. In his office overlooking the Pasig River in downtown Manila, the Japanese commander in the Philippines was being interviewed by reporters hastily sent from Tokyo in pursuit of favorable war news for home-front consumption.

The bullet-headed Yamashita did not disappoint the eager newsmen. "The loss of one or two islands does not matter," he exclaimed. "There is an extensive area in the Philippines, and we can fight to our heart's content. I shall write a brilliant chapter in history in the Philippines."

On January 7, Gen. Douglas MacArthur was on the cruiser *Boise* heading for Lingayen Gulf, 125 miles north of Manila. Around him was the most powerful land-and-sea force ever assembled in the Pacific to that time: 1,000 ships, 3,000 landing craft, 280,000 men. S day on Luzon was January 9. The landing beaches were precisely where General Tojo's rampaging army had invaded the Philippines in December 1941.

All during the long trek from Leyte Gulf, the invasion convoy was attacked by swarms of Kamikazes, and several vessels were sunk or badly damaged; hundreds of men were killed or wounded.

On the voyage, MacArthur, puffing serenely on his pipe, spent a good part of the time sitting in the doorway of the captain's cabin. His was the air of a man whose work had already been done. Carl Mydans, a photographer for *Life* magazine, happened by, and the general remarked: "You know, Carl, this is the same route I followed when I came out of the Philippines in Johnny Bulkeley's PT boat . . . exactly the same route."

At 7:00 A.M. on S day an enormous roar swept across Lingayen Gulf as Adm. Jesse Oldendorf's battlewagons began pounding the beaches. Hard on the heels of the bombardment (at 9:40 A.M.), assault elements of four divisions of Gen. Walter Krueger's Sixth Army stormed ashore. Only a few panicky Japanese stragglers were on hand, and they fired random rifle shots before fleeing into the jungle. Krueger promptly sent two flying columns pushing southward toward Manila.

On S-day-plus-four, two PT boat squadrons and the tender *Wachapreague*, under tactical control of Lt. Comdr. Francis Tappaan, reached Lingayen Gulf. Prowling offshore that night, the Devil Boats had a skimpy bag: four small barges set afire and sunk. A few nights later, Lt. B. M. Stevens's PT 532 and Lt. G. S. Wright's PT 528 fired eight torpedoes at a 6,000-ton freighter, blew off her bow, and caused the Japanese skipper to ground and abandon her.

MacArthur's road to Manila would be a bloody one. General Yamashita, one of the ablest of the Japanese generals, had the same number of troops as did the Americans. He had pulled them back from the Lingayen beaches and deployed them inland. There they would contest every foot of Luzon.

Like a champion boxer, Douglas MacArthur began feinting, bobbing, and weaving, landing one haymaker after the other on Yamashita's sturdy jaw. On January 29, American troops stormed ashore on western Luzon, just north of Bataan, and quickly overran that region of python-infested swamps. Two days later the 11th Airborne Division conducted a combined amphibious-parachute operation at Nasugbu Bay, fifty-five miles south of Manila.

With American divisions closing in from the north, west, and south, Manila was doomed. Late on the night of February 3, a mechanized spearhead of the 1st Cavalry Division plunged across the northern city limits. Later that night, a patrol of Devil Boats, under Lt. Henry Taylor and Lt. Carl Gleason, set out from Subic Bay on an important scouting mission. They would penetrate Manila Bay, where no American vessel had been since Gen. Skinny Wainwright had been forced to surrender his "gaunt ghosts of Bataan" and Corregidor in May 1942.

An intelligence report had informed skippers Gleason and Taylor that Manila Bay was "lousy with Japs." But the perilous part of the mission would be slipping under the big guns of Corregidor, the rock fortress perched in the mouth of the bay. Another hazard was that the Japanese on Corregidor controlled the switch for an electronic mine field guarding the harbor entrance.

The night was moonless, but a bright galaxy of stars was visible in the heavens. Engines muffled, the Devil Boats were creeping toward the bay. Suddenly, a short distance ahead, crew members spotted the dim silhouette of a massive hulk—Corregidor. Pulse beats quickened. Perspiration broke out on foreheads and palms. No doubt at that moment they were crossing the mine field; a flip of a switch could blow them to smithereens.

Onward inched the PTs. It was deathly still; they were abreast the fortress. A muffled cough by a stern gunner brought silent curses from all. The Americans felt as though they could reach out and touch the enormous rock. How many Japanese eyes were watching them? When would the brilliant searchlights on Corregidor flash on? After what seemed an eternity, Corregidor was behind them, and anxious eyes watching to the rear saw that the fortress had been gobbled by the night. Deep sighs expressed the relief of all hands. Throttles were thrown forward, and the Devil Boats raced off toward enemy-held Manila, twenty-three miles away.

In the cockpits, Lieutenants Taylor and Gleason could see a sickly yellow haze over the capital: magnificent Manila, Pearl of the Orient, was burning.

CHAPTER 21 Funeral Pyre at Samar Beach

At midmorning on February 16, while a savage battle was still raging inside Manila at the other end of the bay, Lt. Raymond P. Shafer was bracing himself on the deck of PT 376 (Spirit of '76) and watching in awe as American warships and aircraft pounded Corregidor a half-mile ahead. General MacArthur's attack to recapture the mighty bastion in the bay had been launched.

Ray Shafer was a combination of brains and brawn. He had graduated from Allegheny College, was a member of Phi Beta Kappa and had earned nine varsity letters in sports. A native of Meadville, Pennsylvania, Shafer went on to gain a law degree from Yale University shortly before war broke out. Now all those laurels were of no consequence; what mattered now was for Spirit of '76 to carry out the significant mission it had been assigned in the Corregidor assault.

Above the roar of the guns, Lieutenant Shafer could hear the hum of airplane motors, and off in the distance, he could see a flight of C-47 cargo planes winging toward The Rock. These planes, Shafer and his shipmates knew, were carrying some twenty-two hundred men of Col. George M. Jones's 503d Parachute Infantry Regiment. If Spirit of '76 did its job, perhaps many of these parachutists would survive.

Colonel Jones's paratroopers were to bail out over the dominant terrain feature known as Topside at one end of the two-and-one-half-mile-long island. Topside towered upward for 550 feet, was relatively flat on top, and had sheer cliffs on three sides that dropped away to the bay. The drop zone atop the elevation was so small that a slight miscalculation or a sudden shifting of wind currents could result in a parachutist plunging into Manila Bay. Burdened with seventy to ninety pounds of combat gear and entangled in his parachute risers, the unlucky trooper would drown within seconds unless rescued. Rescue was the role of Spirit of '76 and a few other Devil Boats.

Jumping from the dangerously low altitude of 350 to 400 feet to maximize accuracy, most of the paratroopers crashed with teeth-jarring impact on the cementlike surface of Topside, but some plunged into Manila Bay. PT boats, often under small-arms fire, rushed to the floundering parachutists and fished them from the water.*

Lt. John A. Mapp, skipper of Spirit of '76, spotted twelve to fourteen paratroopers scrambling down a wooded cliff as snipers peppered them with small-arms fire. These troopers had barely missed the drop zone and landed on the cliff's side. Spirit of '76 raced in, and fifty yards from shore put a rubber raft over the side. Lt. Charles Adams and Ray Shafer scrambled onto the raft, paddled ashore as Japanese snipers took potshots at them, and transported the isolated paratroopers back to the Spirit of '76. Minutes later another group of parachutists was spotted on the narrow shelf at the bottom of the cliffs. They were waving their arms frantically at the PT boat. Shafer and Adams climbed onto the rubber raft once more and repeated the rescue mission, again under fire. Altogether the two PT officers had carried twenty-seven paratroopers to safety from the slopes of Corregidor.**

Late that morning, a battalion of the 24th Infantry Division stormed ashore at a point called Bottomside. Far outnumbered by an estimated six thousand Imperial marines and soldiers, the Americans had to dig the tenacious enemy out of foxholes, bunkers, and caves in savage

---

* Late in 1985, Brig. Gen. George M. Jones, who led the parachute assault on Corregidor, told the author that had it not been for the presence of the PT boats just offshore and the daring of their skippers and crewmen, many paratroopers who missed the Topside drop zone would have lost their lives.
** In 1967, Raymond P. Shafer was elected governor of Pennsylvania.

face-to-face fighting. Twelve days later, the last Japanese had died for his emperor.

Thirty-nine months earlier, General Douglas MacArthur had left the Philippines, breaking through the Japanese ring around Corregidor on the first leg of his journey to Australia. Now, shortly after dawn on March 2, the supreme commander and officers of the Bataan Gang (those who had served on his staff since the bleak early days in the Pacific) strolled onto four Devil Boats moored outside Manila. These were emotion-packed moments. Douglas MacArthur was bound for Corregidor, the big rock that he considered the symbol of America's honor, the hallowed old American fortress where, he said, the nation's flag had been ground into the dust.

MacArthur was beaming. He turned to the young skipper, Lt. Joseph Roberts, and remarked jovially, "So this is PT 373. I left [Corregidor] on Bulkeley's Forty-one."

At 10 A.M., the four Devil Boats carrying the high brass edged into North Dock on Bottomside. Douglas MacArthur, with an agility belying his sixty-five years, scrambled onto the rickety dock. This was the precise point where he, his family, and the Bataan Gang had slipped onto John Bulkeley's four leaking PT boats in March 1942. The general stood with his hands on his hips and gazed around at the shell-and-bomb-battered rock. So heavy had been the pre-assault naval and air pounding that MacArthur noted that even the contours had changed.

Inside the heads of the Bataan Gang standing with MacArthur at this dramatic moment in American history (and undoubtedly within the mind of the supreme commander himself) echoed and reechoed the seven uplifting words he had spoken on reaching Australia after his escape from Corregidor: "I came through, and I shall return!"

Symbolic of America's ordeal and triumph in the Pacific were Lieutenant Roberts's four Devil Boats, bobbing gently in the surf a few yards away. Like General MacArthur himself, PTs had been in the thick of things from the beginning.

The day after General MacArthur's triumphant return to Corregidor, Manila fell. The once magnificent city, long known as the Pearl of the Orient, had borne the torments of the damned. Caught in the middle of the savage house-to-house, closet-to-closet fighting, countless tens of thousands of civilians had been slaughtered. Buildings and houses were but blackened, twisted skeletons. By April 16, all of Manila Bay was in American hands.

Hardly had the smoke of battle cleared over Corregidor than General MacArthur launched invasions of seven Philippine islands: Cebu, Guimaras, Negros, Palawan, Panay, Tawitawi, and Zamboanga. The Japanese resisted savagely, fought to the death, even though they knew that their situations were hopeless. Devil Boats played key roles in all of these operations. They scouted shorelines in advance, reporting on Japanese gun positions and installations; strafed and rocketed landing beaches just before assault troops stormed ashore; and patrolled coasts of the invaded islands to wipe out Nipponese trying to flee by canoes and rafts and even by swimming.

While American forces had been fighting in the Philippines, a nasty little war-within-a-war had been raging on and around the islands of Morotai and Halmahera, a few hundred miles southeast of the southern tip of the Philippines. From their base on Morotai, the egg-shaped island separated by twelve miles of water from Halmahera, several PT boat squadrons had been constantly harassing the 37,000 armed Japanese on Halmahera to keep them penned up there.

Devil Boat skippers worked closely with Dutch, Australian, and native scouts, sneaking them ashore at Halmahera and adjacent tiny islands and later retrieving them. On April 6, the PT base on Morotai received word from native scouts that the Sultan of Ternate, who before the war had governed the entire region for the Dutch, was being brutalized by the Japanese and was in danger of execution. A mini-rescue operation was mounted promptly. Shortly after dark on April 8, a team of Australian, Dutch, and native scouts scrambled aboard PT 178 (Torpedo Junction) and PT 364, and the boats set a course for the tiny island of Hiri just north of Ternate, where a rendezvous had been arranged.

It was an especially dark night, a factor for which all of the rescuers were thankful. As the two boats neared Hiri, engines were muffled. Japanese were thought to be on the island, but there was no indication of life. Perhaps fifty yards offshore, the PTs lay to and put two rafts over the side. Silently, several scouts stole into each one and paddled ashore. About a half-hour later they returned carrying the Sultan of Ternate—and his entire harem.*

---

* Official U.S. Navy records fail to confirm the persistent rumor at the Morotai PT base: that the grateful sultan offered to his rescuing skippers the "services" of any of his harem.

During the first week of July, the Morotai base learned of the existence of the *Nanyo Kaihatsu Kaisha* (South Seas Development Company), a "civilian" operation set up by the Japanese to distribute food to their scattered garrisons on Halmahera and the small islands off the west coast. Further probing revealed that the South Sea Development Company stole food from the natives, stored it in warehouses through Halmahera, and had the buildings guarded by native collaborators supervised by a few Japanese officers. When outposts needed food the company hired (or forced) natives to haul it from warehouses in large canoes or in *prahaus*, small vessels some forty feet long and able to carry more than a ton.

Devil Boat skippers, licking their chops over the prospect of taking a crack at the South Seas Development Company, quickly organized a raid. It would be led by Lt. Joe Burk, the holder of the world's record for single sculls (rowing) and a veteran of countless PT actions. In his training days at Melville, Long Island, Burk's classmates had doubted if the soft-spoken, friendly skipper candidate would make the grade when the shooting started. They had had no idea that this mild-mannered, polite young man would turn into a tiger in the South Pacific.

As darkness began to fall on July 5, Joe Burk, a Dutch lieutenant, and thirty-seven native scouts climbed aboard Lt. E. F. Shaw's PT 348 (Merry Mac) and Lt. J. L. Grubb's 351 (The Shadow). Destination: Makian Island. "Boys," Burk remarked matter-of-factly to his crew, "the South Sea Development Company is about to hold a going-out-of-business sale!"

Approaching Makian, the Devil Boats overtook a pair of food-laden *prahaus*. The native crews were petrified. They declared that the Japanese had forced them to man the boats, and that they had orders to take the badly needed food to an isolated Nipponese outpost. Lieutenant Burk took the natives aboard, and several bursts of .50-caliber machine-gun fire sank the *prahaus*. Continuing onward, Merry Mac and The Shadow tied up at a wooden dock on Makian, and Burk led a party of scouts and crewmen to two warehouse buildings belonging to the South Seas Development Company. They set the well-stocked structures ablaze, ransacked a headquarters used part-time by the Japanese, removed bundles of documents, and torched the facility. On returning to the PT boats, Burk ordered five loaded *prahaus* towed to deep water where they were riddled by machine-gun fire and sunk.

Forty-eight hours later, Tiger Joe Burk struck again. This time he took five Devil Boats for a barnstorming tour of the islands off Halmahera's west coast. This jaunt by the PT buccaneers would be a long one—200 miles one way, to the tip of southwestern Halmahera, so deck tanks were loaded with extra gasoline. Overhead would be three fighter-bombers of the Royal Australian Air Force, long a PT boat battle partner.

At Badjo, Obi Island, off the southwestern end of Halmahera, Burk and a landing party burned a South Seas Development Company warehouse and a sago mill. Lt. Steve L. Hudacek's PT 182 blew to smithereens six beached *prahaus* with a 40-mm deck gun. Moments later, a concealed machine gun opened fire and sent a burst into 182. The RAAF warplanes were contacted and they strafed the locale. The Japanese weapon was not heard from again.

Joe Burk's rampaging Devil Boats then headed south, and at the town of Amasing, on Batjan Island, their guns sent broadsides of bullets and rockets into a Nipponese radio station and four warehouses.

Now the boats had reached the limit of their range and turned northward. The group divided, with three boats heading for Moti Island and two to Tidore Island. At Moti the scouts went ashore, set fire to a warehouse, and returned without opposition. It was a different story at Tidore. A landing part of ten men slipped ashore from Ens. William A. Klopman's PT 179 (Betty Lou) and Lieutenant C. C. Hamberger's 180 (Marie). They found no warehouses but broke into an unmanned Japanese headquarters and made off with several armloads of documents.

The ten raiders were trudging through the jungle on the way back to the boats when suddenly a machine gun chattered and streams of bullets whisked past their heads. Before they could react, six Nipponese soldiers wielding rifles and screaming "banzai!" charged toward them. Now a second machine gun opened up from the underbrush. The raiders had stumbled into an ambush. "Haul ass!" someone shouted, and the raiders began a mad dash for the PT boats.

Huffing and puffing, the raiders reached the beach and scrambled onto Marie. The six shouting Japanese riflemen were right on their heels. Manning Marie's bow 37-mm gun, MoMM2 E. D. McKeever opened fire at the enemy pursuers as they burst out of the underbrush behind the beach. All six were cut down. Other guns on Marie poured fusillades into the brush from where the Nipponese automatic weapons had been firing and silenced them. Their work done and not wanting to press their good luck, PTs Betty Lou and Marie abruptly departed Tidore Island and raced out to sea.

On July 10, Lt. Redmond J. Reilly led a pair of Devil Boats on a return courtesy call to Tidore Island. There Lt. William D. Finan's PT 178 (Torpedo Junction) and former Franklin and Marshall football star Lt. Kermit Montz's PT 355 (Hell's Cargo) hit the jackpot. They blasted forty-two *prahaus* sitting on the beach, then crossed to Halmahera's west coast and riddled nine more. Two follow-up raids in the same area resulted in the destruction of some hundred *prahaus*, rigger canoes, sailboats, whaleboats, and anything else that might float.

A final raid was launched on July 30, when Lt. T. J. Lovvorn in PT 177 (Hushee) and Lt. R. C. Fisher's PT 376 visited the town of Toroaoe, on Ternate Island, the domain of the sultan. Cruising along the shoreline, the boats heavily shelled three Nipponese barracks, then the PTs raced off to Kajoa Island. A landing party of six Devil Boatmen and fourteen scouts paddled ashore in rubber boats, stole through the jungle to five warehouses crammed with food, copra, oil, and clothing—all destined for the emperor's soldiers. The five structures were put to the torch. As the pair of boats headed for home, crew members could still see towering plumes of black smoke ten miles out to sea.

By August 1, the enforced going-out-of-business sale of the South Seas Development Company had been concluded. Scouts and natives reported that only one small center was operating, and it had been moved far inland to escape the vengeance of the Devil Boats.

Meanwhile, 2,000 miles north of where Tiger Joe Burk and his mates were forcing the Nanyo Kaihatsu Kaisha into bankruptcy, the Imperial general staff in Tokyo had concluded that Japan's fourteen-year-long dream of turning the enormous expanse of the Pacific into a fiefdom had vanished like a wisp of smoke. But if hope for victory had dissolved, defeat could still be staved off. The empire's forces would continue to fight and inflict such monstrous bloodletting on the foe that the American home front would cry out for a negotiated peace.

So the war in the Pacific raged on. MacArthur's men were bogged down in bitter fighting in the Philippines. The U.S. Marine Corps suffered the most casualties in its history on a flyspeck of coral and sand—Iwo Jima. American soldiers and Marines by the thousands were butchered on Okinawa, while off that bloody battleground hundreds of Kamikaze pilots inflicted the greatest damage and casualties ever on the United States Fleet.

In July 1945, President Harry S. Truman approved dropping an A-bomb, a then revolutionary weapon of unprecedented destructive capacity, on the industrial city of Hiroshima to end the nearly four years of bloodshed in the Pacific. Truman's alternative was to allow a mammoth invasion of Japan to proceed, at an estimated cost of a million American casualties and the deaths of several million Japanese soldiers and civilians.

On August 6, the atomic bomb fell on Hiroshima. The military clique in Japan remained silent. Three days later a second A-bomb flattened the city of Nagasaki. Fanatical Japanese generals pledged to fight on. Bansai!

In bomb-gutted Tokyo, the situation was chaotic. Hirohito for once ignored his generals and took matters into his own hands. He recorded a *kōdō sempu* (distribution of the royal word), and it was broadcast over Radio Tokyo on August 15. Hirohito was considered a god and so sacred a figure that few had ever heard his voice. *Jiro tanaka* (John Q. Public) was stupefied to hear god speaking. Hostilities were to end at 4:00 P.M. (Tokyo time) that day, Hirohito declared. "You must endure the unendurable and suffer the insufferable," he told his subjects.

Throughout the Pacific, American fighting men rejoiced over their unexpected reprieve. But word of Nippon's capitulation touched off a rash of *seppuku* committed by Imperial officers who ripped open their own bellies with ceremonial daggers. One of these was Adm. Takijiro Onishi, founder of the Kamikazes who, before performing the painful ritual, penned a note begging forgiveness from the families of the thousands of Divine Wind pilots he had sent to their deaths.

Hard on the heels of Hirohito's surrender, an American version of *seppuku* was inflicted on the Devil Boats of the Pacific. Their job was done. Due to their plywood construction, they could not be stored away against future need as were steel-hulled vessels. Most of the older PT boats, which had continued to fight due to necessity, were beyond saving anyway: broken frames, dry rot, worms, broken keels, burned-out engines, shell and bullet damage.

From all over the Pacific, these boats were hauled to an isolated beach on Samar Island in the Philippines, doused with gasoline, and set afire. The funeral pyre was an ignominious end for the swift little craft that had been in the thick of the fighting since GM (later a lieutenant) Joy de Jong and TM George Huffman shot down the first Japanese aircraft of the war minutes after the sneak attack on Pearl Harbor began.

None of the Devil Boats' buccaneers were present for the cremation on Samar's beach. Most of the "citizen sailors" had been sent home promptly for discharge. But the battle-scarred boats did not die alone. Imperceptible to the naked eye, an honor guard hovered over the site. Proud and vigilant, standing tall, these were the gray ghosts of the PT boat wars, young Americans who had been cut down in the prime of life while helping to hack out a lengthy and tortuous road to Tokyo.

Epilogue

Nearly all the Devil Boat skippers, most of whom had leapt from college campuses into the perils of the South Pacific, went on to excel in civilian pursuits. A few had already been famous, others became so. In the 1961 inauguration parade in Washington, D.C., a PT boat was hauled down Pennsylvania Avenue as a reminder of newly elected President John F. Kennedy's wartime service. Seated in a VIP box as the chief executive's invited guests were wartime comrades, including William F. "Bud" Liebenow, skipper of PT 157 (Aces & Eights), who had rescued a marooned Lieutenant Kennedy from a Pacific island.

Despite the crushing burdens of the world's most powerful office, President Kennedy never forgot the Devil Boat skippers and blue-jackets with whom he had served in the Pacific. On several occasions Kennedy invited old comrades to lunch with him in the White House. There, with the gusto of any other combat veteran, the president relived those years of peril and triumph.

PT Lts. Raymond P. Shafer and Howard Baker also made it big in politics. Shafer became governor of Pennsylvania in 1967, and Baker served for many years as a senator from Tennessee, including a term as senate majority leader.

Another PT boat citizen sailor, Robert Montgomery, who rose to the rank of lieutenant commander after seeing action in the Solomons, returned to starring in Hollywood movies. He died in 1981. Today his daughter Elizabeth is a screen and television star in her own right. Walter H. Lemm, known to legions of sports fans as Wally, was one of the countless skilled athletes in the PT service and saw heavy duty in the South Pacific. Years later, he was the successful coach of the St. Louis Cardinals and still later, the Houston Oilers. Lemm was the National Football League's Coach of the Year in 1964. PT Lt. Michael Burke supervised the CBS takeover of the New York Yankees baseball team in 1964, later became president of the New York Knicks basketball team and the New York Rangers hockey team.

Commander Selman S. "Biff" Bowling, who was in command of all Devil Boat squadrons in MacArthur's navy (Admiral Kincaid's Seventh Fleet), came home after the war still upset over the Navy's handling of decorations for Lt. A. Murray Preston and other officers and bluejackets who had rescued the downed American pilot in Wasile Bay. Bowling considered that action one of the most daring and perilous rescues of the war. Promptly after the mission, Commander Bowling had recommended Lieutenant Preston for the Medal of Honor, and the two PT boat captains and one bluejacket for Navy Cross decorations. Seventh Fleet staff officers had downgraded the awards. In 1945, Bowling "raised so much hell" around Washington that the higher decorations were restored. Murray Preston received the Medal of Honor from President Harry Truman in the White House.

In 1957, as a captain, Biff Bowling requested voluntary retirement, and left the service to join Texas Industries in Corpus Christi, Texas.

John Harllee, who was in the vanguard of the Devil Boat war in the Pacific from the time he was a PT skipper at Pearl Harbor when it was bombed, eventually attained two-star-admiral rank. In 1960, after leaving the Navy, Harllee served as state chairman (northern California) of a Citizens for Kennedy for President committee. Kennedy appointed Harllee to the Federal Maritime Commission in 1961, and he served as chairman from 1963 to 1969. Since then he has been a maritime consultant, and in that capacity has traveled extensively throughout the world.

There were other PT boat officers in the South Pacific who went to Washington in key positions. Byron R. "Whizzer" White, an all-American halfback at Colorado University and a Rhodes scholar in the late 1930s, was appointed by President Kennedy to the United

States Supreme Court in 1962, a post White was still holding in early 1986. Kennedy also named Paul B. Fay, Jr. (known to fellow Devil Boat skippers as "Red") as Under Secretary of the Navy.

John Bulkeley became the most famous PT skipper of World War II. His bold dash through the tight Japanese naval and air blockade of Fortress Corregidor to carry General MacArthur and his party to safety has endured as one of the most notable military attainments in American history. Certainly for many it was the single most dramatic PT boat feat of the war.

MacArthur's escape (under direct order from President Roosevelt), at a time when the Japanese were trying desperately to capture America's number one soldier, electrified the free world. The feat gave hope to the captive people of the Philippines; it calmed the fearful citizens of Australia and convinced them that their country could be defended; and it provided a prodigious boost to an American home front still shocked and reeling from a series of military debacles in the Pacific and elsewhere. Of equal significance, as Roosevelt had intended, one of history's greatest generals was saved to lead the Allies to victory over Japan.

In retrospect, the escape from Corregidor would seem to have been an impossibility. Not only did the four Devil Boats involved have to elude Japanese warships and aircraft and lookouts on scores of islands along the route, but the navigational obstacles were mind-boggling. Today, when one looks at charts of the six hundred miles of water between Corregidor and Mindanao, he might wonder how the boats made it through the countless reefs, past islands and other hazards, in pitch blackness, in rough waters, and with only primitive navigational aids of a type used by the ancient mariners.

In late 1985, Admiral Bulkeley told the author:

> If one asked me today as a mature individual if it could have been done, I would have to say, 'No way!' Having been young, cocky, and brash, I told General MacArthur previously that it would be a piece of cake, no problem at all.

As a result of MacArthur's escape from Corregidor, John Bulkeley was widely acclaimed at home and became something of a living legend, which he still is today. But some U.S. Navy brass in the Pacific did not join in the Bulkeley acclaim. In mid-1942, the young

skipper had been brought back to the States to receive the Medal of
Honor from President Roosevelt, then spent a year crisscrossing the
nation recruiting top-flight PT boat skippers. ("He did a tremendous
job," Admiral Harllee recalled forty-three years later.) In late 1985,
John Bulkeley told the author what took place when he arrived back
in Australia in 1943 and reported to U.S. Navy headquarters:

> I received a very cold reception from a vice admiral (the
> senior Navy officer in Australia). He was downright nasty. Why
> did I rescue MacArthur? Why didn't I let him die? I couldn't
> fathom the reason for this tirade. Then another admiral took his
> turn and beat me up. Then a Navy captain beat me up. And next
> a commander-somebody-or-other took a turn, but I paid no at-
> tention to him. If I had known that I was going to be beat up
> that way, I would have [asked for duty] in the European theater.

Only years later would John Bulkeley learn the reason for this
unexpected reception: top Navy brass wanted the overall commander
in the Pacific to be an admiral, and with MacArthur out of the way
there would have been a better chance for achieving that goal.

In late 1943, Gen. Dwight D. Eisenhower, preparing to invade
Hitler's fortress, Europe, asked for Lieutenant Commander Bulke-
ley's services, and on D day in Normandy Bulkeley led more than
sixty PT boats and a few score minesweepers. Two months later,
Bulkeley was in charge of twenty-two PT boats and the destroyer
Endicott in the Allied invasion of southern France.

Fifty-two years after graduating from the U.S. Naval Academy,
Rear Admiral Bulkeley remains on active duty. For many years now,
Bulkeley has had the crucial assignment of seeing that the U.S. Navy's ships are battle-ready should the bell ring. In that capacity, he
has been traveling throughout the world almost constantly.

Somehow, Buckaroo (as MacArthur called him) Bulkeley has found
the time to keep in touch with old friends from the Pacific war days.
One of these is Mrs. Douglas MacArthur, who lives in the Waldorf
Astoria Towers in New York City. Another is Mrs. Jack (Dode) Fee,
the young housewife who was three months pregnant when Bulkeley
and his PT men fished her from black Manila Bay when the SS *Corregidor* was sunk by a mine off Bataan, ten days after war broke out.
Jack and Dode Fee were interned in Santo Tomas prison camp in

Manila throughout the war. "We wondered all during that time," Mrs.
Fee said recently, "how our rescuers [the PT boat officers and crew]
fared. How much we owed them for saving our lives." And she said
that it "might amuse" Bulkeley's men today to know that "they didn't
save just me but also a daughter born several months later who is now
the mother of two sons of her own."

In the spring of 1947, seven former PT boat skippers met in the
New York City apartment of Preston Sutphen, Jr., whose firm had
built the boats during the war. They formed Peter Tare (the phonetic
words for PT). Its members are World War II Motor Torpedo Boat
Squadron or auxiliary force officers, and its sole function is to retain
social contact with members. Toward that end Peter Tare holds an
annual reunion at various cities in the United States and abroad.

The year after Peter Tare was formed, a sister organization, PT
Boats, Inc., came into being. Headquartered in Memphis, Tennessee,
PT Boats, Inc. was the brainchild of James M. "Boats" Newberry,
who served with the Devil Boats in the Pacific as a chief boatswain's
mate. At the conclusion of World War II, PT boatmen scattered to
the four corners. But steadily, over the years, Boats Newberry brought
them back together again. His one-page Christmas letter to sixty comrades in 1946 has grown to a forty-eight page semiannual newspaper
today.

Now PT Boats, Inc. is a strong and highly active organization of
nearly ten thousand members. They bill themselves as "The Most
Enthusiastic Veterans Group in the World." And well it might be.
The compact size of the PT boats, the fact that the life of each man
on board often depended upon the courage and ability of his boat-
mates, and because the boats fought alone and isolated or in pairs
deep in enemy-controlled waters, all contributed toward forging strong
bonds of camaraderie that no power on earth can break.

Each year a national reunion attracts more than 1,000 persons,
and twenty regional gatherings average 750 persons each. The Devil
Boat buccaneers of yesteryear have taken a little off the top and put
a little on around the middle. None are as spry as they were in their
World War II heyday. But their fiery spirits still are burning brightly,
and they rejoice in swapping war stories.

In the 1980s, the PT Boat Museum at Battleship Cove, Fall River,
Massachusetts, attracts thousands of visitors each year. The museum

was the final major project spearheaded by Boats Newberry, who, on January 12, 1985, sailed on his last patrol. His place at the helm was taken over by his widow, Alyce Newberry, and daughter Alyce Guthrie who, with the help of a small but dedicated staff, see to it that the PT boat fraternity continues on a forward course with all throttles wide open.

Index